UNFINISHED PEACE

THOUGHTS ON NORTHERN IRELAND'S UNANSWERED PAST

December 2015

UNFINISHED PEACE

THOUGHTS ON NORTHERN IRELAND'S UNANSWERED PAST

To Kathryn
With Many Thanks

Brian Rowan

Barney

COLOURPOINT

For my wife, Val

Published 2015 by Colourpoint Books
an imprint of Colourpoint Creative Ltd
Colourpoint House, Jubilee Business Park
21 Jubilee Road, Newtownards, BT23 4YH
Tel: 028 9182 6339
Fax: 028 9182 1900
E-mail: sales@colourpoint.co.uk
Web: www.colourpoint.co.uk

First Edition
First Impression

A catalogue record for this book is available from the British Library.

Designed by April Sky Design, Newtownards
Tel: 028 9182 7195
Web: www.aprilsky.co.uk

Printed by GPS Colour Graphics Ltd, Belfast

ISBN 978-1-78073-092-9

Contents

Acknowledgements

There are so many people to thank: all those who have made this book possible.

During these recent months of writing, what I have discovered is that there is learning in every day, and in every story that stretches from the conflict period into our unfinished peace.

As a news correspondent, I wrote, onto scraps of paper, many of the IRA briefings on the "Disappeared" – but I didn't come to properly understand the true horror of that practice of hiding bodies, until I read the words that Eimear McVeigh wrote for this book. Eimear is the niece of Columba McVeigh – one of the Disappeared, whose remains have yet to be found.

Then there is the story told by Alice Reid, about her mother Maureen, and her struggles and victories in bringing up ten children after her husband, James was killed in a pub bombing. Alice's poem, a tribute to her mum, offers the very human thoughts and words with which this book ends.

My daughter, Elle, born in September 1994, is as old and as young as the original ceasefires. Today she asks questions, not just about what happened, but why. Elle is a photography student and, for this book, she has photographed people, who have been hurt, are still hurting, and may hurt forever.

I want to thank all those, who wrote their stories for the pages you are about to turn: Dr Lisa Faulkner, Jim Gibney, Harold Good, Alan McBride, Judith Hill, Kathryn Stone, Louise Little, Paul Doherty, Danny Morrison, Roy Dunn, Andrée Murphy, Peter Sheridan, Eamonn Mallie, Deric Henderson, Professor Kieran McEvoy, Jackie McDonald, Jim McVeigh, William "Plum" Smith, Dessie Waterworth, Eimear McVeigh, Sandra Peake, Gary Mason, Tom Elliott MP, Eibhlin Glenholmes, Mervyn Wynne Jones, David Porter, Jarlath Burns, Stephen Douds, Chief Constable George Hamilton, Dr Jonny Byrne, Lee Lavis, Michael Culbert, Winston Irvine, Colin Davidson and Alice Reid.

I also want to thank the former senior IRA leader who spoke to me, on condition of anonymity, about the ceasefire period, August 1994 to February 1996.

As the political battles continue over the unanswered past, and we think about an archive of stories, we can see how it might work, when we read these contributions from very different backgrounds and experiences.

As a journalist, I have tried to follow the working example of David McKittrick, whose writing for *The Irish Times* and the *Independent* made a huge contribution to the coverage of our war and peace. We could all learn something from David, and from the former BBC News Editor and Controller, Robin Walsh. Jim McDowell opened the doors into journalism for me, and colleagues Andrew Colman, Mervyn Jess and Seamus Kelters have been great friends and the source of endless support and advice.

Malcolm Johnston at Colourpoint made this book possible, and, in her structuring and questions, editor Susan Feldstein brought order and greater explanation to its pages.

This book is dedicated to my wife, Val who, many times, pointed me in the right direction and steered me away from wrong places and conclusions. This work I do comes with many strains and tensions, and Val has not just watched out for me, but she has watched over our children, Ruairi, Elle and PJ, and soon-to-be daugher-in-law, Shelley. Thank you, Val.

INTRODUCTION
We are all involved

There are times when you find something even when you are not looking for it, or not consciously looking for it. On this occasion, while I was thinking about writing some introductory words for this book, I found a scrap of paper, on which were some typed thoughts from the late Dr Jack Weir. The former Presbyterian Moderator gave me these notes in 1992, when I had asked for an interview with him at a point in the Northern Ireland conflict when the death toll was approaching 3,000. This is some of what he wrote:

> No shooting or bombing or intimidation should be seen by anyone as a successful operation, but rather as a failure that we have not found a better way – whether we're thinking as loyalists or republicans, unionists or nationalists, security forces or politicians, or most of all, as the plain people of this Province, who have not risen up to cry above all else, "Stop it now!", but have been content to carry on our lives as long as we don't feel involved.
>
> But we *are* involved, for violence and all that leads to and that goes with it doesn't start with the finger on the trigger or the hand that lays the bomb – it starts in people's hearts and minds, in our ambitions and our attitudes to one another. We are all involved.
>
> As John Donne said, "No man is an island . . . any man's death diminishes me . . . And therefore never send to know for whom the bell tolls; it tolls for thee . . ."
>
> And for me, 3,000 times.

Dr Weir's thinking was framed in the circumstances of those times. It was a challenge to all to reflect more deeply and in a different way, and, more than two decades after he handed me that scrap of paper, while many important changes may have taken place, the challenge for all of us in Northern Ireland, and elsewhere, is the same. The past, which is still in our present, will never be satisfactorily answered or addressed with simplistic attributions of blame, and nor can it be reduced to the actions of a few bogeymen.

As we read the words above – from a churchman, who engaged with the IRA in the early 1970s and tried again with loyalists and republicans in the period before the ceasefires of the 1990s – we must ask: what prompted the firing of those guns and the placing of those bombs? The questions are not just about what happened, but why. It is too easy to say, "It didn't have to happen", or, "It shouldn't have happened". It did happen. People died; people suffered horrific physical and mental trauma; countless families were left bereaved and broken. All of us need to deal with that reality. The challenge is that any such detailed scrutiny of the past should not have as its main purpose the staging of some kind of parade of shame, but instead should represent our best attempts to ensure that it will never happen again.

More than 20 years after the 1994 ceasefires, the Northern Ireland conflict – or the conflict in the North – is an unfinished story, whose telling is also incomplete. As yet, there is no past. What happened in those "war" years is still in the present, still vivid, and for some – indeed, many – it always will be. It was the former Speaker of the Stormont Assembly, Lord Alderdice, who once commented that, "the awful pain and damage and scar [are] not necessarily repairable . . . some of it cannot be fixed, whatever you do". So, there is no such thing as trite or as glib or as easy as might be suggested in the notion of simply "drawing a line".

Addressing the past – and the questions it throws up – is a huge challenge. Those questions are not just about Gerry Adams and the IRA, or Billy Wright and the UVF/LVF, or how many republicans and loyalists went to jail. What happened cannot be confined to that limited focus or reduced to that narrow arithmetic. That would afford too many others an easy way out. Things must be seen within a much wider frame – one which encompasses the political and social context out of which the violence grew. The political, governmental, security and intelligence decisions and strategies are all as much part of what happened as the approach and the actions of the IRA and the other republican and loyalist groups. We do not know what the consequences of such an examination of those many players, factors and perspectives will be, but we do know there is not just one past to be considered and scrutinised.

The period under examination in this book begins just before the original ceasefires of 1994, and extends to the present day, 2015, encompassing along the way the stories of policing, prisoners, the dissidents, the Disappeared, the "endgame" decisions and decommissioning, and then the debates, deliberations and protracted negotiations about dealing with the past. It is a reappraisal of events often described as historic in the context of our "Troubles" or conflict, with a narrative that at times travels back to what happened in the 1970s and the 1980s, and at other times propels us forward to what is still happening – and still not happening – today. Those ceasefires, whilst creating an opportunity for a new path, also raised many fears within politics and within policing and among those who had fought the wars. As things developed, promises and commitments became bargaining chips and negotiating points – the future of the RUC being one such example.

As new ceasefires replaced old ceasefires, beyond those crucial and game-changing decisions and declarations, the idea of a South African-type "Truth Commission" was floated and introduced into the mix of the continuing debates and discussions about the best way forward. We are not a population of 50 million-plus, but rather, a small and knowing place. All of us have been close to the news and to what happened. How to address the past became an undertaking for a Consultative Group known as the Eames/Bradley process, then the focus of talks headed by the US Diplomat Richard Haass and Professor Meghan O'Sullivan, and most recently the subject of the Stormont House Agreement, with all its many disagreements that in turn became part of yet more talks. Those talks have not yet produced an agreed way forward, but again became stuck in old arguments including national security and the disclosure of information.

This book is a compilation of my contemporaneous reporting of some of the key events of the recent past, with today's analysis and context and essays added. With the help of others, including some of those who were close to, or inside, some of the big stories and moments as they developed, I will try to read more deeply between the lines and explore some of the key questions. There is no one truth, narrative or answer. There never will be, and this is something that needs to be understood and accepted by us all.

While what happened cannot be reduced to any individual – to Gerry Adams or anyone else – it is how leaders such as Adams decide to cooperate with any process that will determine the responses of others – including those we don't see, in the hidden corridors of intelligence and national security. At an Easter Commemoration inside Milltown Cemetery in April 2010, the Sinn Féin President spoke about the past and its many questions:

> I am also very conscious of the human cost of the war and the great hurt inflicted by republicans . . . I have acknowledged this and my regret for this many times. And I do so again today. There are victims and citizens who want to know the truth about what happened to loved ones during the conflict. That is their right. I cannot demand truth for victims of British terrorism, collusion or unionist terror, without supporting the same

right for victims of republican actions. That is why Sinn Féin supports the establishment of an effective independent and international truth-recovery process. I certainly would be prepared to be part of such a process and I would encourage others to participate.

The IRA and its leadership know much about decades of conflict, and have the answers to many of the questions about the war. Others, too, have information and explanations and answers. What is needed now is the gathering and pooling of that knowledge, and then the sharing of it in the most constructive way. The IRA, loyalist, security and intelligence wars won't really be over for any of us until that happens. Of the many sides identified by Adams in that Easter speech, how much each one will be prepared to reveal and disclose is still uncertain. Do the British and Irish Governments want a detailed examination of the past; are those in security and intelligence and in politics prepared for public scrutiny; are the IRA or those in the various loyalist paramilitary groups ready to divulge what they know? We still do not know.

At some point, addressing the past will be about how we get an agreement on these multiple, contested and competing narratives and truths and explanations; about how we come to some better understanding and appreciation of the experiences of others; and about how we open our minds to a willingness to reflect, not just on what happened – but why.

When they are happening, wars and conflicts are about enemies; about killing; about trying to win and not lose. They are about orders being given and being carried out and, for those like myself, tasked with reporting what is happening, about recording the events of there and then. It is only afterwards that we can come to ask more questions and try to better understand. This is when fixed narratives can become disturbed. There was nothing romantic or glorious or glamorous about the trenches and the battlefields of this place in that span of years that stretched from the late 1960s.

In this book, you will read the thoughts of some of those who have had lead roles – whether very publicly or in a quieter, more discreet way – in the transition from conflict to the better place we are today. I am grateful for their writing and contributions, and to the many others who have spoken to me both privately and openly over the years. For me, the war and peace of this place has been, and is still, a long journey of learning.

Brian Rowan
November 2015

CHAPTER ONE
October 1993: A Foot in the Rubble

"After each of these atrocities, the cry was, 'Never again!' – but here we were, yet again."
Former Methodist President, Harold Good, writing for this book and reflecting on the time of the Shankill bomb and the preceding period.

"Although I didn't know her, as I watched the TV programme, I was 13 years old again, sitting on the cold floor of our school assembly hall, as teachers struggled to pay tribute to a pupil; a child. . . I was reminded that so many young girls here never became brides, or indeed, [that] many fathers weren't there to walk their daughters up the aisle."
Academic Dr Lisa Faulkner, thinking back to the period of the Shankill bomb.

During the years of the conflict, there were many times when this place seemed to walk or rush to the very precipice, and then pause, or stop or step back. Why things never tipped over into something much worse is one of the many unanswered questions of the past. Perhaps, on different occasions, people were held back, or pulled back from the brink, as a result of some of those many discussions that were never publicly seen nor heard.

The last week of October 1993 was one of those times. It was a bloody week, remembered for the Shankill bomb on Saturday, 23 October and the Greysteel shootings, which took place seven days later. Much of what happened in between these two atrocities – and before and after – is forgotten or lost in the small print of those dark years of the conflict. In the typed note handed to me by Dr Jack Weir in 1992, as mentioned in the Introduction, there was another important reflection. "My first reaction must be one of sorrow – and shame," wrote the former Presbyterian Moderator. "It is sorrow, not only at the tragic loss of lives of men and women, and even children, but also at the much larger crowd of those behind them, those bereaved of loved ones: those bearing in their minds and bodies the wounds and disabilities inflicted by this ongoing violence; homes shattered and honest businesses destroyed," he continued. "It is shame – that it has gone on so long, [that] there still seems to be no end in sight – and [that] for most of us, these casualties become no more than statistics." In these words, carefully crafted and chosen to chisel into our awareness – and lack of awareness – there is an abrupt awakening: a jolt which forces us to confront the reality of the much wider circle of human suffering which each individual death brings.

As Dr Weir typed these thoughts in 1992, that cold statistic – the toll of deaths – had reached 3,000. He was right, about how names and people became forgotten in the tallying up of the dead; this was something that happened again and again, and now happened once more in October 1993. There were ten deaths in the bomb on the Shankill, and eight people were killed in the gunfire and the madness of the Greysteel shootings, just a week later. Yet, for all the horror of that statistic, it represented just part of the story of those seven days in 1993.

In remembering headlines such as Shankill and Greysteel, so much of what else happened, even during that seven-day period, is either ignored or forgotten. Between those two Saturdays in October, six other people lost their lives – Martin Moran, Sean Fox, James Cameron, Mark Rodgers, Gerard and Rory Cairns. Shot in their homes and at work, they were the softest of targets in a bloody play of revenge. Their names, those shootings, are often forgotten, overlooked amidst the "bigger" events of the time.

There are other things we so often forget – such as the people who are sent to those scenes that are the places of both sorrow and shame. Here, the carefully chosen words of Dr Weir evoking such places are echoed in other words – those spoken by Gary McColl, a police constable who was tasked with searching for the dead and the injured in the rubble of the Shankill bomb:

> I remember an old man being recovered, and his head was the first thing to appear from the rubble – that was quite a frightening experience. He was [still alive], because I remember seeing his eyes blinking, and a member from the ambulance crew put an oxygen mask over [his face]. Unfortunately, by the time he left the rubble, he had died ... We continued to remove rubble from where we were standing and, unfortunately and unknown to anybody, we were standing on other bodies. As the rubble was being removed – and it will stay with me until I die – I saw a young girl's foot.

In this interview, about 15 months after the tragic events of that October day in 1993, this police officer was telling his story publicly for the first time. As he described the images locked in his memory, his words were like the turning of a key, opening up that scene to the thinking and seeing of others.

"I knew it was a young girl's foot," he continued, "because [I could see] her shoe size was about 3 or 4, as it poked through the rubble." He recalled how at that point, he had wanted to stop searching – but he had to continue. His stark, shocking testimony is a reminder that there is so much detail missing from the public narrative of what happened in Northern Ireland/the North during the conflict years; so much we either blank out or redact, or just don't want to know or remember.

Among the ten people who died in that explosion was one of the bombers, Thomas Begley. Another IRA member, Sean Kelly was found with the injured in the rubble, and he and Begley have become the bogeymen of that day of slaughter. Yet they too are only part of the story. While Kelly and Begley carried out the attack, it is clear that they were not responsible for its planning. Who shaped the events of that day? Who thought through this premeditated attack on loyalists on a busy Saturday on the Shankill Road?

At that time, the IRA had become obsessed with trying to kill Johnny Adair: they had been hounding and hunting him for months, and on occasion had deployed for the purpose several units armed with AK47 rifles and a .38 Special revolver. In that blind obsession, everything else became blurred. It was well known that the UDA had an upstairs office in the same block of buildings as Frizzell's fishmonger's shop on the Shankill Road. If the IRA believed that Adair would be in that office on that Saturday, he was never going to be allowed enough time to get out before the bomb went off and, therefore, there was never going to be sufficient warning given to allow innocent passers-by to get to safety.

On the designated day, the IRA carried the bomb into the fishmonger's shop below. But the UDA office was empty at the time of the explosion, and those killed were uninvolved men, women and children – the youngest victim just seven years old. There was never going to be enough time to clear the area and, so, the IRA had calculated on killing civilians in an attempt to kill loyalists, and in particular the Shankill UDA leader, Johnny Adair.

This has never been said or admitted by the IRA, but it is part of an ugly truth. Perhaps it is something they would still deny. That organisation will never disclose the names of those who ordered and directed this attack, or reveal the identity of the man who made the bomb, or disclose the names of those who knew what was to happen that day. These details will, it seems, never be part of the record. But might they at some point acknowledge that, in planning this bombing and the Remembrance Day bomb in Enniskillen in 1987, and other bomb attacks, they knew there would be civilian deaths? This would mean some more of the truth being brought to light, even if all of the details will never be disclosed; it is the type of question to be further explored as the setting up of an Independent Commission for Information Retrieval continues to be discussed. What level of exposure of all the facts can we hope for; how can we optimise our chances of obtaining as much information as possible – and not just from the IRA, but from the many other parties who had a part to play?

As a journalist, I had been inside that UDA office on the Shankill Road many times, to meet and speak with senior loyalists. I remember clearly the pungent smell of fish there, when you entered the front door of the building to climb the steps to the upstairs office – but I had never really given much thought to Frizzell's, the nearby fishmonger's shop. Yet, since 23 October 1993, the fish shop has been a constant in the telling and the retelling of the events of that day, and the slaughter on the Shankill Road. Neither would I have thought of, or been aware of, the police constable, Gary McColl, who would later tell his harrowing story of searching through the rubble at the scene. There were so many in the rubble, so much activity at that scene, so much to think about – and so much that, at the time, we had to try to block out. We attempted to lock those scenes out of our thinking, or at least tried to, but they are always there, somewhere in our minds and remembering.

Dr Lisa Faulkner, now an academic working in the area of conflict transformation, was just 13 and about to head into Belfast with friends on that black day in 1993. They heard the Shankill bomb explode and, more than two decades later, a television documentary brought Lisa back to that time.

Dr Lisa Faulkner, writing for this book

As Brian Rowan shared his harrowing experiences of the Shankill bomb on the TV programme, *The Troubles I've Seen,* his words not only filled our living room, but took me and my fiancé away from our wedding planning, as I was transported back to that day in October 1993. Whilst I wasn't on the Shankill Road, nor did I know any of the victims, it is one of the many atrocities which remind me of our dark past – a past marred by suffering and carnage, which I feel fortunate not to have endured for too long.

On that Saturday afternoon, I had met two friends at the bus stop outside the Everton Complex on the Crumlin Road. We were intending on going "down town", which entailed junk food of some kind and a movie in the cinema on the Dublin Road. I was enjoying my new-found "freedom", since starting the Girls' Model Secondary School the month before. As my memories fade with the passage of time, I am not sure what made us leave the bus stop – it may have been that one of us needed more money, or that we forgot to ask for permission to go into town. However, as we crossed the Ardoyne Road a few minutes later, I can remember the distinct noise of the bomb, followed by an unearthly quiet. We knew that we would not be venturing anywhere after all. As I walked down my long street, I can remember people emerged wearily from their homes, asking their neighbours, "Was that a bomb?" All the while, the atmosphere became increasingly eerie and tense.

As the enormity of it all emerged, I failed to see beyond Leanne Murray [one of the victims], as quite simply, I kept thinking, "That's just like me or my friends being killed." At 13 years old, Leanne and I were the same age, we both attended the Girls Model and I am sure we both had our books "backed" with some kind of boy band poster or another. Although I didn't know her, as I watched the TV programme, I was 13 years old again, sitting on the cold floor of our school assembly hall as teachers struggled to pay tribute to a pupil; a child.

As I went back to the wedding planning that evening, I was reminded that so many young girls here never became brides, or indeed, [that] many fathers weren't there to walk their daughters up the aisle. Such programmes help us to remember those who will never be forgotten by their nearest and dearest; however I am also grateful that in 20 years' time, those who are 13 today will not be reliving such harrowing experiences.

After the explosion on that Saturday back in October 1993, I remember seeing Johnny Adair and other loyalist leaders on the Shankill Road, and I remember the statements that followed the bombing: siren words that were the warning signals of another bloody week to come. The fear was palpable, as we all tried to anticipate what might come next. And we did not have to wait long to see the inevitable play-out and the loyalist response, which the IRA would have also known was certain to come.

Alan McBride's father-in-law, Desmond Frizzell owned the fishmonger's shop and was killed in the blast. So, too, was Alan's wife, Sharon. In the days after the tragedy, there was huge controversy when Gerry Adams was one of those who carried the coffin of Thomas Begley at the bomber's funeral. Adams had of course carried the coffins of many IRA men and women, as had another of Begley's pallbearers that day, the Belfast republican, Jim Gibney.

Jim Gibney, Sinn Féin, writing for this book

1993 was one of those many, many grim years of the conflict. It opened with an attempted loyalist wipe-out of an entire Catholic family in Dungannon. The UVF, which we now know was being directed by British Intelligence agencies, burst into a home and shot dead a father and son, Patrick and Diarmuid Shields. Then after the funeral, Diarmuid's girlfriend, Julie Statham, an only daughter, took her life because she could not envisage a future without [him]. Loyalist assassination squads were prevalent, having been reorganised and rearmed by the British.

The IRA attempted to thwart them, but one of its major attacks resulted in tragedy, a huge loss of life that heightened sectarian tensions. In October that year the IRA set out to kill senior leaders in the paramilitary UDA – including Johnny Adair – who regularly met in an office above the shop on the Shankill Road. However, when the IRA active service unit struck, [the UDA] weren't there. Worse still, the bomb exploded prematurely and killed nine civilians, and an IRA Volunteer on the operation, Thomas Begley. In the following week, loyalists killed 14 people, the vast majority of them Catholics.

Back in 1993 Sinn Féin was involved in secret talks, both with the British and with SDLP leader John Hume, aimed at attempting to resolve the ongoing conflict. [In the aftermath of the Shankill bombing,] the question put by the political opponents of the Republican cause, scenting a major difficulty for republicans, was whether Gerry Adams would acknowledge young Thomas Begley, the IRA Volunteer, who had also died that day.

There was not a scintilla of doubt in Gerry Adams' mind that he would attend the funeral and carry the coffin of Thomas Begley. There was not a scintilla of doubt either in the minds of the leadership team around Gerry Adams, advising him. There was not a scintilla of doubt in my mind that I would attend Thomas's funeral and carry his coffin. Gerry Adams, Tom Hartley and I carried Thomas's coffin together. We did so because we were part of him politically and emotionally; part of his lifelong experience of injustice; part of his lifelong experience of resistance. We were there to be with his grieving family, his grieving community – IRA and civilian. Thomas died as an IRA volunteer on active service.

I had been carrying the coffins of IRA volunteers since I was a teenager in the Short Strand in the early 1970s. I carried the coffins of my teenage friends who were IRA volunteers. I was proud to do so, and I was proud to be a pallbearer at Thomas's funeral. I was however concerned enough to raise a doubt about the impact Gerry Adams carrying Thomas's coffin could have on the fledgling peace process. My concerns were essentially, would Gerry Adams' presence at Thomas's funeral strengthen those very powerful forces in the British Government, in unionist circles and in Irish society, [who were] opposed to peace, and consequently prolong the war and the agonising loss of life – so obvious in the tragic deaths of all those in Frizzell's fish shop on the Shankill Road. I raised my concerns, and Gerry Adams and the others in the room listened, and [they] attended Thomas's funeral and also carried his coffin, as I did.

The huge loss of life in Frizzell's fish shop was a human tragedy on a massive scale. And we knew it and felt that for the families who lost relatives at the time, and we still do. There was a significant risk involved. Gerry Adams was involved in negotiations with the Irish, British and US Governments, and I and others were in talks with a range of individuals from the Protestant Churches. But it was right for Gerry to attend the funeral and carry Thomas's coffin. It was the right thing to do for the Begley family. It was the right thing to do for Sean Kelly, who was on the IRA operation with Thomas Begley and was badly injured. It was the right thing to do for peace in Ireland. A peace that we have enjoyed for nearly 20 years, and which has transformed the politics and people on this island.

Others could not and did not understand this decision in relation to Begley's funeral. They thought it was wrong: insensitive and thoughtless. In the immediate aftermath of the bombing, Alan McBride, having lost his wife and father-in-law, hounded Gerry Adams, following him and picketing him. But many years later, in 2007, he made his peace with the Sinn Féin leader, in a letter he wrote to him after the funeral of the loyalist politician David Ervine, who died suddenly in January that year.

"David Ervine's funeral was very important to me," McBride would later comment. "I thought, 'We are so close'." He was talking about the significance of Adams and others attending Ervine's funeral, and how close he then thought Northern Ireland was to peace after the many years of violence.

"I wrote a letter to Gerry Adams, basically just acknowledging his journey . . . I firmly believe he is totally committed to peace-building," McBride would later tell the *Belfast Telegraph*. He revealed that the Sinn Féin leader had replied – in a handwritten letter – asking if they could meet. It would take a while for that to happen but, with time, corners can be turned into different places, allowing for different relationships and understandings.

Alan McBride has turned many such corners and made decisions that have been hugely difficult, including a decision to be filmed meeting Adams for a Channel 4 documentary about the Bible. Before this happened, the two met privately – a meeting which was facilitated by the former Methodist President, Harold Good. I covered the story of this highly significant meeting in a *Belfast Telegraph* piece at the time:

A long way from the horror on Shankill
(*Belfast Telegraph,* 7 December 2009)

Harold Good – the pastor and the preacher – was the obvious choice. He knows both men and is trusted by them. He also knows the importance of quiet conversations in a developing peace. At the meeting place last Wednesday, he was with Alan McBride when Gerry Adams arrived with his aide, Richard McAuley.

"We did shake hands," Mr McBride told this newspaper, and then, as they chatted "in a very natural discussion", he had a glass of water and a banana, and Gerry Adams had coffee and a scone. For most of the time they were together, Reverend Harold Good and Richard McAuley listened as the other two men spoke. This was their conversation.

"A meeting such as this is hugely symbolic of what is possible," the churchman told this newspaper. "As I sat and listened, I thought of the journey which both have made in their own way to come to this place," he said.

That place is a long way from that bomb and that rubble on the Shankill Road in October 1993, and from the statements made that day by the IRA and the UFF. Hopes of peace appeared to have been buried in that blast – but within 12 months, both the IRA and the loyalists had declared their ceasefires.

The long journeys of Gerry Adams and Alan McBride brought them to [this] meeting place last Wednesday. "We can understand that there are those on all sides of this conflict who would find this kind of meeting very difficult, and we respect that," Mr Good said. "These are very personal journeys for people to make in their own way and in their own time, and this must also be respected," he added.

Sixteen years after the bomb, a story of extraordinary journeys is beginning to be told.

Reverend Good remembers the day of the Shankill bomb too of course. He remembers driving to the Mater Hospital in north Belfast, and remembers how helpless he felt when he got there. It was also a day that brought back other grim memories, ones which have never been lost in the conflict rubble.

Harold Good, former Methodist President

For me, it was a reliving of the horrendous bombing of the nearby Balmoral Furniture store in 1971 when, with bare hands, I joined in the search for survivors under the rubble. We retrieved four bodies, two of them but babes. After each of these atrocities the cry was, "Never again!", but here we were, yet again [in 1993 and this latest bomb on the Shankill].

When the dust had settled, but not the anger, I too was horrified to see the pictures of Gerry Adams carrying the coffin of the bomber. Sixteen years later, at a very public event, I was speaking about what might bring healing to our land, emphasising the need for confession, grace and forgiveness. At the front of the hall sat Alan McBride, whose young wife Sharon and her father had been killed in the bomb. At the back sat Gerry Adams.

Alan asked me if I thought this would be the opportune moment for him "to make his peace" with Adams. This would not have been the time or place but, not long after, both Alan and Gerry Adams came to my home. It was my sacred privilege to sit with them as they spoke. If ever there was an "uncomfortable conversation", this was it.

It is for Alan to say what this conversation meant to him but, as I heard it, this was a conversation about mutual understanding, acknowledgement and apology. For me, it was a sign of what can happen, and a signpost for how we might begin to deal with the past in a way that would bring release and healing.

These words from Harold Good initially take us back in time – into the darkness and the dust and the despair of the conflict years – and then, they take us inside the room of that Adams and McBride meeting, without ever breaching the confidentiality of precisely what was said. "He [Adams] acknowledged my pain, my hurt and he apologised to me," Alan McBride would later say. In the mayhem of 1993, with all the talk of war and in the midst of the noise of the shootings and the bombs, and the anger and condemnation, we would never have considered such a conversation possible. Yet it happened – and what we can learn from this is that these stories of bombings and shootings do not end with what happens on any particular day, but that they can evolve and develop into other happenings on other days.

This is not to suggest that this type of meeting can or will work for everyone. In the same way that Gordon Wilson did not for a moment suggest that he spoke for all the victims of the IRA's Remembrance Day bomb in Enniskillen, so Alan McBride speaks only for himself and of what happened to him as an individual. Others have no desire to meet with Adams or other republican leaders, and continue to hope for justice, however remote that prospect. For McBride, it was a difficult, very personal decision and one that caused his mother-in-law, who had lost both a husband and a daughter, a great deal of pain. He spoke about this in an interview with me on 21 June 2015, at a "Day of Reflection" event at the WAVE Trauma Centre, where he works. WAVE describes itself as a broad church, bringing together victims and survivors from a wide variety of backgrounds with often diverse views and opinions. That date – the summer solstice, the day of most light and least darkness – is now used by the Centre and others as a time of quiet remembering.

Alan McBride, WAVE Trauma Centre

Obviously it was something I struggled with myself, for many, many years, but I just knew the time was right. We had this conversation in Harold Good's house, which I think went well – [and] lasted a couple of hours. We spoke about everything. Gerry Adams actually opened by apologising for the Shankill bomb. We did not agree on the conflict. I thought that it should never have happened. He thought that it was inevitable . . .

When the story [of my meeting with Adams] broke then on the Monday, my mother-in-law heard about it – on the news. I didn't get to tell her about the interview, because this was a prelude to a programme that we were making together for Channel 4, and it wasn't to come out until February [2010]. So I thought, actually, that I would have time over Christmas to talk to her about it, because she wasn't very well.

So, she was angry with me, to be quite honest. . . And I think for very good reason. Obviously she saw me as somebody that had betrayed her daughter's memory. I mean, Gerry Adams obviously carried the coffin of the bomber, and she just found me meeting him to be very, very difficult. And my mother-in-law and I would be very, very close. So, it was a very painful conversation when I went up to see her [about it], and she was crying. Then, a couple of days later, she was at Stormont with me for the launch of a book that I had put together for WAVE. I had invited Gerry Adams to [the launch] . . . He came into the room when she was there, and I just knew that she was going to find that so difficult.

So, I got in touch with Harold Good, who was also there, saying, "Could you get word to Gerry Adams and tell him if he could just go?", which he did. I emailed Adams later on that night, to apologise . . . He understood entirely and was quite gracious in just saying, "Look, listen, I understand".

People have a difficult journey to make in these kind of issues, and even families aren't together on it . . . Because I was going to have to make this programme with him [Adams], I didn't want the first meeting to be a very public affair – on camera. I wanted to have this private conversation with him first and foremost, and I did. I regret not paving the way for my mother-in-law to have heard about the meeting. I regret that it broke very suddenly. But I think, at the end of the day, if you're trying to build peace and promote tolerance, and trying to normalise this place again . . . I think meeting Gerry Adams, for me, was quite a significant step, and perhaps for others quite symbolic. I also know, of course, that not everybody will agree, and I got a lot of criticism from certain quarters for doing it but, from other quarters, I got some praise and recognition: "Look, this was a brave thing to do" . . . People will have their own opinions about that.

Alan's words tell more than one story and extend far beyond the events of a single day; they recount not just his meeting and conversation with Gerry Adams and what it meant for him to be in the room, but also how this then played out within his family circle and beyond: the fresh hurt caused; his mother-in-law's sense of the "betrayal" of the memory of her lost loved ones. Every one of these actions and reactions is a book of chapters revealing many experiences and emotions, and the pages keep turning through time. The story of the Shankill bombing is not about one day and one bomb and those deaths in October 1993; it extends above and beyond this, to include what happened before that day, what has happened since, and what will happen in the future. That event in October 1993 had, and continues to have, multiple repercussions; each individual's experience of those repercussions reveals further facets of the story – emotions, experiences, subsequent decisions and actions. The beginning is before that day, and we still don't know the end, or if there will be such a moment or discernible point to come. This is why the conflict is an incomplete book: the story is unfinished, there are crucial details yet to be filled in, with none of us knowing at this point whether there will ever be a full stop.

CHAPTER TWO
August 1994: First Steps to a Different Place

"As a result of my faith, my upbringing and my experience, I believe that the suffering of those from all sections of society – who lost their lives, their loved ones, their limbs and the lives they once had or dreamt of – cannot be justified."
Louise Little, granddaughter of the late Gusty Spence, writing for this book.

"'We are all victims here, love'."
Kathryn Stone, Victims' Commissioner 2012–2014, recalling words spoken to her in a casual conversation.

"In the very heart of communities, where labels and stereotypes have been strongest, lies the secret to unlocking the next phase of the peace journey."
Judith Hill, UTV journalist, writing for this book.

We may imagine that we believe what we see and hear. Yet so often we interpret, or misinterpret, what we see and hear in terms of our own preconceived ideas about a situation. You can become fixed in a personal experience – for example, in my case and in the case of numerous journalists reporting on conflicts international and local, it is common to become locked into a working practice, with a specific language and approach that can soon become routine. Killings, bombs, bullets, coded statements, clandestine meetings and briefings become the way of things; the abnormal becomes normal. Within that tunnel vision, it is difficult to see around corners, much less to think out of corners. We all can become trapped in certain experiences and beliefs and doubts. We understand and misunderstand; we know yet do not know. None of us sees or hears everything, and much of our learning comes afterwards and not in actual time.

So, in that period of the Shankill bomb and the reprisals that soon followed, despite intimations of potential peace initiatives, it was difficult for most of us at the time to see and believe in the possibility of ceasefires being in the offing. It all looked the ugly same. Yet, as a peace process develops, so we come to better understand how things can change and indeed how quickly that can sometimes happen. Not so long after the carnage of October 1993, those ceasefires did materialise, through the perseverance and faith and powers of persuasion of those – including some who were closest to the violence – who opened their minds to a different way.

On 31 August 1994, I was one of a small number of journalists in Belfast and Dublin who had been called together to hear the words of an IRA statement being read – in my case, in the whispered tones of a woman representative. Sitting at a table with my journalist colleague, Eamonn Mallie, we wrote as the woman continued with her quiet, measured delivery. These were words of breaking news and major headlines; words that could not have been imagined or thought possible those few months earlier, in October 1993.

IRA Statement, 31 August 1994

Recognising the potential of the current situation, and in order to enhance the democratic peace process and underline our definitive commitment to its success, the leadership of Óglaigh na hÉireann have decided that, as of midnight, Wednesday, 31 August, there will be a complete cessation of military operations.

- All our units have been instructed accordingly. At this historic crossroads, the leadership of Óglaigh na hÉireann salutes and commends our volunteers, other activists, our supporters and the political prisoners who have sustained this struggle against all odds for the past 25 years.

- Your courage, determination and sacrifice have demonstrated that the spirit of freedom, and the desire for peace based on a just and lasting settlement, cannot be crushed.

- We remember all those who have died for Irish freedom and we reiterate our commitment to our republican objectives. Our struggle has seen many gains and advances made by nationalists and for the democratic position.

- We believe that an opportunity to secure a just and lasting settlement has been created.

- We are therefore entering into a new situation in a spirit of determination and confidence; determined that the injustices which created this conflict will be removed, and confident in the strength and justice of our struggle to achieve this.

- We note that the Downing Street Declaration is not a solution, nor was it presented as such by its authors.
- A solution will only be found as a result of inclusive negotiations.
- Others, not least the British Government, have a duty to face up to their responsibilities.
- It is our desire to significantly contribute to the creation of a climate which will encourage this.
- We urge everyone to approach this new situation with energy, determination and patience.

When I look at them now, I see how my pencil-written notes of that meeting, initially quite neat and deliberate, become a scrawl, spread across five jotter pages. Perhaps this indicated an impatience on my part, an eagerness to get on with things. The news that we had been waiting for was contained in the opening sentences of the IRA statement – but we could not leave our table until the entire text had been read out and transcribed. Within minutes of the completion of our task however, the words of this much-anticipated IRA statement were being analysed in news reports across the world.

Radio Ulster News Report (Brian Rowan), 31 August 1994

At a few minutes past eleven o'clock this morning, the waiting and the speculation ended, when a statement from the IRA leadership finally materialised. It said that, from midnight tonight, there would be a complete cessation of military operations. All of its so-called units had been instructed accordingly. The IRA said it believed that an opportunity to secure a just and lasting settlement had been created.

The Downing Street Declaration was not a solution and a solution could only be found as a result of inclusive negotiations. There was no qualifying clause in the statement, reserving the right to defensive action, and nor was the cessation of IRA activity tied to a fixed duration. But politicians are questioning whether or not this is a permanent end to the IRA campaign. In a few hours' time, when the decision of the IRA comes into effect, a new situation will begin to unfold and many will be hoping that real and meaningful progress can be achieved.

These many years later, we have a better understanding of that day and that statement: that after the "Long War", this was the beginning of the long making of peace – a protracted process of, at times, broken steps, and a journey that would be punctuated and interrupted by the loss of yet more lives. That day in August 1994 was the start of something – yet, in our reporting of that day, we may have thought that we were much closer to some kind of resolution or ending than we actually were. What we would find out instead was there was no grand plan on the part of the governments which would take us to the next stage; there was no big political thinking or strategic responses at the ready, to advance the situation beyond the IRA statement. Some of the players were more ready, more thinking and more open to new possibilities, but others were stuck in the same old and fixed positions.

So, that important and significant declaration on 31 August 1994, which became the stuff of world news would, eventually, become lost in a cloud of political confusion and endless arguments over semantics. What did "a complete cessation of military operations" mean? Why was the word "permanent" not used? How and when would the decommissioning of arms be achieved? These questions and concerns soon overshadowed all else, and became the sticking points around the IRA's words. After all the killing through so many years, there was an understandable suspicion – a lack of trust that led to the endless dissection, picking and scratching at the detail of this IRA statement. How could it be believed? Why should it be believed? The political scepticism was immediate and obvious, and was mirrored by the profound and widespread doubts of those in the security and intelligence services.

"The security forces are very worried about a ceasefire being used for the movement of materials [and] setting up booby traps," a senior NIO official told me in 1994, six days before the IRA announcement. Pointing to one of the slogans of that period – "Time for Peace, Time to Go" – he asked, "What's changed?" To his mind, republicans were still expressing the same "Brits Out" approach, only now in a different form of words. "They are not finished," he told me.

The past 20-plus years have been a process of change and challenges – and the word "crisis" is often present, or not far away. That IRA ceasefire was a first brick, and one that would eventually crack, without ever completely crumbling. On its own, the statement of 31 August 1994 was never going to be enough. For so many people, there were too many reasons not to believe it. We see that better now, with the benefit of hindsight: time gives us a clearer view, a much wider frame in which to see and analyse.

What we can better appreciate now, from the vantage point of the present, is that in this first ceasefire declaration, the IRA was also talking to itself, trying to persuade and convince the body of its membership. The ceasefire initiative was a leadership decision, which then had to be filtered down throughout the organisation, and explained and justified to all in its ranks. In other words it was a high-level, Army Council decision, which by no means all in those ranks below would have agreed with. Events beyond 1994 would tell us that it was too much for some, including at a senior level within the IRA.

In an interview for the *Belfast Telegraph* in August 2014, the 20th anniversary of the IRA declaration, a senior republican spoke to me about the general feeling within the movement at this time: "Maybe some people in the leadership thought it [the ceasefire] was permanent, but it wasn't the prevailing attitude in the mainstream. There was no inevitability that this was the end." I had been told by others that he was one of the last to be brought over the line in terms of a willingness to explore a political alternative to what the IRA called "the armed struggle". "The jury was out for a lot of people," he continued. "It was uncharted waters."

The Downing Street Declaration represented the positions of the then British and Irish Governments – Prime Minister John Major and Taoiseach Albert Reynolds. It was their road map; what they thought was possible. While the Declaration's position and proposals failed to meet IRA expectations, loyalists would come to regard it as part of a developing picture that was causing concern among their ranks.

On the evening of 23 October 1993, just hours after the Shankill bombing, a statement from the UDA was issued, which contained the following words: "John Hume, Gerry Adams and the nationalist electorate will pay a heavy, heavy price for today's atrocity, which was signed, sealed and delivered by the cutting edge of the Pan Nationalist Front." In the days which followed, more killings ensued, this time instigated by loyalists, along with more statements that included this recurring "pan nationalist" theme, indicating that their violence was a response, not only to republican violence but to certain ongoing political initiatives.

On 26 October 1993, James Cameron and Mark Rodgers were killed in a gun attack on workers at a council yard as part of the threatened loyalist response to the Shankill bomb; a statement issued in the aftermath of these murders included the menacing assertion: "This is only the start of the heavy price to be paid by the Hume/Adams talks and the nationalist electorate. Our attacks will widen and intensify." This reference to the nationalist electorate put the entire Catholic community in the loyalist firing line. It was now clear that the idea that loyalist violence was merely reactive, within some tit-for-tat frame of reference, no longer fitted with the facts.

By the end of 1993 and beginning of 1994, it seemed that there was to be no let-up in a trend which had been ongoing for several years: a resurgence of loyalist violence, the targeting of the Catholic community in numerous attacks and, alongside this, a very specific targeting of republicans. This had included attacks on offices and on the family homes of Sinn Féin members. One example of this was the shooting in May 1993 of Alan Lundy, as he was carrying out work to construct a porch as an additional security measure at the west Belfast home of Alex Maskey, then a Sinn Féin Councillor.

In the period leading up to the 1994 IRA ceasefire, loyalists had been watching a dialogue develop between the Sinn Féin President, Gerry Adams and the then leader of the SDLP, John Hume – and this fed their existing fears about the "Pan-Nationalist Front" as an emerging political threat. Around the same time, reports were beginning to surface about secret, back-channel contacts between the British Government and the republican leadership. For loyalists, there was a stench of sell-out in the air: a mood which can be read between the lines of a statement from UDA prisoners in January 1994, which was issued as a direct response to the Downing Street Declaration. Here is part of the text of that statement:

From UDA Prisoners' Statement, January 1994

. . . Given also that the Joint Declaration was brought about in no small measure by the actions of the Provisional Movement, in the background of many secret discussions and deals with the IRA, neither government has given us reason to place our trust in them.

Similarly, we do not feel we could ever trust the Republican Movement, and we have severe reservations as to whether any ceasefire would be genuine. We doubt the ability of the Republican Movement to control a complete cessation of violence, and believe that republican splinter groups would emerge to continue the conflict.

We feel the present situation to be very serious and volatile. While fully exploring the present "scenarios for peace", we believe now, more than at any time in the history of the present conflict, our organisation should prepare for war . . .

This statement was an expression of fear in a period of uncertainty, at a time when consideration was being given to opening a gate into some other place or possibility, a gate beyond what had become the practiced and normal way of things, however violent and abnormal this reality was. Now the many different parties in this conflict were being challenged to think and see things differently, even in a fog in which many had been lost. It was a big ask.

Early in 1994, in the course of my work as a reporter, I was given a handwritten note outlining the thinking of the UDA-linked Ulster Freedom Fighters at that time. Each point was numbered, and the initials UFF written as "_ _ _". Here is an extract of the text:

UDA/UFF Leadership Position, 1994

4. If PIRA reject [the Downing Street] Declaration, then nothing changes as far as we are concerned. Our war against the Pan-Nationalist Front will continue.

5. For the _ _ _ to finish our military campaign, the PNF must cease to exist, their cutting-edge PIRA must cease their campaign of genocide against the Protestant people, and their blowing up of our towns and cities must cease. Finally, all Dublin interference must end.

6. The _ _ _ exists because the Government has abdicated its responsibilities to defend the State, its citizens and their rights, by a continued policy of containment and appeasement to nationalists . . .

And yet, after the IRA ceasefire declaration of August 1994, despite all of the concerns and doubts, loyalists put down the next brick for the foundations of peace, by declaring their own ceasefire on 13 October 1994.

Combined Loyalist Military Command Statement, 13 October 1994

After a widespread consultative process, initiated by representations from the Ulster Democratic and Progressive Unionist Parties, and having received confirmation and guarantees in relation to Northern Ireland's constitutional position within the United Kingdom, as well as other assurances, and, in the belief that the democratically expressed wishes of the greater number of people in Northern Ireland will be respected and upheld, the CLMC will universally cease all operational hostilities, as from 12 midnight on Thursday, 13 October 1994. The permanence of our ceasefire will be completely dependent upon the continued cessation of all nationalist/republican violence: the sole responsibility for a return to war lies with them.

In the genuine hope that this peace will be permanent, we take the opportunity to pay homage to all our fighters, commandos and volunteers who have paid the supreme sacrifice. They did not die in vain. The Union is safe. To our physically and mentally wounded, who have served Ulster so unselfishly, we wish a speedy recovery, and to the relatives of these men and women, we pledge our continued moral and practical support. To our

---

My first reaction must be one of sorrow - and shame.

It is sorrow not only at the tragic loss of lives of men and women, and even children, but also at the much larger crowd of those behind them, those bereaved of loved ones, those bearing in their minds and bodies the wounds and disabilities inflicted by this ongoing violence, of homes shattered and honest businesses destroyed.

It is shame that it has gone on so long, how there still seems to be no end in sight -- and how for most of us these casualties become no more than statistics.

But there is also a deep sense of failure in these figures

the utter failure of this violence to do anything more than lead to further violence and destruction, enmity and division, bitterness and hatreds, fears and suspicions -- xxxxxxxxxx

and of how urgently we must try to impress on all who engage in, support or find excuses for this violence the utter futility of such policies for achieving peace or justice, or anything but the reverse

and recognise how easily it becomes addictive, with the delusion that success may come with stepping up the violence, having one more heave.

No shooting or bombing or intimidation should be seen by anyone as a successful operation, but rather as a failure that we have not found a better way -- whether we're thinking as loyalists or republicans, unionists or nationalists, security forces or politicians -- or most of all as the plain people of this province, who have not risen up to cry above all else "STOP IT NOW" but have been content to carry on our lives as long as we don't feel involved.

But we are involved, for violence and all that leads to and that goes with it doesn't start with the finger on the trigger or the hand that lays the bomb, but it starts in people's hearts and minds, in our ambitions and our attitudes to one another. We are all involved.

As John Donne said, "No man is an island ... any man's death diminishes me. And therefore never send to know for whom the bell tolls, it tolls for thee" -- and me, 3,000 times

"We are all involved." Dr Jack Weir, writing in 1992. *(Elle Rowan)*

Check Against Delivery:

April 4th 2010

Peace; Equality; Jobs and Unity

A chairde,

Tá mé lán sásta seasamh anseo libh inniu ar Domhnach na Cásca seo le smaoineadh ar ár gcomrádaithe a chuaigh romhainn agus a caint faoi an todhcaí.

Is cuimhin linn an méid a thug ár laochraí cróga ar son saoirse na tíre seo, an méid a chaill siad.

Cuidíonn seo linn nuair a bhíonn fadhbanna againn nó nuair a bhíonn muid traochta.

I want to welcome you all here today.

Easter Sunday is a special day. Especially here in Belfast.

It is a day to remember, to honour, and to celebrate all those republicans of our generation and other generations who gave their lives in the struggle for Irish freedom and justice.

Belfast republicans are proud of our patriot dead; we are proud of their families, we are proud of our struggle and we are proud of our history.

Belfast is where the United Irish men and women committed to ending the connection with Britain.

This is the city where James Connolly organised the working men and women, and particularly the women against sweat shop exploitation.

In 1916 he went from the Falls Road to join with the Irish Volunteers, the Irish Citizen Army, Cumann na mBan and Na Fianna to take on the might of the British Empire.

This is the city where Sean MacDiarmada joined the Irish Republican Brotherhood.

1

extraordinary sacrifices and displayed great courage in pursuit of freedom and justice and Irish unity.

I am proud to have been part of all that.

During this phase of the struggle some of us had to leave our families and homes, go on the run, adapt many ruses, go under false names.

We relied totally on the support of the people to protect us.

And we, in turn, protected the people as best we could.

We did not divulge their names, their roles, their actions.

That is still my position. That was the bond of comradeship and loyalty which was forged between us.

And let no one think that I will bend to the demands of anti-republican elements or their allies in a hostile section of the media on this issue.

I am also very conscious of the human cost of the war and the great hurt inflicted by republicans.

I have acknowledged this and my regret for this many times. And I do so again today.

There are victims and citizens who want to know the truth about what happened to loved ones during the conflict.

That is their right. I cannot demand truth for victims of British terrorism, collusion or unionist terror without supporting the same right for victims of republican actions.

That is why Sinn Féin supports the establishment of an effective independent and international truth recovery process.

I certainly would be prepared to be part of such a process and I would encourage others to participate.

I am glad the war is over.

4

"I am glad the war is over." Gerry Adams' speech, Easter 2010. *(Elle Rowan)*

Left: "If ever there was an uncomfortable conversation, this was it." Rev Harold Good, describing a private meeting between Gerry Adams and Alan McBride. *(Elle Rowan)*

Above: "Significant and symbolic." Alan McBride, commenting on that conversation with Gerry Adams. *(Elle Rowan)*

Top and above: Gerry Adams and Alan McBride, both pictured at a West Belfast Festival event, August 2015. *(Photograph courtesy of Antrim Lens)*

Left: "I had been carrying the coffins of IRA volunteers since I was a teenager." Belfast republican Jim Gibney *(Elle Rowan)*

Above: The 1994 IRA
ceasefire – republican
steps into a different
place. *(MT Hurson)*

Right: "Seize the moment":
An Phoblacht report on the
1994 ceasefire. *(Elle Rowan)*

Opposite: "Who a person is,
is more than a single layer
of experience or action."
Louise Little. *(Elle Rowan)*

Above: "I was 13. Teenage times had begun." Judith Hill, thinking back to the 1994 ceasefires. *(Elle Rowan)*

Right: Twenty years after the ceasefire – Brian Rowan and Judith Hill at the West Belfast Festival, 2014. *(Courtesy of Alan Meban)*

Left: "The past cannot be parked." Paul Doherty. *(Elle Rowan)*

Top: UFF statement in response to Shankill bomb, October 1993. *(Elle Rowan)*

THE NORTHERN COMMAND OF THE UFF ISSUED THE FOLLOWING STATEMENT

THIS AFTERNOON THE LOYALIST PEOPLE OF WEST BELFAST HAVE BEEN AT THE RECEIVING END OF A BLATANTLY INDISCRIMINATE BOMB ATTACK SUPPOSEDLY AIMED AT THE LEADERSHIP OF THE UFF. THE NUMBER OF WOMEN AND CHILDREN KILLED AND INJURED IS STILL UNCLEAR LEADS A LIE TO THE FALSE CLAIMS. AS FROM 1800 HOURS TONIGHT ALL BRIGADE AREA ACTIVE SERVICE UNITS OF THE UFF ACROSS ULSTER WILL BE FULLY MOBILISED. JOHN HUME/GERRY ADAMS AND THE NATIONALIST ELECTORATE WILL PAY A HEAVY, HEAVY PRICE FOR TODAY'S ATROCITY WHICH WAS SIGNED SEALED AND DELIVERED BY THE CUTTING EDGE OF THE PAN NATIONALIST FRONT AND FINALLY TO THE PERPRETRATORS OF TODAYS ATROCITY WE SAY THIS. THERE WILL BE NO HIDING PLACE TIME IS ON OUR SIDE AND TO HUME IS THIS PART OF YOUR PEACE PROCESS.

Right: UDA prisoners' statement in response to the Joint Declaration, 1994. *(Elle Rowan)*

U.D.A - P.O.W's RESPONSE TO JOINT DECLARATION.

This document was compiled at the request of the U.D.A. inner-council. It contains a summary of the concerns and opinions of U.D.A. P.O.W.s on the Joint Declaration - Downing Street, 15th December 1993.

Each U.D.A. P.O.W. was in the first instance, asked to participate in a series of meetings within U.D.A. wings H.M.P. Maze. The meetings of groups of between eight to ten P.O.W.s were held during the period 19 - 20 December 1993.

We recognize that the Joint Declaration, Downing Street, 15 December 1993, contains some positive points. Particularly the reaffirmation in paragraph 4 to "uphold the democratic wish of a greater number of the people of Northern Ireland..." and "to exercise their right of self - determination on the basis of consent..."

However, given previous assurances by the British and Eire Governments, especially prior to the signing of the Anglo - Irish agreement on 15 November, 1985; we find it very difficult to place our full confidence in the Joint Declaration.

Given also, that the Joint Declaration was brought about in no small measure, by the actions of the Provisional Movement. In the background of many secret discussions and deals with the I.R.A. Neither Government has given us reason to place our trust in them.

Similarly, we do not feel we could ever trust the Republican Movement, and we have severe reservations as to whether any cease-fire would be genuine. We doubt the ability of the Republican Movement to control a complete cessation of violence and believe that Republican splinter groups would emerge to continue the conflict.

We feel the present situation to be very serious and volatile. While fully exploring the present "scenarios for peace" we believe now, more than at any time in the history of the present conflict, our organisation should prepare for war. Not only should we be aware of, and prepare for internment; in the event of the situation deteriorating further, we are of the opinion that our organisation should work to their own agenda.

Contrary to media speculation, amnesty is not an issue, and is "of very low priority" to U.D.A. P.O.W.s. All P.O.W.s are agreed, that the investment they have put into the cause, should not be bartered in any discussion, and we stress we do not want the council to feel constrained by it in their deliberations, in any way. The consensus of opinion is that the present situation is much too serious to even think of amnesties.

We realise that our own council will have to make many serious and difficult decisions in the coming months. We are extremely happy with our councils handling of the situation to date, and we pledge our full support and allegiance for them to continue to do that which is right; regardless of what this may entail for us.

It is difficult to summarise our response to the Joint Declaration; however, one U.D.A. P.O.W. stated:

"We'll be dammed if we do,
We'll be dammed if we don't,
And, we'll be dammed if we
Let them do it to us!"

4. IF PIRA REJECT DECLARATION THEN NOTHING CHANGES AS FAR AS WE ARE CONCERNED. OUR WAR AGAINST THE PAN NATIONALIST FRONT WILL CONTINUE.

5. FOR THE --- TO FINISH OUR MILITARY CAMPAIGN THE P.N.F. MUST CEASE TO EXIST THEIR CUTTING EDGE PIRA MUST CEASE THEIR CAMPAIGN OF GENOCIDE AGAINST THE PROTESTANT PEOPLE AND THEIR BLOWING UP OF OUR TOWNS + CITIES MUST CEASE. FINALLY ALL DUBLIN INTERFERENCE MUST END.

6. THE --- EXISTS BECAUSE THE GOVERNMENT HAS ABDICATED ITS RESPONSIBILITIES TO DEFEND THE STATE, ITS CITIZENS AND THEIR RIGHTS, BY A CONTINUED POLICY OF CONTAINMENT AND APPEASEMENT TO NATIONALISTS.

7. THE --- TOTALLY REJECT ANY SUGGESTION THAT OUR CAMPAIGN IS RANDOM. OUR VOLS HAVE DEMONSTRATED THAT WE CAN STRIKE DEEP INTO THE HEART OF REPUBLICAN AREAS AT IDENTIFIED TARGETS BOTH NORTH AND SOUTH OF THE BORDER. OUR VOLS HAVE ALSO CARRIED OUT ATTACKS ON EIRE POLITIC TARGETS IN EIRE. WE HAVE DEMONSTRATED OUR DESIRE FOR PEACE AND STABILITY WITH OUR PARTICIPATION IN THE 12 WEEK CEASEFIRE IN CONJUNCTION WITH OUR COMRADES IN THE CLMC. AT THE BEGINNING OF THE BROOKE TALKS. MORE RECENTLY, AGAIN THROUGH THE CLMC, WE HAVE PRESENTED SIX POINTS WHICH WE FEEL COULD BRING ABOUT PEACE + STABILITY.

Left: Handwritten briefing from loyalists with the initials 'UFF' excluded, 1994. *(Elle Rowan)*

Right: Pages turn from conflict to ceasefire. *(Elle Rowan)*

NEW ULSTER DEFENDER

War Commentary

Reported actions of the Ulster Freedom Fighters

Ulster Defender

A Progressive Democratic Process...

Ceasefire

On the 13th October 1994 the Combined Loyalist Military Command - comprising the leadership of the UDA, the UVF and the Red Hand Commando - announced a universal cessation to their military operations.

It was no accident that the C.L.M.C. choose representatives from the Ulster Democratic and Progressive Unionist parties to announce the historic decision they had taken nor was it coincidental that Fernhill House on the edge of the Glencairn estate in West Belfast, which was the headquarters of the old UDA, was chosen as the venue for the press conference called by the two parties.

Since 1989 both the UDP and the PUP have made themselves available to the CLMC to provide their views on political developments in the province. It is widely known that representatives of both parties are considered to be honest brokers who are determined that our country comes before party or personality and are trusted to provide the loyalist leadership with an honest appraisal of how they see political developments affecting the loyalist people of Northern Ireland. This in itself must be considered as novel as most unionist representatives in Ulster are not famed for allowing the betterment of their country to stand in the way of personal or party advancement. This was never better indicated than in the recent underhand and cowardly campaign of black propoganda which has been directed at members of the UDP and the PUP, from "unionist" sources fearful of electoral challenge, since the CLMC ceasefire.

The increasing political influence of the UDP and PUP on the thinking of the CLMC was first evidenced in 1991 when the loyalist leadership suspended their military campaign to facilitate the Brooke talks. The loyalist ceasefire held solid despite severe provocation by the IRA who launched a bombing campaign against Protestant housing estates in an attempt to goad the loyalists into retaliation. The 1991 ceasefire only ended when the Brooke talks collapsed in failure. But an important signal had been sent out by the CLMC, and that was that they were indeed serious when they talked about accepting - and indeed were willing to facilitate and encourage - an agreed settlement worked out between the elected representatives of Northern Ireland. The problem, as ever, was that the elected representatives here, almost without exception, seemed almost incapable of agreeing on what day of the week it was never mind what was best for the country. Indeed there are still some amongst them who can barely hide their disappointment that the violence has been ended.

Against this political backdrop and with the IRA's sectarian murder campaign continuing unabated the CLMC returned to war - with a vengeance.

With the coming together of the SDLP, Sinn Fein and the Dublin government in a pan-nationalist front, the CLMC in December 1993 called on all unionist and

3

"The first thing we had to think about was how to demilitarise."
Retired RUC officer Roy Dunn (right), photographed with former
Chief Constable Sir Hugh Annesley. *(Roy Dunn personal collection)*

Roy Dunn (right) at his policing graduation. *(Roy Dunn personal
collection)*

Left: RUC Information Forum 1995. *(Elle Rowan)*

AGENDA - RUC INFORMATION FORUM ON POLICING
WEDNESDAY, 15 MARCH 1995

9.30 am - 10.00 am	Arrival and Registration
10.00 am - 10.15 am	Welcome and Opening Address The Chief Constable - Sir Hugh Annesley, QPM
10.15 am - 10.25 am	Crime Assistant Chief Constable R C White, BEM, LLB
10.25 am - 10.35 am	Drugs D/Chief Inspector A Green
10.30 am - 10.55 am	Question Session
10.55 am - 11.30 am	Coffee Break
11.30 am - 11.40 am	Recruiting and Equal Opportunities Chief Inspector J Lindsay
11.40 am - 11.50 am	Complaints and Discipline Assistant Chief Constable A O Hays, OBE, BA
11.50 am - 12.15 pm	Question Session
12.15 pm - 1.30 pm	Lunch
1.30 pm - 1.40 pm	Special Branch Assistant Chief Constable R Flanagan, BA
1.40 pm - 1.50 pm	Community Affairs Chief Insp
1.50 pm - 2.00 pm	The role Superinte
2.00 pm - Close	Final Qu

Below: "The outstanding issue for comment, and one largely unheralded, is that in the face of rampant terrorism the RUC has managed to deliver a normal policing service at all." Then Chief Constable Sir Hugh Annesley, speaking at the RUC Information Forum. *(Elle Rowan)*

Over the last 6 months, as you know, Northern Ireland has experienced the momentous change of almost complete peace after a quarter of a century of terrorist violence. The process that brought us to this point had many strands, but that we are here at all is due in large measure to the sacrifice, commitment and success of the RUC, so bravely supported by the Army. As we continue to review our approach to policing in this new situation, some of our critics might like to ponder this:

'it should not be a surprise that occasionally our actions have led to criticism. The outstanding issue for comment, and one largely unheralded, is that in the face of rampant terrorism the RUC has managed to deliver a normal policing service at all - which it so clearly has done'.

Today I publicly salute r
military colleagues, mem
public who so stoutly su
countless lives, and for averting atrocity a
intelligence, that 4 out of every 5 planned terrorist attacks were thwa
can take it that throughout the campaign of violence, virtually every anti-terrorist
success had a Special Branch dimension. It must too be stressed that these
successes were achieved in a completely even handed way right across all
paramilitary groupings. In the quite proper drive to be more open about our work,
we will never of course say or do anything which would risk exposing to danger
those who have been pivotal in standing between order and anarchy.

What then does Special Branch do? Well, simply stated, our major objectives are:-

1

Above: "We will never of course say or do anything which would risk exposing to danger those who have been pivotal in standing between order and anarchy." Then Head of Special Branch, Ronnie Flanagan. *(Elle Rowan)*

Above: "I never went to my bed at night wondering who I might shoot, kill, bomb or maim." Peter Sheridan, former Assistant Chief Constable. *(Elle Rowan)*

Left: "Not one person has been held accountable for any of it." Andrée Murphy of Relatives for Justice, speaking about collusion. *(Elle Rowan)*

Secretary of State, you have now the platform to make the two statements that we long to hear: that the future of policing lies with the RUC and that the future of my members lies within that RUC.

Thank you.

Top: Reassurances sought at the Police Federation Conference, June 1995. *(Elle Rowan)*

Right: Reassurances given by then Secretary of State, Sir Patrick Mayhew at the 1995 Police Federation Conference. *(Elle Rowan)*

Below: Twenty years later, handshakes that were once unthinkable. Deputy First Minister Martin McGuinness and PSNI Chief Constable George Hamilton at the West Belfast Festival, August 2015. *(Photograph courtesy of Antrim Lens)*

SECRETARY OF STATE'S SPEECH: POLICE FEDERATION CONFERENCE

INTRODUCTION

Mr Rodgers, Ladies and Gentlemen;

I wonder whether, if challenged, a statement obtained in that style and in the presence of about 160 police officers would be admitted as a voluntary statement. At least there is an audio and video recording of the interview.

But the question is academic. For there will be no subsequent resiling from the statement I am about to make.

(i) The future of policing in NI does rest with the RUC; and

(ii) Your members' future as police officers does lie within the RUC.

I will go further. It will be an RUC whose Chief Constable continues to provide one pillar of a tri-partite structure for its control and administration, and his operational independence will continue to be assured.

I am delighted to have the opportunity to address this, my fourth Police Federation Conference.

As the ceasefires continue to hold, and the full horror of the daily litany of terrorist atrocities is, we hope, becoming established as a thing of the past, we must not lose our sense of perspective. All our present challenges and uncertainties pale into insignificance beside the memory - the living memory - of that which called forth the sacrifices made over the last 25 years by the officers of the RUC and its Reserves, their comrades in the armed forces, and their families. We will not forget those sacrifices; indeed our remembrance of them provides the spur to our endeavours to build, on a firm foundation of democracy, trust and mutual respect, an established and enduring peace.

prisoners, who have undergone so much deprivation and degradation with great courage and forbearance, we solemnly promise to leave no stone unturned to secure their freedom. To our serving officers, NCOs and personnel, we extend our eternal gratitude for their obedience to orders, for their ingenuity, resilience and good humour in the most trying of circumstances, and we commend them for their courageous fortitude and unshakable faith over the long years of armed confrontation.

In all sincerity, we offer to the loved ones of all innocent victims over the past 25 years, abject and true remorse. No words of ours will compensate for the intolerable suffering they have undergone during the conflict.

Let us firmly resolve to respect our differing views of freedom, culture and aspiration, and never again permit our political circumstances to degenerate into bloody warfare. We are on the threshold of a new and exciting beginning, with our battles in future being political battles, fought on the side of honesty, decency and democracy against the negativity of mistrust, misunderstanding and malevolence, so that, together, we can bring forth a wholesome society in which our children, and their children, will know the meaning of true peace.

This statement, read at a news conference by Gusty Spence, represented joined-up loyalist thinking – both military and political. The Combined Loyalist Military Command, or CLMC, represented the Ulster Defence Association, the Ulster Volunteer Force and the closely-associated Red Hand Commando. They chose to speak through the voice of Spence, but his words stretched across loyalism to also represent prisoners, as well as the small political parties, the UDP and the PUP. These parties would then become the new voice of loyalism in the political developments that would follow: people such as David Ervine, Gary McMichael, Billy Hutchinson, Davy Adams and William "Plum" Smith. At this early stage, there was a sense of momentum, as one statement or initiative prompted or encouraged another and, in no time, the focus of the pages of the loyalist magazines turned from a commentary on the war to the news of a ceasefire.

In August 2014, I was invited, with fellow journalists Eamonn Mallie and Charlie Bird, to speak at the West Belfast Festival, Féile an Phobail, on the theme of the 31 August Declaration, on which we had reported those 20 years previously. Our audience included people much better placed than we were to contextualise that day: one-time senior and significant IRA figures, but who cannot yet tell their stories or give their perspective on events. There is no mechanism as yet in place to release them to make their contributions to the conversations on the past: there is still ongoing investigation and, with that, the prospect of arrest, prosecution and perhaps even jail. In similar vein, are the loyalist leaderships going to name those who gave the orders for the attacks that spanned the decades of conflict? Are they going to name those who were sent to carry out these attacks, or those who determined their organisation's strategies, and who wrote or dictated the words of their statements? The answer to those questions is no. Any answering or explanations of the past, especially before a structure is set securely in place, will not come with that kind of specific or individual detail. This needs to be understood.

That Festival event in August 2014, at which I and fellow correspondents spoke, was chaired by the Ulster Television journalist, Judith Hill. Although Judith was just 13 when the ceasefires were announced, it was felt that she would be able to bring the thinking of a different generation to the discussion; something she has also done below in a contribution for this book, which focuses on the value of authentic story-telling and the possible next steps of the peace journey.

Judith Hill, Reporter, UTV

Those ceasefire images – of cars with flags being flown out the windows, and men sitting at tables, reading out prepared words from sheets of paper – are grainy in my mind, but they are etched there. I was 13. Teenage times had begun. Back then, my teenage self didn't know that I'd end up reporting on news here, and on the evolving journey of peace. Back then, I'd no appreciation of the thousands of behind-the-scenes conversations that made those grainy images possible. Back then, few were to know that it would take another four years for a peace accord to be signed. That day came one day [after] my 17th birthday. Adulthood beckoned.

As a journalist, the peace process has been my reporting context. Unlike the generation before me, it's not so often to the bullet and the bomb that we react. But everyday news can still often reflect a negotiation between the past and the present, as those with influence – and all of us actually – try to work out what this peace thing is. But as that working out continues, authentic storytelling needs to be right at the core of it. In the very heart of the communities, where labels and stereotypes have been strongest, lies the secret to unlocking the next phase of the peace journey. For many, it hasn't felt safe to storytell yet. Fear and control can go hand in hand; they need to lose their hold.

My career as a journalist has progressed as the peace process has unfolded, and sometimes unravelled. It makes me wonder (and it's an odd question): if the peace process was a person, what phase of life would it now be in? If we're counting by birthdays – it's hit the big 2-1. So, what's next? I hope that what is next will see communities – and all of us – own our stories and not be bound by them. That there will be freedom in communities for people to bravely share their testimonies. So that heartfelt stories get the free space they deserve and need to change each of us, while changing this place we all call home.

Interestingly, in its October 1994 statement, the Combined Loyalist Military Command made reference to "innocent victims" and, more than two decades later, a battle continues over the very definition of victimhood, and how to distinguish between who was hurt and who did the hurting. There are those who argue vehemently that the two should and must be separated. At the time, Gusty Spence told me he intended his comments to be interpreted in the widest possible sense: "I was speaking about every injustice that had been perpetrated: by Protestant on Catholic, or Catholic on Protestant, or government on people." Today's debate is focused on how far the term "victim" should stretch or be stretched.

Kathryn Stone, who was Victims' Commissioner in Northern Ireland in the period 2012–2014, has heard and deeply reflected on all of the arguments.

Kathryn Stone, NI Victims' Commissioner, September 2012 – July 2014

Who is a victim? Who isn't? Millions of words must have already been swallowed up, arguing, debating and discussing this. It occupied most of my time as Commissioner for Victims and Survivors. Indeed [this question] was argued, debated and discussed long before me and will be argued, debated and discussed long after me.

The African-American civil rights activist, Maya Angelou said: "People will forget what you said. People will forget what you did. But people will never forget how you made them feel." So, how do I feel, a year, and more, on from leaving? I feel privileged and proud to have served; but saddened to see little progress. Every person I met was important: every injured or bereaved person; every person trying to care for someone broken by their experiences; all of them, important. Every tiny fragment made up the picture. Every group I visited knew what pain felt like and expressed it in raw, visceral ways. It was often incredibly difficult to listen to, but was no less legitimate than the group up the road, who represented "the other". I left certain that no one had more right to victim status than anyone else. For every victim's reaction, there was an equal, opposite one.

A commitment to working towards reconciliation and better understanding has to be the goal of any funded group: no commitment and no demonstrated outcomes, no money. I sat with victims who mourned the loss of their loved ones, their independence and the life they once had. It mattered to me that they were respected as individuals, whatever their faith or politics. Demonstrating this must be the ambition of any shared society. Without that fundamental understanding, there will be no sustainable peace process – and no peace of mind for victims and survivors.

Gusty Spence's granddaughter, Louise Little, was 16 when the ceasefires were declared in 1994. Today, she believes this argument over the definitions of "victim" and "perpetrator" is much too narrow; that there are other layers that should be carefully explained and explored.

Louise Little, granddaughter of the late Gusty Spence

As a result of my faith, my upbringing and my experience, I believe that the suffering of those from all sections of society – who lost their lives, their loved ones, their limbs and the lives they once had or dreamt of – cannot be justified.

Some difficult experiences continue to teach me about the "layers" of people, and that it can be unhelpful to define people as a single layer of their experience or role, or as simply innocent or guilty. As a mother is not only a mother, so a victim is not only a victim, nor a perpetrator of violence only a perpetrator of violence. Who a person is, is more than a single layer of experience or action. I believe that at the core, at the beginning of a person, before understanding, experience of life or conflict, there is an innocence. Simple and pure. This core of a person always exists, but the layers of life, the experiences and understanding that are added to [it], shape what each person becomes, how they are perceived and understood, and what they do.

Often, we select the layer of the person we want to focus on, and magnify it – this becomes the definition of who they are: a victim, an ex-prisoner, a police officer, and so on. But it doesn't reflect the experiences that went before or those that came after. Nor does it allow for the possibility that people can and do change. While the layers of their lives: their actions, deeds or inactions, do not dissolve away, they are more than that single layer or experience.

> To seek to understand the person, and to learn from the past, is to create a new layer of understanding in oneself – to dare to dig deeply, and carefully, into the layers of life.

More than two decades after the original ceasefires, such questions dominate the continuing debates and arguments over the past. Should the "combatants", all of them, be considered as falling under that description, "victim"? What about the roles of the military, the British Security Service MI5 and the RUC's Special Branch within the conflict? What about the part played by agents, and those who handled and managed them? How should we even describe what happened – was it a war, a terrorist campaign, a conflict, or something else? Who decided on the label, "the Troubles"? These are just some of the many unanswered questions.

What is clear, is that we still live in a place of sides, of angry words, of divided communities, even though so much has changed. However, there is a lot that is unchanged, and this thing that we label as "the past" is still very much with us. Some think that the questions from the past might die with the conflict generation. This is a flawed analysis; the false hopes and unrealistic wishes of some. Stories, experiences and questions are passed from one generation to the next, until they are acknowledged and addressed.

In 1974, 20 years before the ceasefires, Jim Doherty was killed by a UVF bomb. His son, Paul is still asking questions – questions which confirm that the past cannot be outlived, and that many will continue to wait, however long, for a day of answers and answering – for accountability and some acknowledgement.

Paul Doherty, son of 1974 pub bomb victim, Jim Doherty

On 2 May 1974 at 10.07 p.m., the UVF set off a no-warning bomb in a bar on Belfast's Ormeau Road, killing six men, including my Dad. Why? Perhaps it was to protect the union, the thinking being that by the brutal intimidation of innocents, perhaps republican violence would subside. History teaches us this is a flawed strategy. Revenge, retribution for lost British/Protestant lives perhaps – but this is futile, reminiscent of Jihadist violence and just as productive. Recreational killing, rite-of-passage or [the] marking [of] territory, whatever the reason, none of them are just.

Four boys, aged 16 and 17, were convicted of the bombing, [but] they didn't plan it or assemble [the device]. To get to the truth and come to terms with the past, we need to hear from those who did. We cannot ignore our past: it forms us, shapes our future and occupies our present.

Yet the space for dealing with the past does not exist in Northern Ireland.

Our current politicians are incompetent, that's one view, and, while it may be true of some, it surely cannot be the case for all. Rather, I believe, they are frozen in time, rigid with fear of losing power, of diminishing the green or orange head count. Therefore, their masters continue to be the hard-line voters on both sides of the sectarian divide. So long as that continues and the vacuum of real political debate persists, no progress can be made in moving this society forward. But there is no alternative, I hear you say: well, that is true – no viable one currently.

So what must happen, in the absence of leadership from our elected representatives, is that society must lead them. Create the debate; marginalise the hard-line politicians; open up the past; let the truth quench the drought of intransigence, thereby dragging our politicians with us. The past cannot be parked, put into storage or left for future generations to hypothesise or write essays about. It is a live issue, an urgent one that cannot be outlived; it must be dealt with.

These are words that place the past in the present, demonstrating that it is still here, more than 20 years after the first of the ceasefires, and 40 years after Paul's father was killed. Still with us and still waiting for some process; some creative thinking and some courage; some leadership and some new way. In the delay in finding an agreed way of talking about and recording the past, important memory is being lost. David Ervine, Gusty Spence and Jim McDonald, all of whom had seats at that loyalist top table on 13 October 1994, are now dead. So too are the unionist political leaders of that period: James Molyneaux and Ian Paisley. The then Taoiseach Albert Reynolds has also since died – a man who was critical to that period, because he was someone at a high political level prepared to take the necessary risks and to make deals, authorising conversations within both the republican and loyalist communities and ultimately persuading Prime Minister Major and President Clinton of the possibilities for peace. Gone too is Father Alec Reid, who so often acted as a key conduit in facilitating meetings and communicating messages in the crucial behind-the-scenes dialogues that were happening pre-1994.

With their passing, their stories, understandings, explanations and context have been lost. Significant contributions are missing, and others are left to try to fill in the gaps. And, without any agreed process, there is still silence on the part of the living too – the people who would have been key to the IRA and CLMC decision-making of 1994, some of whom had significant doubts at that time, and about what developed afterwards. All of this means that the record is missing important information and, in the long wait for some agreed and structured process on the past, memory and detail are being lost. This is what happens when processes are delayed or become stuck or are deliberately stalled.

Now, more than 20 years after the first of the ceasefire statements, and that meeting with the IRA's spokesperson, we can see 1994 much more clearly – what it meant and did not mean. There was not just one ceasefire, but two, that many parties worked very long and very hard for. They were a beginning towards some better end; not perfect or complete, but the first steps out of a war mindset that were probably the hardest to take.

Since then, it has been a long and arduous path. We have had more killing, struggles over decommissioning and demilitarisation, the tug-of-war between prisoners' rights and those of victims, the devolution of politics and policing, and the continuing threat posed by dissidents. That takes us through to today, where the past is as yet unaddressed, and the political institutions at Stormont still stumble and falter, constantly having to be stabilised. More than 20 years on, these are today's realities. Those announcements in 1994 and what they represented, despite all the flaws, should never be taken for granted. Just look around the world at escalating conflict in so many places, and you can see the progress that has been made here in Northern Ireland/the North. More needs to be done, but so much has already been achieved.

CHAPTER THREE
February 1996: The Ceasefire Cracks

"In 1994, the Provisional IRA called a 'ceasefire' to their paramilitary campaign. . . At the time it was believed that this was finally the end of hostilities, and we as police officers could begin to change our policing strategies and style to suit a more normal peaceful society."
Retired RUC Chief Inspector, Roy Dunn, writing for this book.

"Eventually its [the IRA leadership's] patience snapped and it resumed the campaign (though not at full blast), until a new government – one willing to negotiate – came to power."
Former Sinn Féin Publicity Director and IRA leader, Danny Morrison, writing for this book.

"We took a unilateral decision [to declare the 1994 ceasefire], but if your analysis is that there's no dividend, no return, how do you justify continuing that strategy?"
A former senior IRA leader, in conversation with the author in 2015.

The ceasefires were delivered into a vacuum and not into structured peace negotiations. There was no talks table, nothing to indicate that inclusive negotiations were about to begin. Instead, what followed was a stand-off over what should happen next, and whose move it was next. Those first steps into a new place were also steps into uncertainty, away from that old, familiar territory of conflict and killing, declarations of war and condemnation, within which some were more comfortable and sure of themselves. Now things were different, with a new set of challenges, and in some ways it was a bit like learning to walk all over again.

So, in the early days of the ceasefires, responses and reactions to the new situation were not sure-footed but, rather, stuttering and stumbling – and perhaps even stubborn and intransigent. Was anyone really ready for this new day? There was some cosmetic tinkering with security, there were some exploratory talks involving government officials and Sinn Féin and loyalist representatives and, almost immediately, there was a move to try to achieve the decommissioning of arms. We know now that the way in which this was approached, and the terms in which it was framed, were all wrong. Indeed, it could be argued that these were unthinking – and even provocative. There was talk of the need for "decontamination" and "quarantine", for the establishing of some kind of certainty that the ceasefire was intended as permanent, with a call for the decommissioning of arms as proof of this.

This was the mud in which the process became mired. At this time, back in the mid-1990s, all the focus was on the IRA as an organisation and the arms in its arsenal and, for republicans, the demands being made in this regard felt very much like an attempt by the other "side" to force a surrender from them, as a means of securing a victory by other, or different, means. Eventually, the foundation brick of the ceasefire would crack. Danny Morrison, former Publicity Director of Sinn Féin and a one-time senior IRA leader, watched that ceasefire come and go.

Danny Morrison, former Sinn Féin Publicity Director

We had been down the road of so many failed ceasefires, had been so case-hardened, wary and disillusioned, that it was obvious to me that the Movement would not have embarked on this one unless it represented a defining moment. Pat Sheehan and I were together in H4 [the Maze prison], when Radio Ulster announced [news of] the IRA statement. Pat was into the fifth year of a 20-year sentence, having previously served ten years; he had been "on the blanket", and was the last and longest on hunger strike, when the hunger strike ended in October 1981. Although all prisoners had a vested interest in a political settlement and early release, most IRA prisoners viewed the ceasefire – its potential and its dangers – from a selfless, principled position, tempered by pragmatism and the reality of there being a military stalemate.

I had privately, much earlier, come around to the belief that the IRA should cease fire and that the struggle had to risk its future on politics exclusively. Nevertheless, in September 1994, all of us POWs were so incensed at the subsequent list of demands from the British and unionists – which appeared to be a deliberate attempt to scuttle the peace initiative – that we all would have understood, had the IRA removed its offer from the table and resumed its campaign. Indeed, the commitment to armed struggle would have been reinforced. But that would have been to react emotionally and not strategically. Instead, the leadership remained steady. Eventually, though, its patience snapped and it resumed the campaign (though not at full blast), until a new government – one willing to negotiate – came to power.

Ironically, certain IRA leadership figures, whom I would have anticipated opposing the peace process, supported it. Others, whom I would have predicted enthusiastically supporting a ceasefire, went on to organise a dissident campaign, which was never going to be able to replicate the tempo of the IRA campaign, and which has proven to be militarily pathetic and futile.

Twenty years ago, a Tory government undermined the peace process. In 2015, another Tory government, by threatening to remove a cornerstone of the Belfast Agreement – the European Convention on Human Rights – [has] thereby [brought] back powerful memories of September 1994.

Now, when we follow the paper trail of this period – the weeks and months that followed the 1994 ceasefire announcements – the mistakes appear much more obvious. At the time, the UUP, then the largest of the unionist parties, produced a document entitled, "Dealing with Terrorism – Disbandment, and Decommissioning of Weapons". The ceasefires were but a few months old and, already, in this Paper, unionists were suggesting an International Disarmament Commission. At this early stage, part of what they wanted to do also was to "portray the IRA as it really is", that is, "an intact, well-armed terrorist organisation", with a view to exposing it to "the full glare of world attention". Too much was being expected too soon – and it was being demanded by the wrong people.

In the same period, speaking in the United States, the then British Secretary of State, Sir Patrick Mayhew delivered this assessment of the IRA:

Sinn Féin undoubtedly does have a democratic mandate in Northern Ireland, though a lot less than Mr Hume's nationalist party, the SDLP. But it is inextricably linked with the Irish Republican Army and that Army [is]:

- still in being;
- still maintaining its arsenal;
- still recruiting;
- still targeting;
- still training;
- still researching improvised weapons;

[and] not least, . . . still seeking funds to maintain its operations, and still carrying out, on a greater scale than before the ceasefire, brutal punishment beatings in the community.

At this time, Mayhew wanted three things: a willingness in principle on the part of the IRA to disarm progressively; an understanding on the methodology or modalities of that; some actual decommissioning as a tangible, confidence-building measure, and to signal the start of a process. He concluded: "That is how Sinn Féin can remove their self-imposed disqualification, and take their place at the talks table, where a lasting settlement can be negotiated upon equal terms." We now know that it would take more than a decade from this point for the IRA to formally end its armed campaign and to participate in significant acts of decommissioning. These processes would be spread over years, and not months.

So, what is our learning from this period, the lessons that can be shared with other conflict zones? One lesson is that these big questions are best addressed within negotiations, and not before. Dialogue works better than demands. You have to think outside and beyond the "enemy" relationship, and not just about what has happened – however painful – but what is now possible. The needs of all have to be considered – not just of some. The fact is that Mayhew and the unionist leadership failed to recognise how the republican community had also been hurt.

Did anyone really believe that the IRA would respond positively to the demands of the British Government and the unionist political leadership? Adams and McGuinness had already delivered the IRA ceasefire against the wishes of some. This is an important point, made in Danny Morrison's earlier contribution. The adoption by unionists and the British Government of what they may have considered to be perfectly reasonable positions ended up tipping the debate inside the IRA against Adams and McGuinness. They could no longer hold the ceasefire line. The Government and unionists did not believe in the ceasefire, did not believe the IRA, did not believe Adams and McGuinness; republicans did not believe the British or the unionists. The ceasefires had not pushed anything into the past. Instead, they had brought many things into sharper focus: the violence, the many hurts and the trauma of the preceding decades. The wars – all of them – were still too raw, too real and too present in people's minds and, to this day, for the many victims of this conflict, that remains the case.

There were all sorts of worries back in 1995, on the part of many different groups. The new ground on which we found ourselves brought with it new fears. Some of these, for example, were expressed at the Police Federation Conference in June that year, in a speech made by its Chairman at the time, Les Rodgers, in the presence of then Secretary of State, Patrick Mayhew. The

Federation represents thousands of officers up to and including the rank of Chief Inspector.

To this day, I have my notes from that Conference, detailing the questions and answers of that day – questions that would have different answers on another day. As such complex processes as the search for peace develop and progress, nothing is ever certain or absolute, no matter how convincingly it is said at the time. This has also been part of our learning. These are the shifting sands of peace-building, where what gets washed in may then be washed away again. This day at the Police Federation Conference would be no different. The delegates heard declarations made that seemed certain and unequivocal – only for these to be unsaid and undone again, on another date and another day.

Radio Ulster News Report (Brian Rowan), 6 June 1995

In his address, the Federation Chairman, Les Rodgers spoke of, "an uneasy and still hardening peace", and he went on to make three points. First, he said weapons must be decommissioned. Secondly, he emphasised that the Federation would not accept an amnesty or early release for convicted terrorists. And, thirdly, he said there should be no dismantling of the emergency legislation for the foreseeable future. Les Rodgers finished by addressing the Secretary of State. He told Sir Patrick he had a platform to make two statements: that the future of policing lies with the RUC; and that the future of Federation members lies within that RUC. The Secretary of State is due to reply shortly.

These occasions are, of course, stage-managed and choreographed. One speech knits into the next, and there are no dropped stitches. Mayhew was never likely to respond negatively to the questions put by Les Rodgers from such a public platform. And so, on the same day, the expected and the rehearsed answers were duly supplied by the Secretary of State: "The future of policing in Northern Ireland does rest with the RUC; and . . . your members' future as police officers does lie within the RUC."

All of that would change with time and in the course of negotiations, as we now know. But this Federation speech was an expression of real hurts, especially in its opposition to a prisoner amnesty or early release. "They can be released to begin their lives anew when they have served their sentences fully," Les Rodgers asserted. "The walk to freedom is more than their thousands of murdered and injured victims can take. They and their families are the ones who really got the life sentences, and whose lives cannot be put back together again. The innocent are still paying the price for terrorism, and so must the guilty."

At the time of that speech, almost 300 police lives had been lost in the conflict and, now, while others sought IRA demobilisation and disarmament, there was a republican demand for the RUC to be disbanded. These were the continuing tugs-of-war – and tugs-of-peace – and much of what we were hearing was a spilling out of emotions, an expression of real concerns about betrayal – as well as a preoccupation about who would "win" and who would "lose"; who was right and who was wrong.

New governments and the negotiations of a political process would eventually move things into a different place. Previous commitments and guarantees were forgotten, as if they had never been made. So, despite Mayhew's words back in 1995, the RUC as an entity would go, to be replaced by the Police Service of Northern Ireland (PSNI). This did not mean that the RUC disappeared from the narrative of the conflict. Quite the opposite has been the case. Today, 20 years on from Les Rodgers' speech, parts of the RUC are being scrutinised like never before. Suggestions about collusion between the authorities and paramilitary elements, which were rife long before the ceasefires, have come to be believed, and indeed, have been substantiated. These 20-plus years later, there is an unrelenting probing of the "dirty war", and specifically the roles of RUC Special Branch, British military intelligence, the British Security Service MI5 and the hundreds of agents they ran.

Numerous killings, going as far back as the 1970s, are now under a spotlight, with questions about who knew what, and when. Collusion is no longer dismissed as mere propaganda, but its existence is now understood to be a fact of the conflict. However, in this examination of past practices, there are concerns among former officers that the entire Force is being tarred with the collusion brush. Back in 1995, there was of course no such thing as Twitter, no such method of instant, public communication on a broad public platform. In 2015 however, 20 years later, we got an idea of the continuing hurt and anguish felt by police officers today, in a Twitter exchange between the current PSNI Chief Constable, George Hamilton and former RUC officer, Roy Dunn. Dunn had tweeted: "Please defend the 99 per cent of RUC officers who always tried to keep everyone alive, whatever their faith", to which Hamilton responded: "I was one of them and also remember many who were intimidated out of [their] homes by violent people from both sides!"

Roy Dunn had served in the RUC for over 30 years, retiring at chief inspector level. His tweet was a reaction to a television documentary investigation of a Special Branch unit, as he later explained: "Sadly, there was no one on the programme to defend the RUC, and answer these allegations . . . I thought it was so sad that, once again, the good name of the RUC was being dragged through the mud, and [that] there is no one left to defend it." Dunn's thinking will be shared by many who served in the RUC and who see this digging into the past as one-sided, or lop-sided. Dunn's own policing career was not in Special Branch.

Roy Dunn, retired RUC Chief Inspector

I joined the RUC in 1969, and served until I retired as a Chief Inspector in 2001. . . I never came across any so-called "collusion", as my colleagues and I really did try our best to keep everyone alive, irrespective of who they were . . .

I recall the murder of a man living off Broadway, close to the entrance to the Royal Victoria Hospital. We had been performing a Vehicle Check Point (VCP) on Broadway a short time before the murder. We lifted the check point and moved away from that area to another location. An hour or so later, the murder took place – and local politicians suggested that police lifted the check point to facilitate the murder and [that] this was, "yet another example of collusion between police and loyalist paramilitaries". This was very hurtful, as it was totally untrue. It was later established that the killers used a "clean scout car" to check the area, prior to them coming in. It had nothing to do with collusion.

In 1994 the Provisional IRA called a ceasefire to their paramilitary campaign . . . At the time, it was believed that this was finally the end of hostilities, and we as police officers could begin to change our policing strategies and style to suit a more normal, peaceful society. The first thing we had to think about was how to demilitarise. We firstly had to learn to patrol without army accompaniment both on foot and in vehicles. It was necessary to take everything incrementally and at a slow rate of progress, because there was always the threat of a hostile crowd surrounding isolated police officers, and inflicting serious injury. The murder of the two army corporals in Andersonstown in 1988 was never far from our minds.

. . . I look back on my time in "B" Division with great fondness. Of course, I lost some fine colleagues to terrorist attack, and one to a road traffic collision with a military vehicle . . . My colleagues and I always did our best to keep everyone alive and well, and to thwart any potential terrorist attack. We were always closing the Peaceline gates, as we wanted as much as anyone else to prevent loss of life. There was never any talk or indication of collusion, as we would never have allowed or condoned it.

Dunn's words speak of his personal experiences as a policeman and his 30-plus years of service. There is no mechanism out there, no official archiving process yet established, to enable him to record that account in any formal way. The telling of his, and of many other similar experiences, would bring us some wider understanding and appreciation of the nature of policing in Northern Ireland in the period before the ceasefires, and afterwards. However those stories will not expunge from the annals of the conflict the reality that others were engaged in collusion, nor will they silence the loud calls for some kind of accountability to be established.

There are very good reasons why some of what happened – before the ceasefires and since – has been described as the "dirty war". The following testimony, from Andrée Murphy of the Relatives for Justice Project, provides us with further insights.

Andrée Murphy, Relatives for Justice

Collusion used to be contested . . . It used to be branded republican propaganda. Since the ceasefires, that projection and lie has changed utterly. In the run [up to] the IRA ceasefire of 1994, the family homes and family members of republican activists were deliberately targeted. It was a clear military tactic that was presented in the media as "more tit-for-tat attacks/killings". It was nothing of the sort.

Women suffered particularly during this period. When family homes were targeted, safety was destroyed and homes became a site of violation. For women, in their predominant role as mothers, homemakers and sustainers, this was an unnoticed and often unreported violation that had long-term effects. Following the [loyalist] importation of South African weapons, 12 women were killed. Katrina Rennie and Eileen Duffy, Tess Fox, Marie Theresa Dowds de Mogollon, Sharon McKenna, Philomena Hanna, Sheena Campbell, Karen Thompson, Moira Duddy, Theresa Clinton, Roseanne Mallon and Kathleen O'Hagan were murdered. All of these killings point to state collusion.

[In the] 21 years since our ceasefires, families have uncovered the conclusive fact that the collusive role of the State in loyalist paramilitaries was nothing short of all-pervasive, and that the State allowed members of its own forces to be killed in order to protect agents within republican organisations. A British Prime Minister has stood up in the House of Commons and acknowledged that there was state collusion in the murder of a human rights solicitor [Pat Finucane]. Not one person has been held accountable for any of it. In the context of that impunity, cover-up and delays in providing information to families remain the order of the day. While the fact that collusion occurred is no longer contested, continual denial and pretence, that [it] was an aberration rather than a concerted military tactic, continues as the dominant narrative. If the state continues to cover up collusion, then that policy continues.

Like Roy Dunn, Peter Sheridan has over 30 years' policing service – in his case, spanning both the RUC and the PSNI. Sheridan is now part of a peace-building organisation, Co-operation Ireland. There was a time when the IRA was targeting and planning to kill Sheridan, yet, in the evolving peace negotiations, he, along with former PSNI Chief Constable, Sir Hugh Orde, took part in talks with republican leaders, Gerry Adams and Martin McGuinness. Those talks, in 2004, took place in Downing Street and were also attended by Tony Blair – a first direct conversation about demilitarisation, and the importance of republican support for policing. Sheridan, who retired as an Assistant Chief Constable, accepts the reports that have found and pointed to collusion, and that it was part of what happened. He asserts however that it was never part of his policing service or thinking.

Peter Sheridan, former Assistant Chief Constable

In contributing to this book, I want to make it clear that during my 32 years of policing service with the RUC, and in later years with the PSNI, I never went to my bed at night, wondering who I might shoot, kill, bomb or maim, nor did I ever get up in the morning, thinking of someone as my enemy. I wondered where the next robbery would be, where the next road traffic collision would happen and whether anyone would be killed or injured in it. I wondered whose house I would visit that day that had just been broken into. I did not consider anyone to be my enemy.

I believe that the vast majority of police officers who I worked with were honourable, decent people, who wanted the same as I did. They were like the majority of people in Northern Ireland. They [might] have had a different cultural background to me, they [might] have attended a different school or church, but they weren't that different when it came to caring about people, wanting to help others or doing the right thing.

However, I cannot walk away from the fact that I met some rogues, scoundrels and downright criminals along the way. I cannot walk away from the comments of the former head of the Metropolitan Police Service, Sir John Stevens, when in 1999 he reinvestigated the murder of Patrick Finucane and allegations of collusion. In his report, he concluded: "My enquiries have highlighted collusion, the wilful failure to keep records, the absence of accountability, the withholding of intelligence and evidence, and the extreme of agents being involved in murder. These serious acts and omissions have meant that people have been killed or seriously injured." Similarly, Nuala O'Loan as Police Ombudsman, concluded in one of her enquiries that her investigation established collusion between certain officers within Special Branch and a UVF unit in north Belfast and Newtownabbey.

I am clear that those honest, decent police officers are as horrified by these findings as I am – but I am also clear that their honesty and decency during a 30-year conflict should not be forgotten, in favour of those police officers who betrayed good policing.

The peace process casts people in many unexpected roles. Sheridan, the police officer with over 30 years' service, who took part in those Downing Street talks with Adams and McGuinness, would years later be instrumental in paving the way for a first meeting and a handshake between McGuinness and Queen Elizabeth. In that sense, he has very much been on the inside of events that have changed relationships. Back in the mid-1990s, however, there was not the sense of momentum or the will for significant change that are so essential to peace-building. Yes, several years after that 1995 Police Federation Conference, the release of hundreds of prisoners – both republican and loyalist – began as part of a wider political deal, but it would take time – and, for some, too much time – to achieve the type of general momentum that was necessary for creating the right conditions for peace.

Amidst the doubts and the delays of the mid-1990s, the IRA ceasefire ended, in the mayhem and the shock and the headlines of a bomb in London. Reading back over the documentation and records of that period now, the warning signs and words can be seen – including a statement from the IRA in late September 1995, in which the demand for decommissioning was described as "ludicrous".

Radio Ulster News Report (Brian Rowan), 29 September 1995

This statement from the IRA could leave no one in any doubt about where it stands on the decommissioning issue. The IRA described the demand as a deliberate distraction and stalling tactic by the government, which it accused of acting in bad faith. The demand, the IRA said, was ludicrous, and there was no possibility of it being agreed to.

Some sources also see significance in the opening lines of the IRA statement, in which it said its complete cessation of military operations was delivered in August last year, because of the opportunity it believed existed "at that time".

Many republicans would argue that since then, the situation has changed – and not for the better. Indeed, one source spoke of the process, "drowning and no one throwing it a life jacket". There is no question that this is a difficult time for the process but, in the background, efforts are continuing to try to break the stalemate.

These words now seem particularly stark. At the time, despite all the difficulties, there was probably still a sense that things could and would be salvaged, but actually, the course was one leading to that London bomb just a few months later. In between, a series of killings was carried out in the name of Direct Action Against Drugs (DAAD): a front or cover name for the IRA. Four of those killings happened in December 1995, leading to a police assessment that was, by now, a statement of the obvious. They had taken the opportunity to "seriously assess the intelligence and the information" available to them. Having looked at "the meticulous planning and ruthless execution of these murders", their conclusion was as follows: "We believe that they [the murders] were carried out either by, or on behalf of, the Provisional IRA." At the time, there was a mountain of speculation pointing to IRA involvement in the deaths, and the IRA had not moved to deny any of this.

We now know that what we were witnessing was the prelude to the ending of the IRA cessation and the subsequent London Docklands bomb. But on the day it happened, 9 February 1996, it came to many people as a sudden shock. The news literally exploded in the British capital. There was not just a statement to announce the ending of the cessation of military operations, but also the horror of this IRA bomb, delivered to underscore the seriousness of the situation and the anger at that time. It was about what the IRA could still do, what it was still capable of, even after those many months of ceasefire. In the explosion, more lives were lost: those of Inan Bashir and John Jeffries.

In the course of my research for this book, I met one of the IRA's most senior leaders at that time, and asked him to contextualise that period – from the declaration of the 1994 ceasefire to the Docklands bomb of 1996. He spoke about a number of factors: the internal management of the IRA organisation; the absence of all-party talks; the demands of the British Government and unionist leaders, and the language within which those demands were framed.

Senior IRA leader, speaking on condition of anonymity

Using terms like "decontamination" was an affront – a provocation. You had to have high levels of communication, brief your people, manage any grassroots problems and motivate them to get involved in campaigns. We learned from the 1975 ceasefire that you just can't leave activists to turn their thumbs. You need focused projects that they can invest their energies in – one such project being "Disband the RUC"; another, "Start the All-Party Talks".

At that time, the [internal IRA] conversation was: "There is an alternative to armed struggle" and [so] you need to see that alternative. In the absence of any establishment projects [such as all-party negotiations], republicans established their own. We took a unilateral decision [to declare the 1994 ceasefire], but if your analysis is that there's no dividend, no return – how do you justify continuing that strategy? What do you do to change that; change the dynamics?

February 1996 [the Docklands bomb] – very, very few people would have known [about it]. If you didn't need to know about it, you didn't know. Say you tried to do that [the bomb], and you were caught, you were f***ed, because you'd played your ace card. Part of the strategy was to [target] the British economy. The message was: "We still have the capacity to strike at the financial heart of London. We can strike without you having any foresight or knowledge."... The Blair Government coming in changed things.

Precise knowledge of how the ceasefire would be brought to an end would have been limited to very few within the IRA. It is clear from the words above that the primary consideration was to keep the planned bomb attack in London under the radar. The IRA knew it was going to get one chance at this. Interception of the bomb, or the attack being interrupted or disrupted by police or intelligence officers, would have represented a huge failure and setback. More knowledge inside the organisation would have meant more talk, and an opportunity for the RUC Special Branch or MI5 to pick up a signal. The senior republican who spoke to me for this book would not have done so in 1996: he would not have shared such context or analysis. At that time of the Docklands bomb, he was one of the IRA's principal leaders. He has since made the transition from the IRA into the republican political peace project. Yet today he still speaks on the condition of anonymity in relation to that IRA role.

Back in 1996, at the time of the Docklands bomb, the public comments from the IRA were all about blame: "Instead of embracing the peace process, the British Government acted in bad faith, with Mr Major and the unionist leaders squandering this unprecedented opportunity to resolve the conflict ... The blame for the failure thus far of the Irish peace process lies squarely with John Major and his Government."

Radio Ulster News Report (Brian Rowan), 10 February 1996

The combination of the London bomb and the statement, announcing an end to the IRA's complete cessation of military operations, has taken the peace process into its darkest phase yet.

It's difficult to see any logic in the actions of the IRA. The bombing, and what the republican group said in its statement, will strengthen rather than weaken the demands for decommissioning and will further delay any prospect of all-party talks.

The RUC has already indicated that some security measures removed in the wake of the ceasefires will be reintroduced, including, where necessary, military support.

What lies ahead is difficult to predict, but any further attacks could destroy the fragile peace of the past 17 months.

While loyalist sources are saying there'll be no knee-jerk reaction to what has happened, some are also warning that any further attacks could have serious consequences. These sources are saying that it's up to the Catholic/nationalist population to make clear to republicans that there's no mandate for a resumption of violence.

At times like this, there are such blizzards of words – words of analysis, interpretation, condemnation, concern, and confusion. The learning of that period is not about what we saw, but what we did not see. What would begin to emerge over a period of time was a story of internal discontent and dissent; a questioning of the direction the IRA was taking, and of the decisions linked to the Adams/McGuinness peace strategy. This would lead to cracks within the organisation, a failed attempt to overthrow Adams and McGuinness, and, ultimately, the emergence of violent dissident republican groups. Those things I will explore in more detail in a later chapter. Back in February 1996, however, John Major chose measured words in response to the IRA statement and bomb. A door was being kept ajar.

Statement by the Prime Minister, 10 February 1996

The evil act at Docklands struck at the heart of 17 months of peace in Northern Ireland. Innocent people had their lives shattered in a most violent and shocking way. My heart goes out to them and their families. We all owe a debt, too, to the emergency services, who coped so magnificently.

Where there was optimism, a dark shadow of doubt has now been cast. The IRA once again callously threaten the desire for peace. They will not be allowed to prevail. Too many lives have already been saved, too much good has come out of the ceasefire, to allow that to happen.

I intend to carry on the search for peace with the Irish Government and the democratic political parties. The IRA and Sinn Féin must say now that their campaign of violence has stopped, and [that] they will never resume it again.

We will be vigilant about security, both on the mainland and in Northern Ireland. We will assess carefully and coolly this challenge to the peace process and the way ahead. The prize of peace is too precious to be squandered.

I have visited Northern Ireland many times. I have seen the changes that the ceasefire has brought: the lightness of mood among the people, the increasing prosperity, the happiness, the freedom to walk down a street without fear.

I am determined to entrench their freedom as a permanent part of peace in the life of Northern Ireland. Nothing less will do.

The ceasefire would not be restored during John Major's reign as Prime Minister. In Northern Ireland and elsewhere, people watched as the IRA engaged in sporadic attacks in Britain, and we listened to the words of the Combined Loyalist Military Command.

Since the summer before the Docklands bombing in fact, that leadership had been alert to what was being said by republicans and to what could happen. In July 1995, the CLMC had stated: "The entire population of Northern Ireland, Great Britain, the Irish Republic and America will not easily forgive any group which undermines the peace process, [and] anticipates or precipitates a return to war." Just weeks later, it elaborated: "While the IRA's commitment to peace remains questionable, loyalists must remain prepared. The CLMC wish to reassure the people of Northern Ireland that, provided their rights are upheld, the CLMC will not initiate a return to war. There shall be no first strike."

After the Docklands bomb, the mood and tone inevitably darkened.

From CLMC Statement, 12 March 1996

From a position of confidence, strength and sophistication, we have withstood the recent provocation of IRA bombs on the mainland, which have killed our innocent British fellow citizens. These atrocities cannot be permitted to continue, without a telling response from this source. We are poised and ready to strike to effect. We will give blow for blow. As in the past, whatever the cost, we will gladly pay it. Now is the time to draw back from the brink.

The British and Irish Governments tried to find a formula for talks that would bring all the sides, including republicans, to some negotiating process. The plan was an election to a Forum, and then negotiations and, within that frame, the hope was that the ceasefire would be reinstated. Through a series of briefings, the IRA spoke out against this new plan. As we now know of course, Sinn Féin contested the May election and increased its share of the vote to over 15 per cent. However the IRA viewed the proposed upcoming talks as little more than a decommissioning conference and, in briefings, ruled out any short-term prospect of a renewed ceasefire. In words which were delivered in the jaws of the planned talks, they also reiterated that the arms question should be set in a much more long-term context. The two briefings – at which I was the only journalist present – were delivered by the leadership spokesman, "P. O'Neill", not by way of formal statements but in comments to be attributed to "a senior IRA source". I, of course, knew whom I was speaking to and knew the authority with which he spoke.

The first briefing took place in a house to which I was taken and the second, at a table at a café in a shopping complex in west Belfast – the same place, in fact, where the IRA ceasefire statement had been read almost two years previously. By now, the mood was very different however: it was one of defiance.

As soon as those briefings were reported in June 1996, every word of their content was dissected and analysed: an indication of the importance of the moment and of this particular political juncture. I would soon learn that the policing and intelligence worlds were also listening very closely. In a chance meeting in the BBC foyer around that time, a senior RUC officer asked me who I had been speaking to. I ignored his question, as he knew I would, but, as I got into a lift, he mentioned an initial, which I again ignored. He did not raise the name with me again but, in a later conversation, designed to assure me that my phone was not being listened to, he hinted at an interception of a conversation involving Gerry Adams and the man then operating as "P. O'Neill". These are the kind of mind games that can be played at such times.

So there was, as I have said, huge interest in the contents of these IRA briefings which would soon be reported publicly. John Hume queried some of the detail of these reports. He still believed that it might be possible to achieve another ceasefire before the planned date for talks on 10 June 1996. It was proposed that at those talks, participants would be asked to make a formal declaration of commitment to principles of democracy and non-violence, and that the focus would be to try to achieve progress on the arms question, with some actual decommissioning to take place during the process of all-party negotiations.

However, that day would come and go, without a ceasefire. Sinn Féin was barred from participation and, by the weekend 15 June, the IRA's intentions became clear. This time the message was not in words, but rather delivered by means of a huge bomb in Manchester. In a blizzard of blowing glass and debris, scores of people were injured – and the loyalists were being taken ever closer to their breaking point.

Two days after the bomb, on Monday, 17 June, I met two of the UDA's then "brigadiers" on the Shankill Road, to hear the words of a statement issued on behalf of the Ulster Freedom Fighters (a cover name):

UFF Statement, 17 June 1996

The weekend bombing in Manchester carried out by the IRA is a further demonstration that republicans do not seek a political resolution to the conflict.

It is the UFF's considered view that an IRA resumption of conflict in Northern Ireland is imminent.

We have alerted our personnel accordingly, and remain prepared for all eventualities.

The UFF has a binding duty to ensure that the loyalist community is not rendered defenceless from republican attack.

However, we are fully committed to the current peace process and to a political resolution of the conflict through dialogue in a peaceful atmosphere.

To this end, we offer the opportunity to the IRA to immediately reinstate its ceasefire.

There would however be no new ceasefire until more than 12 months later – July 1997. There were more bombings and killings by the IRA, including at Army Headquarters in Lisburn in October 1996. During this time, bombings and killings were also carried out by loyalists, in what they came to term a "measured response". There was also, significantly, the issuing of orders and threats in the name of the Combined Loyalist Military Command relating to two men who had once held senior rank within the UVF and the UDA.

The men named in a CLMC statement on 28 August 1996 were Billy Wright and Alec Kerr, who were being accused of "treasonable and subversive activities" – that is, of disobeying the ceasefire orders of the Combined Loyalist Military Command. The two men were ordered out of Northern Ireland and warned of "summary justice" if they ignored this "directive". Kerr is now living in exile. Wright stayed, and was shot dead by the INLA inside the Maze prison in December 1997. Beyond the naming of the two men, this statement was an indication that loyalists were also struggling to navigate their collective participation in the peace process, as well as the mood among some within their organisations. Both before and after the Wright killing, there was a surge of violence on the part of loyalist paramilitaries, some of it involving Wright's dissident organisation, the Loyalist Volunteer Force; the UDA or UFF was also involved in this activity, although it tried unsuccessfully to cover its tracks.

Over time, things changed, with new governments coming into power in both Britain and in Ireland. The new Prime Minister, Tony Blair, and Taoiseach, Bertie Ahern managed to construct a negotiations process that had Sinn Féin on the inside before any proposed beginning to arms decommissioning would be undertaken. The loyalists were also inside these talks, as were the principal unionist and nationalist leaders at the time, David Trimble and John Hume. With former US Senator George Mitchell as Chair of the negotiations, there was an important international dimension to the proceedings – Mitchell's presence carrying all the weight and expectations of the US President, Bill Clinton.

Those talks eventually delivered the historic Good Friday Agreement, in April 1998. However, they were not conducted in a peaceful climate. Sinn Féin's agreement to the Mitchell principles of democracy and non-violence caused a schism within the IRA, leading to the first acts of dissident republican violence. There was also a surge in loyalist violence as we have seen and, while the eventual Agreement delivered much in terms of a political structure and Commissions to address policing and prisoner releases, it still left a lot unsolved, unanswered, unforgotten and unforgiven. In the chapters which follow, we will look at some of these very difficult areas: the emotionally charged debate about prisoners' status versus victims' rights: collusion in a sharper focus; the emerging dissident threat; the secret graves of the "Disappeared". In all of this lies the poison that seeps from our past and that, on occasion, still threatens to flood our present.

CHAPTER FOUR
The Prisoners: Sleeping with the Victims

"One has only to inspect the violent and murderous history against the community by the prisoners – every one of them convicted after the due process of the law – to conclude it is inconceivable that public opinion would be ready to accept early release of those responsible for such atrocious crimes."
Editorial in *Police Beat,* the magazine of the NI Police Federation, February 1995.

"If they cannot recognise that the releases of political prisoners are an integral part of building peace and reconciliation, then perhaps they would be as well keeping their mouths shut, as they are adding little to the positive dynamic for peace in this editorial."
Sinn Féin's then Prisons' Spokesperson, Pat McGeown, responding to the above editorial in February 1995.

"I explained how serious and determined our prisoners were, and that to ignore them could result in more dead bodies on the streets . . . I told her not to piss up their legs, and she asked me what I meant. I said, 'Don't tell them any lies.'"
Loyalist Jackie McDonald, recalling a meeting in London with then Secretary of State Mo Mowlam in January 1998.

"We were about to be released as POWs [prisoners of war], and the world could be in no doubt about that. Of course we knew full well that the struggle was far from over; that this was only the beginning of a new phase or new chapter . . ."
Jim McVeigh, the last IRA "OC" in the Maze/Long Kesh, thinking back on his release in July 2000.

In the years after the Good Friday Agreement, the prisoners – the men and women who were serving long, conflict-related sentences – were now a big part of this evolving story. What would happen to them? Would the gates open? If so, what would the likely timeframe be? These questions asked for answers. The ceasefires were not a magic wand, of course. They did not bring the immediate release of prisoners but, rather, prompted a long and emotional debate about what should and should not be done.

To properly understand the prisoner issue, you need to understand something of the context in which it unfolded: the history of Maze/Long Kesh prison; the sense in which many had long regarded it as a prisoner-of-war camp; the battles which had been fought by those inside to secure, and retain, their political – or "special" – status. My own career as a reporter does not encompass those years of turmoil in the 1970s and early 1980s, when the prisoners' struggle to retain political status gave rise to the "blanket" and "dirty" protests, and then the hunger strikes. Pat McGeown, quoted above, died in October 1996, about 20 months after he issued that response to the Police Federation editorial. McGeown was a key player in those prison battles, and in the 1981 hunger strike. What I know about those events has been informed by what I have read about them, and by what I have been told by others with direct experience of them. My journalist colleague, Eamonn Mallie watched the situation unfold as a witness in actual time, and met the Belfast republican, Bobby Sands in 1979 – two years before Sands' death on hunger strike. For several years before this, tensions within this jail had been simmering towards a dramatic boiling point.

Eamonn Mallie, Journalist and Author, writing for this book

1976 would prove an eventful year in the Maze Prison: a year which would effectively change the course of history in Northern Ireland. In July 1972, Special Category Status was introduced . . . which meant prisoners were treated very much like prisoners of war, not having to wear prison uniforms or do prison work. In 1976, the British Government brought an end to Special Category Status . . . for those convicted after 1 March. Early in that year, the IRA leaders in prison [had] sent word to the IRA's Army Council, to begin killing prison officers, pledging: "We are prepared to die for political status. Those who try to take it away from us must be fully prepared to pay the same price." Prison officers were now being targeted.

On 14 September 1976, newly convicted prisoner, Kieran Nugent began a "blanket protest", refusing to wear a prison uniform. I interviewed him some years later, when he said, "I told the screws they'd have to nail the uniform on me." He was a hard man. In March 1978, this blanket protest escalated, when some prisoners refused to leave their cells, to shower, or use the lavatory . . . The blanket protest escalated into the dirty protest, with republicans refusing to "slop out", and choosing to smear excrement on the cell walls.

A visit to republican prisoners by Archbishop Tomás Ó Fiaich guaranteed world headlines for the cause of republicanism. On 31 July 1978, Dr Ó Fiaich said: "One would hardly allow an animal to remain in such conditions, let alone a human being. The nearest approach to it that I have seen, was the spectacle of hundreds of homeless people living in the sewer pipes in the slums of Calcutta. The stench and filth in some of the cells, with the remains of rotten food and human excreta scattered around the walls, was almost unbearable. In two of them, I was unable to speak, for fear of vomiting."

The following year, and after the IRA bomb attack that killed Lord Louis Mountbatten at Mullaghmore in County Sligo, Mallie himself was allowed a visit to the jail, where he met two prisoners: one, a loyalist and the other, Bobby Sands.

Eamonn Mallie, Journalist and Author

The images you see on posters – of a youthful Sands with flowing locks and a broad smile – are not compatible with the reality which I met in the person of Roibeard Ó Seachnasaigh, in 1979. The future Fermanagh and South Tyrone MP was pathetic-looking in demeanour. His gaunt, drawn, wan and emaciated face was partially eclipsed [by] long, dark, lank hair. His eyes still haunt me. They darted about endlessly, as if another blow was about to be landed from God knows where. Sands wore the outward signs of a caged and condemned man, forced to fight for his very existence.

The fluency with which Bobby Sands spoke Irish was remarkable. This was no "gaoltacht" Irish. Here was a prisoner who was a master of his native tongue . . . Not a word of English was spoken for the duration of my visit. He was razor-sharp and deadly hubristic in outlook. "How could the blowing up of an old man and members of his family on a boat in Mullaghmore be moral?" I challenged. Bobby Sands was having none of this sermonising by me: "He [Mountbatten] knew Ireland's problems, but did nothing about them. He came to Ireland and availed of its hospitality," he retorted. No quarter given on IRA activity.

I bade farewell to the enfeebled Sands, who then, in 1979, was totally anonymous to the world outside the Maze. [He] wrote me a long letter in Irish to thank me for my gaol visit. I didn't see Bobby Sands again, but the portrait of his pity is fixed forever on my retina.

Over 18 months later, the name Bobby Sands resonated around the globe, as the man who had won a Westminster seat in defiance of the Iron Lady, Margaret Thatcher, and sacrificed his life on hunger strike. . .

Sands would be the first of ten hunger strikers to die in those turbulent months of 1981, in a battle of wills between the prisoners and the Iron Lady. However that year, 1981, decided nothing and ended nothing. There were other cards yet to play, other moments that would test all the sides in this conflict. It was far from being the end. Another journalist colleague, Deric Henderson, who also reported on events during that period, evokes the bleak horror of the time.

Deric Henderson, former Press Association Ireland Editor, writing for this book

The skies were heavy, and the mood was antagonistic and resentful, as the mourners sheltered under trees and umbrellas by the side of a freshly dug grave, which awaited the remains of Kevin Lynch. Even before the Requiem Mass had ended, the grounds just across the road from his family home in Dungiven, were packed. [In August 1981] Lynch, 25, a member of the Irish National Liberation Army, was the seventh republican hunger striker to die, and, with no sign of a resolution to the issues which for years had dominated life inside Long Kesh, tensions here were probably as high as at any time during this particular stage of the conflict.

"Show me your Press Pass. Where is it? Hand it over!" It wasn't so much a request, more an angry demand. And if I was asked once, then I must have been challenged ten times for proof of identity by various individuals, [who were] growing increasingly wary of the Fourth Estate, and especially their bosses in Belfast, Dublin and London, who by this stage had effectively lost interest.

The death of Bobby Sands, just over two months earlier, was a monumental event which invited unprecedented international media attention, but by the time Lynch died – after going without food for 71 days – this was a story struggling to stay on the front pages. And [so] the graveyard at St Patrick's Church was deeply hostile territory for visiting journalists. There was a poisonous atmosphere, and it was an awful place to be.

Margaret Thatcher wasn't prepared to yield. I'll never forget the look in her eyes and the venomous tone, as she chided those of us sitting across a table [from her] at Stormont Castle, when we dared question her political judgment as Sands embarked on his mission. "They're playing their last card," she claimed.

There was just this sense of hopelessness and although there was no shortage of engagement, there was a feeling of inevitability. Days standing outside those dreary prison gates and long, long nights hanging around the foyer of the then Greenan Lodge Hotel (now the Balmoral Hotel) at Blacks Road, west Belfast, as the men from the Irish Commission for Justice and Peace busied themselves in an upstairs room, trying to agree some sort of compromise and maybe a settlement. The families were getting desperate as well. Kevin Lynch died before the [hunger strikers'] relatives formally intervened to demand an end to the suffering.

Every time I travel [through] the Glenshane Pass, I glance in at that graveyard and reflect on that August afternoon all those years ago. The republican hunger strike may have been a defining period in Irish history, especially for the IRA and the then faint voices of Sinn Féin. But it was also a horrible, horrible time.

Today that fight remains etched in the minds of so many who were part of it: those who watched it; those who witnessed it; and those who wept at what happened, both inside and outside that jail.

From the 1990s onwards, I as a journalist reported many times on the happenings within the Maze Prison and Crumlin Road Jail: the battles for segregation (i.e. the separation of republican and loyalist prisoners); the killings; the discovery of an advanced escape tunnel, and how a republican, dressed as a woman, walked from a supposedly high-security jail. I have monitored the prisoners' attitudes to political developments, watched the early releases that flowed from the Good Friday Agreement and witnessed the establishment of a Sentence Review Commission.

Through different pairs of eyes, the releases will have been perceived very differently: as walks to freedom or walks of shame; as a betrayal in terms of political decisions taken and deals made; as a denial of justice. That post-Good Friday Agreement emptying of the Maze/Long Kesh prison stemmed from decisions taken by governments and parties that clearly distinguished between "political" prisoners and other, "criminal" prisoners. However loud the denials, that difference has always at some level been recognised – and the decisions taken in 1998 acknowledged and confirmed this.

It is too easy to only blame the prisoners of this war for what happened – for the killings, the injuries and the missing limbs, the bombs, the demolished buildings, the graves and headstones, the empty chairs. The prisoners – now labelled "ex-prisoners" – are the names and faces that can easily be attached to all of those things. This in itself raises another question. For how long in this developing peace process will that description – former or ex-prisoner – continue to apply?

Another expression we often heard being used was when someone was referred to as being "involved". The word was used in a very narrow sense, meaning republicans and loyalists. It was not used however to describe those in governments, or politics, or the security and intelligence services – and yet, in the course of the conflict, all of these too were "involved" in countless decisions, actions, policies and directions that were a key part of what happened here.

Who, for example, was "connected" to or "involved" in the many, now uncontested acts of collusion? Who knew about this aspect of the "dirty war"? Why was there no legal framework in place for agent-handling – something which is described in a review of the Pat Finucane killing as, "a wilful and abject failure" on the part of successive governments? In his Review, Sir Desmond de Silva QC concluded: "I believe that the Government was fully aware of the entirely unacceptable fact that there was no adequate framework in place for agent-handling in Northern Ireland in the late 1980s." Who should answer for this?

Agents did not just provide information to the various intelligence agencies. We now know that, in a number of high-profile cases – both loyalist and republican – they were active participants in violence. Indeed, some have been described as "serial killers". There are continuing arguments about the extent of collusion, and whether it was a tactic, policy, strategy or an instance of "mission creep", but the collusion-deniers are no longer a credible voice. "Involved" means so many things in so many different spheres of this conflict and, if the past is to be only about blame, where does that begin and end? It is too easy, too comfortable and too limited to start and finish with the prisoners.

The prisoners' collective story – told from all the different perspectives – is still only part of the narrative of the conflict, and there are many other parts. Something happened here that drew thousands of people – British and Irish, loyalist and republican, military, police and intelligence – into a battle that extended over several decades. Certain politicians are still trying to occupy that old ground today – to make it the fighting place of the present, in terms of establishing victimhood, and managing and restricting blame. For these people, it seems to be about trying to control the past, and trying to close doors to any wider scrutiny and examination.

Many ex-prisoners I know and have spoken to are ordinary people, whose prison experience had its roots in extraordinary happenings and circumstances. They are not unthinking, mindless people. I will never forget the words of a loyalist, an ex-prisoner himself who had been given a life sentence, and who spoke to me about the sense in which prisoners "sleep with the victims". In other words, they must sleep with what they did, constantly replaying their actions, thinking and turning in the darkness of every night. The same man took his own life after his release.

The late Gusty Spence once described Maze/Long Kesh as "a miserable, desolate place [with] lights, watchtowers, guards [and] sensory devices . . . all those things which would accumulate in such a prisoner-of-war camp". Here again we have that distinction being made between conflict and criminal prisoners. Spence also talked about "ghosts", and said: "[There is no one] who has spent a long time in prison, who does not have nightmares . . . Whenever you wake up, the shadow of the bars is on the wall." He remembered the rain, more of it than in other places, and he talked about the "trail of tears to Long Kesh" – a reference to the visiting families. Yet he also accepted that those involved in paramilitary organisations could not "exonerate themselves from the heartache and the anguish that they have caused". Spence was always able to think beyond the next sentence, and he developed that thought by asking the question: "What ghosts does society have to exorcise?" What he meant, of course, was that there are others, who were not in jail, who are not ex-prisoners, neither loyalist nor republican, who cannot absolve themselves of blame. Of course, they still try to do so. It is always easier when it is someone else's fault.

When I spoke to him over a decade ago, former prison governor, Duncan McLaughlan remembered the H Blocks of the Maze as, "very claustrophobic . . . [with] low ceilings . . . oppressive". The lights always had to be on. It was, "a strange place to work, [an] uncomfortable and an unsafe place to work". "A prison should be a place where there is no fear, where there is dignity, self-respect and, I think, the Maze worked against many of those things." The authorities were not in charge. Yes, they held the keys, they had security arrangements in place that contained the prisoners, but staff were not in control of the wings. "With the Maze, you had a cohesive group of prisoners who operated from an ideological base and, as we know, the Maze became a battlefield in the fight between principally the republican movement and the government," McLaughlan commented. In those circumstances, staff worked "on the fringe" of the prisoners.

Duncan McLaughlan went on to observe: "There are many notorious prisons in the world . . . Alcatraz, Devil's Island – none has had any significant effect or influence on the life of the community in which it was based. Maze is the one exception to this. It is a significant exception, and it became inextricably bound up in the political difficulties of Northern Ireland. It didn't cause the Troubles, but it became part of them and it contributed to them . . . If you are in for a political offence and someone says, 'No, you are a criminal', then you are going to resist, and that decision [to end special category status, in 1976] was a step too far."

Duncan McLaughlan believed the "vast majority" of prisoners would not have been in jail, had there not been a conflict, and concluded: "And that marks them out as different". Others, of course, will have a completely different view. The prisoners will always be criminals, terrorists, killers, bombers, murderers – those responsible for death and destruction, and for the deep wells of tears which have been, and still are, wept in mourning and in remembering the dead.

As early as the beginning of 1995 – just months after the ceasefires – the Presbyterian Minister Roy Magee, who has since died, was pressing the Northern Ireland Office for a Commission to examine the early release of prisoners. Magee had previously had a conduit role in the process – communicating messages and exploring possibilities with the Northern Ireland Office and in Dublin – and had helped to pave the way to the loyalist ceasefire of 1994. The Commission, he believed, should gather all relevant opinions, including from the families of the victims of violence. Magee wanted findings brought forward within six months to help inform the debate on early releases and said that, while politicians would be consulted, the Commission should not be politically-led.

The editorial in the Police Federation magazine, *Police Beat,* left no one in any doubt as to its position. Under the headline, "Properly Convicted", the piece declared: "One has only to inspect the violent and murderous history against the community by the prisoners – every one of them convicted after the due process of the law – to conclude it is inconceivable that public opinion would be ready to accept early release of those responsible for such atrocious crimes. It is not just that this premature release makes a nonsense of the seriousness of their crimes and atrocities – it also insults the feelings and undiminished grief of the families of the victims. The ceasefire is barely six months old. Talk and especially any move to release these prisoners, is irresponsible and undermines the rule of law."

Sinn Féin's Prisons Spokesperson, Pat McGeown responded: "For them to use the logic that political prisoners have been convicted by some fair and just due process of law is a nonsense, and ignores reality. Political prisoners have been convicted using special draconian laws, special inhuman interrogation centres and special no-jury courts." As detailed in Chapter Three, the Police Federation position was consolidated at its Annual Conference four months later, in June 1995. So there were these two very different perspectives of the prisoners and their role in the conflict, with some regarding them as products of the circumstances, and others as criminal murderers. The same argument, between these very different points of view, continues today. All opinions must be heard. There will never be one truth which all recognise, and there will never be an agreed narrative. The gap is too wide to close.

Also in June 1995, the Northern Ireland Association for the Care and Resettlement of Offenders (NIACRO) held a two-day conference in Belfast. Part of the aim of the conference was to bring international thinking to the discussion. NIACRO made clear it did not want to act as some kind of mediator on the prisoner issue but, rather, wanted to help inform the debate: "In a divided community like Northern Ireland, it is important too that respective communities and diverse constituencies have an opportunity to be heard. We have endeavoured to build into the programme opportunities for those differing Northern Ireland perspectives to be voiced. In addition, we have tried to include opportunities for audience participation, in the Open Forum sessions on each conference theme." The content and structure of the conference was informed by a research report written by Brian Gormally and Kieran McEvoy – the latter is now a Law Professor at Queen's University.

At that time, the Chair of NIACRO was Harold Good – the Methodist preacher and pastor mentioned in Chapter One for his facilitation role in a meeting between Gerry Adams and Alan McBride. Good has been involved in many quiet initiatives, both before and after the ceasefires. Ten years after this NIACRO-hosted event, he would be one of two church witnesses to the IRA's decommissioning initiatives and, later, would involve himself in a reconciliation project known as "Uncomfortable Conversations", which I will look at in the closing section of this book.

The debate around prisoners, their role and their release, would grow from these early seeds into political discussions, which would eventually help to shape some of the key tenets of the Good Friday Agreement. Kieran McEvoy, whose research with Brian Gormally had provided the basis for the NIACRO conference, watched as the thinking and strategies evolved.

Kieran McEvoy, Queen's University Law Professor, writing for this book
In the early 1990s, as discussion on the possibility of paramilitary ceasefires intensified, a number of us began to look more closely at the issue of prisoner releases. From the outset, it was clear that the early release of prisoners would be part of the broader political conversation about how to deal with the changed circumstances. However, it was equally clear

that such conversations would be extremely difficult, not least for those victims directly affected by violence.

At the time I was working as Information Office for NIACRO – a large voluntary organisation which campaigned on behalf of and provided services to prisoners and their families – mostly those convicted of "ordinary offences". Together with my then colleague, Brian Gormally, we managed to secure funding to conduct a comparative project on the process of early release of prisoners in South Africa, Israel/Palestine, Spain and Italy, as well as to conduct historical work on prisoner release in Ireland. Our view was that we could inform the public conversation about this extremely difficult and sensitive matter – providing technical and legal information in an accessible format – and allowing people to make up their own minds, albeit from a more informed position.

The research looked at a number of themes which featured in all of the jurisdictions, including the legal frameworks used; whether releases should be done on an individual or a collective basis; whether they should be linked to other issues (e.g., decomissioning of weapons); and the views of victims. We concluded that prisoner release was legally doable, that victims had a range of views on the issue, and that it was not possible to have a successful peace process without such releases. Broadly, the Northern Ireland experience suggests that we were right.

McEvoy makes a very valid point. A sustainable peace would not have been possible, had this issue not been resolved. The eventual releases, following on from ceasefires and political agreements, became an essential block in peace-building. They had to happen, and the decisions made around this strategy had to think beyond the angry words and emotions and resistance.

In the period leading up to the Good Friday Agreement in April 1998, the Maze prison had once more been headline news – as one story after another destroyed any notion of this being a place of impenetrable security. In March 1997, an IRA escape tunnel, stretching some 30 metres, had been discovered under an exercise yard and about the same distance – 30 metres – from a perimeter wall. An inquiry was ordered and the report exposed the gaping holes in the prison's security systems.

Statement from NIO Prisons' Press Office, 28 April 1997
The report recognises the unique challenge faced by Governors and staff at Maze Prison. They have to run an establishment in which a large number of highly dangerous and determined terrorist offenders is concentrated.

It notes that prisoners are housed in segregated blocks and submit themselves to the discipline of the paramilitary factions. Through intimidation and constant pressure upon staff, these prisoners had, over a period of years, in effect gained control within the wings to which they were confined. Recently searches have been carried out only infrequently . . .

It was in these very dangerous circumstances that PIRA prisoners in H7 were able to break through the concrete floor of Cell 18 in "A" wing, dig through a metre of hardcore and infill, and then tunnel through soil at a depth of two metres . . . Most of the tools and materials used to construct the tunnel were improvised from cell furniture and handicraft materials. The tunnel was lined and supported with wood acquired by dismantling cell furniture, cut-down metal table legs and lengths of wood supplied to the prisoners for handicrafts. Soil was deposited in two cells at the end of the wing. Prisoners were able to achieve all of this because of the effective absence of staff from wings, and the steps which prisoners had taken to obscure the line of sight down the wings from the centre of the H-Block.

In a news report that day, I gave this assessment of the conclusion reached in the report:

Radio Ulster News Report, 28 April 1997

There are no surprises in this report. The Inquiry team has come up with the type of recommendations everyone had expected. The report emphasises the need for what is termed "a purposeful staff presence" on the wings of the Maze. It recommends that prisoners should be locked up twice a day to facilitate headcounts and cell checks. And full searches of the blocks which house republican and loyalist prisoners will be carried out on a frequent and unpredictable basis. Movement of prisoners between blocks is to be strictly controlled . . . The report suggests that in future, cell furniture be constructed out of soft materials, and a fresh risk assessment is recommended for all handicraft tools. The Secretary of State, Sir Patrick Mayhew, says he entirely endorses the report and has asked the Chief Executive of the Prison Service to take the recommendations forward as a matter of urgency.

In the months that followed, however, prisoners made a complete mockery of the notion of improved or enhanced security within the wings of the Maze. Late in the evening of 10 December 1997, news began to emerge of an escape and, approaching midnight, a short statement from the authorities provided some more detail:

Statement by the NI Prison Service, 10 December 1997

The Northern Ireland Prison Service tonight confirmed that an IRA prisoner Liam Averill from south Derry, serving a life sentence for murder, escaped from Her Majesty's Prison the Maze this afternoon. It is thought that he took advantage of a Christmas children's party attended by the wives and children of prisoners to leave the prison in the guise of a visitor. All emergency procedures have been activated and an inquiry into the circumstances will be set up.

The political talks that would eventually produce the Good Friday Agreement were of course ongoing at this time, and headlines about the escape brought the jail, and the prisoners, back into focus. It was a reminder of the many complex issues that had to be addressed in these negotiations. This was not just the story of another embarrassing security breach at the Maze prison, but something that had wider implications too. In the reactions and commentary that followed the escape, William "Plum" Smith, who chaired the 1994 loyalist ceasefire news conference and was Prisoners' Spokesman for the UVF and Red Hand Commando, talked about the ongoing efforts to win over public and political opinion on the issue of early releases, and said that the escape would damage that work. Republican thinking on the matter, as expressed by one source, was much more relaxed, however – prisoners will always attempt to escape: an opportunity had presented itself, and had been taken.

As further details emerged, including the revelation that the prisoner in question – a convicted killer – had made good his escape by disguising himself as a woman, the story of the breach became ever more humiliating for the prison authorities.

Radio Ulster News Report (Brian Rowan), 11 December 1997

Prison sources say 147 visitors were allowed into the jail for yesterday's party and it is thought Liam Averill, disguised as a woman, mingled with some of them, as he covered a distance of 600 yards or so undetected during his escape.

The incident is being viewed as another highly embarrassing breach of security at a jail where earlier this year an IRA escape tunnel was discovered.

The Secretary of State is set to order an inquiry, and one question requiring an answer is whether the visitors were counted in and counted

---

out of the jail. Additional head counts and cell checks were introduced at the jail earlier this year.

160 Maze prisoners are due to begin 10 days' Christmas home leave in about a fortnight's time. While some are questioning the wisdom of allowing that leave, it is believed the prison authorities will let the prisoners out.

That leave involved more prisoners being given more time at home than ever before – but all of this was still happening too slowly for loyalists and republicans, who were demanding much more. Their focus was on releases – not temporary leave – and that Christmas, as the prisoners emerged through the turnstiles into the prison car park, there was an indication both of growing impatience, and of potential danger. A statement from loyalist prisoners was read to reporters. It warned that over the Christmas period, UFF/UDA prisoners would be re-assessing their position in terms of support for the talks process, and claimed that process was operating to a republican agenda. One of the UDA prisoners who spoke went on to describe the ceasefire as "shaky", and said that the current situation represented the most dangerous phase since the process began.

Within days, the news would turn to a killing inside the Maze on 27 December 1997, and then, to a surge in loyalist violence. We were now indeed in a very dangerous and volatile phase. Billy Wright – the dissident loyalist who had defied orders from the Combined Loyalist Military Command (CLMC) to leave Northern Ireland – was the target of the shooting, in a gun attack carried out by prisoners linked to the Irish National Liberation Army (INLA). Wright had become a problem in the loyalist efforts towards peace. His killing in jail as he sat in a prison van became the subject of a protracted inquiry, which concluded that there was no evidence of state collusion in his death. Yet this shooting, like many others, may never be fully explained or understood, as I suggested in a piece written several years later for the *Belfast Telegraph*.

Why death of "King Rat" is dark and dirty riddle
(*Belfast Telegraph*, 14 September 2010)
Maybe Billy Wright was just too big for loyalists to kill – too big a player in Ulster's war for the guns of the UVF, UDA and Red Hand Commando to be fired at him.

And maybe, then, the INLA did what those organisations could not – or would not – do.

The Wright murder inside the Maze Prison on 27 December 1997 came in a gun attack led by Christopher "Crip" McWilliams – serving a life sentence for the murder of a Belfast bar manager, Colm Mahon six years earlier. McWilliams had been put out of the bar, and returned with a gun. So, the stories of the two killings are very different. The Wright shooting was part of a decades-long conflict; one of the so-called "spectacular" operations. The killing of Colm Mahon had nothing whatsoever to do with that long war.

Billy Wright was one of those big loyalist characters – in that category with Adair and Stone. His "war story" was inside the UVF, inside a unit based in Portadown and attached to the mid-Ulster "Brigade". That was until the mid-1990s and the declaration of the Combined Loyalist Military Command ceasefire.

Wright, like Adair and Stone, could not cope with the "peace". The pages in his story are about killing; about drugs; about Drumcree and that marching stand-off in his hometown; about the "dirty war" and suggestions that he was an agent; about the UVF and then the LVF; about the jail shooting, suspicions of collusion and then the public inquiry. Whether his reputation and reality matched up depends on whom you speak to.

The day of his killing is one I remember in fine detail – one of those shock-and-headline days – the shock being that Wright was killed inside a supposedly high-security jail. At the Maze, INLA and LVF prisoners shared an 'H' Block. They were enemies, too close to each other; within touching and shooting distance . . .

. . . I called one of Wright's associates, Mark Fulton, who was on his way to the prison. The news that was emerging on the outside was true. In the emergency control room at the jail, a report of the shooting [had been] received at 9.59 a.m. By 10.53 a.m., Wright was pronounced dead . . .

. . . [In August of the previous year, Wright had] dismissed the directive [of the loyalist leadership, who had ordered him out of the country]; [he had] publicly defied them. And, then, in a place where he would have believed he was safe, the INLA caught up with him. And, in that confined space in a prison van, he had no chance.

The UDA brigadier, Jackie McDonald – who was part of that leadership that ordered Wright and Kerr out of the country – has many different stories to tell about the Portadown loyalist. He says Wright once offered him two army-issue SA80 rifles, almost as a "trophy" if the UDA would carry out a killing on his behalf – an offer McDonald says was declined. Then, there are other stories: Wright threatening McDonald with "summary justice" and, when the ceasefire was announced, Wright telling a loyalist audience to dump their guns and "make a few bob out of selling drugs". He had enemies and he had friends.

Years before his killing, the IRA claimed a spy within its ranks had been given "a plan for the assassination of Billy Wright" – a plan provided by a handler with a clear purpose. He [the agent] was told, "When the IRA kill Wright, you'll be well in there", the IRA claimed in a statement in 1992. And years after the killing in the Maze, a Special Branch officer told me that, using sources within the UVF, they had "influenced the move to expel Wright [in 1996]". Wright was part of a mixed-up war – a man who lived and operated in open and hidden places. He was part of the killing and was, in his turn, killed. As in so many other cases, we know part of his story – but not all of it. And we never will.

Prison security – or the lack of such – became the focus of the Wright inquiry. Along with the other headline incidents about the prison at the time, everything was pointing to the fact that the Maze or Long Kesh was not a prison in the sense that most people would understand the term. This was a prisoner-of-war camp in all but name; a place where often the tail wagged the dog. As we journalists walked onto the wings of the Maze some days after the Wright shooting – to meet first the UDA, and then the IRA prison leaderships there – it was clear to us who was in charge.

This was 8 January 1998 – just four days after news emerged of a UDA prisoner vote to withdraw support for the peace process. Already there was a political effort underway to try to get the prisoners to reverse that decision. The talks that were happening on the outside needed the loyalists inside the tent, so to speak, and the prisoner vote was now threatening that participation and presence. The Ulster Unionist leader David Trimble went into the jail to meet them, and on 9 January, British Secretary of State Mo Mowlam would do likewise, after being persuaded to do so by a loyalist delegation, including the UDA "brigadier", Jackie McDonald, who had previously met her in London.

Jackie McDonald, Loyalist Leader, writing for this book

In the days leading up to the Good Friday Agreement, there was a lot of uncertainty, anger and discontent within loyalism because of serious issues with the RUC and the attitude of the British Government. UDA prisoners in the Maze had threatened to withdraw their support for any agreement, and there was pressure on the leadership on the outside to somehow defuse the situation. As a result, a UDP [Ulster Democratic Party] delegation, led by Gary McMichael, and including myself, [was] invited to Labour Party Headquarters in London to meet Mo Mowlam, the then Secretary Of State.

It was VIP treatment [once] we landed at Heathrow . . . as Mo had squeezed us into her very busy schedule. Gary and our delegation, representing all areas of the organisation, outlined just how serious the situation was in the Maze, and the possible impact that might have on the situation on the streets of Northern Ireland. We explained to Mo and her colleagues that she would need to visit the prisoners and listen to their concerns – but her advisers were warning her of the dangers of such a visit, and tried to convince her not to go.

I explained how serious and determined our prisoners were, and that to ignore them could result in more dead bodies on the streets. She left the room and spoke to Tony Blair, who was in Japan at the time, and returned to tell us she had been given the okay to go. Again, her colleagues advised against it, saying if she spoke to UDA prisoners, she would have to speak to others in the prison.

Fair play to her, she said she was going ahead. I told her she would have to go next morning as we were meeting the prisoners in the afternoon, and she agreed. I told her not to "piss up their legs", and she asked me what I meant. I said, [she should not] tell them any lies, because they would see right through her. We then asked her what we could tell the media who were waiting outside, and Mo told us to let them know that she was meeting UDA prisoners in the Maze next morning to discuss their concerns, and of course she did just that. The prisoners accepted what she told them – and you know the rest.

As regards "the rest", the loyalist prisoners were eventually talked into a change of mind but, in this period, it was evident how fragile the peace process was. The responses to the Wright killing brought many guns back into play on the part of the LVF, the UDA, the INLA and the IRA. As a consequence, the UDA-linked Ulster Democratic Party and Sinn Féin were both suspended from the political talks for a period. At this time we were also seeing the first bombings by dissident republicans – something I will look at in detail in Chapter Five. It was against such an unpromising backdrop that the political talks continued and were able to make progress – ultimately towards the historic deal that came to be known as the Belfast or Good Friday Agreement. With the subsequent creation of a Sentence Review

Commission, the prisoner releases began – a trickle at first, in a process gradually gaining momentum, as the cells of the Maze/Long Kesh were emptied of this category of prisoners. The first releases took place on Friday, 11 September 1998.

Radio Ulster News (Brian Rowan), 12 noon, 11 September 1998

Three loyalists came out first about twenty minutes ago – Matthew McCormick, Daniel Annesley and Gary Hall. They didn't speak to reporters here in the Maze car park, and were driven away. There is no one here on the loyalist side with any public role, but I spoke to a senior loyalist figure from Belfast. He said they didn't want any triumphalism and wanted this to be low-key. On the republican side, there are members of the pressure group Saoirse here. They've been pushing for prisoner releases, and Gerry Kelly and Brendan McFarlane, who escaped from this jail in 1983, are also here to meet those republicans coming out, and those releases should come soon.

This was the beginning of something much bigger. By July 2000, over 400 prisoners had been freed, and this essential, if controversial, element of peace-building was completed. The voices of opposition were heard but not heeded; they could not stop what was happening. In the jail car park that day, 28 July 2000, the IRA, UDA, UVF and Red Hand Commando prisoners each released a statement about their thoughts on this day and what it meant for them.

IRA Prisoners' Statement, 28 July 2000

. . . We walk free from this prison camp, as have our comrades before us, proud republicans, unbowed and unbroken. We are determined to pursue and achieve the goals for which so many gave their lives: that is, the establishment of a united democratic socialist republic. As republicans who have experienced suffering, we understand well the hurt of others. We offer the sincere hand of friendship to everyone who is prepared to help build a new future for all of our people. The New Ireland we seek is an equal and democratic one. An Ireland that truly cherishes all of her children equally.

In the words of Nelson Mandela, also a former political prisoner: "We understand that there is no easy road to freedom. We know it well. None of us acting alone can achieve success. We must act together as a united people, for national reconciliation and for nation building. Let there be justice for all. Let there be peace for all."

These words were delivered to waiting reporters that day by Jim McVeigh, the last IRA "OC" or Officer Commanding in Maze/Long Kesh. Now, in a contribution for this book, McVeigh thinks back to that period and the time before it, and forward, to what has happened since and the place we have now reached: a determination that there will be, in his words, "no going back to those days of bitter conflict".

Jim McVeigh, last IRA "OC" in Maze/Long Kesh

It's hard to believe that we were released 15 years ago. Notwithstanding all the ups and downs of the peace process, there's no doubt in my mind that we are all in a much better place, as a consequence of the difficult decisions that were taken back then.

As I write this, the institutions established by the Good Friday Agreement are under threat, because of the difficulties arising from Tory cuts and the issue of welfare reform. Ironically it is a measure of how things have changed, that we are exercised by such matters, rather than simply issues of nationality or symbols. Whatever about those difficulties, there will be no going back to those days of bitter conflict.

I remember vividly the evening before our release. As I lay on the bed in my H Block cell, I spent most of the night thinking about each of the hunger strikers, and the terrible suffering that had occurred within the H Blocks. I thought about the many friends and comrades who had been killed during the course of the conflict. I had spent 16 years within the H Blocks, and had witnessed the transformation in prison conditions as a consequence of the sacrifices made by so many. I felt proud that we had endured and had triumphed; that the system of brutality and criminalisation designed to break republican prisoners had been defeated. Thatcher had been defeated.

We were about to be released as POWs, and the world could be in no doubt about that. Of course we knew full well that the struggle was far from over; that this was only the beginning of a new phase or chapter in our struggle. Many republicans had grave reservations about the peace process, about the ceasefire and the GFA. I had long come to the conclusion that the course that we were now on was the correct one. But it would be fair to say that we were far from convinced that everything would be plain sailing. We were determined to use the opportunities presented by the ceasefire to build a popular political struggle that could and would deliver our political objectives.

I'd thought about my mother, Rosaleen who had passed away a few years earlier. Between 1972 and 1997, when she died, she had visited three of her sons in various prisons. She had visited us, worried about us, cried for us and fought for us. Like so many women, she had been politicised by the experience of the prison struggle. The sheer courage and doggedness of thousands of women like her had defeated the British policy of criminalisation. It broke my heart to know that [my mother] would not be there to greet me. That I would not have the opportunity to spoil her in her old age and repay, at least in part, the love and care she had shown me and my brothers over those long years in prison. I now had two sons myself and I was determined to help shape a different future for them.

I'm glad to say that the decisions we took then have brought us to a different place, a better place. There are many difficulties within the political process, and we face many challenges. I'm now a Sinn Féin councillor and the leader of the biggest political party in Belfast City Council. I could never have imagined the political space I now find myself in, but I have never forgotten that day in the [prison] car park and the statement I read . . . I'm content that, as Bobby Sands said, our revenge should be the laughter of our children.

McVeigh's statement on behalf of the IRA prisoners was just one of several read to assembled reporters on that summer's day in 2000. There were of course others from the loyalist organisations too.

UFF/UDA Prisoners' Statement, 28 July 2000

Today is an important day for the peace process and the process of conflict resolution. For the first time, there are no UFF prisoners of war incarcerated behind these walls. The journey that has brought us to this point has been very difficult, and there are still many challenges ahead.

It is a testimony to the determination of the UFF command and to our political colleagues in the UDP, that the peace process has produced a political agreement, the prisoners of war have been returned home, and one hopes that conflict is finally behind us . . .

As we leave Long Kesh for the last time to embark on a new future, we are mindful of the many victims of the Troubles. All sides have suffered greatly and we acknowledge the hurt felt by the victims of this war and their families. In all sincerity we reiterate the sentiments expressed in the CLMC ceasefire statement, by offering our abject and true remorse to the innocent victims of the conflict . . . It is our hope that we will prove to be the last generation forced to war in defence of our community. . .

UVF/Red Hand Commando Prisoners' Statement, 28 July 2000

At this time of the Agreement's implementation, which includes the release of serving political prisoners from organisations who subscribe to peaceful transition, we would remind concerned organisations and individuals of our commitment to non-violent means of addressing the political conflict in Northern Ireland. This was demonstrated by our support for a declaration of ceasefire in 1994, and our becoming proactive in our support for our political representatives in the negotiated process. Ulster Volunteer Force and Red Hand Commando prisoners have supported the peace process, the negotiated agreement and [the] democratic developments which continue to emerge. We acknowledge the overwhelming desire for peace given by way of referendum on the Good Friday Agreement by the people of Northern Ireland ... We remain forever conscious of the casualties of the conflict and, in respect for all surviving families, we return to our communities with dignity, ... with sensitivity and an ongoing commitment to the democratic process.

The 28 July 2000 releases were much different than that first low-key day of releases in September 1998. On this July date, almost two years later, over 80 prisoners were freed from the Maze and elsewhere; bigger names linked to bigger headlines and events in the conflict period. It all looked and felt more dramatic; more of a defining moment.

For the prisoners this was a new day, but of course for the families of the victims, it will have been a reminder of older days – past days which were still very much part of their present. Back in December 1998, there had been an indication of just how raw and emotional this issue was for some, when during the Christmas home leave releases, Michelle Williamson, whose parents were killed in the IRA Shankill bomb, chained herself to the turnstile in the prison car park in protest. William "Plum" Smith – spokesman at the time for UVF and Red Hand Commando prisoners – understood how difficult this matter would be for some. He was at the jail on that last big day of releases in July 2000, some two years after he had taken part in the Good Friday Agreement negotiations and the talks that had set in motion this process regarding the prisoners.

William "Plum" Smith, former UVF/Red Hand Commando Prisoners' Spokesperson

In most conflicts or wars, when a peace agreement has been reached, the prisoners of that conflict are returned to their respective communities

– and Northern Ireland was no different. As Chairman of the PUP and Prisoners' Spokesperson, I made it quite clear at all times that there could be no wholesome agreement which did not include a deal on prisoners. Whilst the constitutional position of Northern Ireland was paramount, we would not abandon the men who were languishing in prison.

Two weeks prior to the signing of the Agreement, we had still not come to [a consensus], and I went public, stating that unless there was an agreement on prisoners, then there would be no agreement. We then entered into more talks: this time Mo Mowlam sat in, along with her civil servants and aides. The argument centred around the release period [i.e., when it would start and be completed] . . . Mo Mowlam was saying three years, which was too long as far as we were concerned. We demanded two years. She left, saying she would have to contact Tony Blair, and the meeting was adjourned while she did that. After a few hours she recalled the meeting, and told us that two years had been agreed by the Prime Minister. We then discussed and agreed [upon] the mechanisms [by which] that would be delivered.

On the eve of the Good Friday Agreement, I insisted [on being] accompanied by a senior member of the CLMC to go into the prison to speak directly to the prisoners, and this was granted. When the final day of releases approached, we had a meeting between the UVF, RHC and PUP [about] how we would handle this historic occasion . . . The world's press would be outside the gates, and we were cognisant of the pain and hurt this could cause if prisoners and supporters started to cheer, just like football team supporters whose team had scored. We then came up with the idea that our prisoners would not come out the front gate but another gate, and we hired transport to ferry them away – [which] also meant there were no supporters hanging about.

We celebrated the occasion in a dignified way, by honouring the Quaker workers who had manned and managed the Visitors' Centre voluntarily for thirty years. A delegation of EPIC – the UVF/RHC ex-prisoners' organisation – presented the workers [in the Centre] with flowers and presents, and at the same time recognised the pain and hurt of all victims.

To this day – more than 15 years after the releases were completed – this place of many stories, the Maze prison, remains controversial. There were plans for a peace and reconciliation centre on the site, where some remnants of the prison have been retained (including a hospital, H Block and watchtower). That plan however became stuck in a political logjam. There were concerns expressed about the site becoming a "shrine to terrorism" or a "shrine to the hunger strikers".

Given what happened there across the decades, the jail is a place of huge historical significance. It brings to mind both the fine detail and bigger picture of the conflict years. We remember the lives lost, the lives taken, and a roll call of names synonymous with bombs and bullets, death and destruction.

Whatever happens, even if it is physically demolished, this edifice to the conflict won't be erased from our minds. It has too big a presence and significance in the physical and metaphorical landscape to be ignored or forgotten. The prison was and is, as Duncan McLaughlan once said, "inextricably bound up" in stories of struggle, turmoil, political battles and armed conflict. The stories of the thousands of republicans and loyalists who were held there over the years are part of our history, part of what happened and of what needs to be told, explained and understood.

Back in that prison car park in July 2000, a former loyalist prisoner who had been held in the jail said it should be "razed to the ground". Around the same time however, Laurence McKeown, one of the republican hunger strikers from 1981, made a very different argument and pitch: "There have been so many lives tied up with [the Maze/Long Kesh], both people who were actually [there] either as prison officers or prisoners, and families who've been travelling to that place for years. The idea of just wiping it clean or demolishing it isn't the way. I think it should be retained as a place where people can go. You don't wipe things clean by denying that they existed, and nor do I think that, by retaining some place such as an element of Long Kesh, you keep on the ghosts of the past. I think what you do is allow a space for those ghosts to quietly disappear."

Dessie Waterworth, who worked as a prison officer in the blocks of the Maze for more than two decades, sees things differently again. He remembers the protests, the stench when the jail was "an open sewer", how security was compromised and the escapes; he remembers too his murdered colleagues.

Dessie Waterworth, retired Prison Officer, in an interview for this book
When I arrived, the first thing they said to me was: "Anything you were taught, forget about it. You are now in the Maze." We were detailed to work in the H Blocks, and that was generally 3, 4 and 5, which were the protest Blocks. Whenever Block 6 came on stream as a dirty protest block, I worked in A and B wings . . . All you could call it was an open sewer, cells covered in excrement, urine out of the doors at night, unwashed

prisoners. We had no special gear to wear, just our ordinary uniform of shirt and trousers . . .

There was a murder campaign against staff. In 1976 three staff were killed; in 1979, ten staff were murdered. That was meant to terrorise the staff, to stop us doing our duties. It actually had the reverse effect: we did our jobs. They were also attacking our homes. During the hunger strike, we supplied them with their meals and they refused them and, as far as we were concerned, that was their choice. But the staff were blamed again. We had no faith in the Northern Ireland Office . . .

In the early 1980s, after prisoners were separated and given their own wings – loyalist wings, republican wings – staff were removed from the wings to the top grille. That gave up control inside the wings . . . Searches weren't carried out; structural checks on doors and grilles – meant to happen every day – did not happen. Prisoners were not counted and numbers were returned and recorded daily in the journals as "assumed". This all led to the escape in September 1983 . . . Staff complained, but were ignored . . . It could have been made the secure prison it was meant to be. After any major incident, such as the escape, the discovery of the tunnel, the murders, we took back control and it worked; it was secure. But the prisoners complained and controlled movement/escorts stopped, and security went out the window again.

I think H Block 6, the hospital and the tower [the retained buildings] should all be taken down and put into a big grinder . . . so everyone who has done time gets an egg-timer if they want a memory of the Maze.

I worked with some of the bravest men and women in the country. They were doing a job that no one else would do, and deserve proper recognition. I also think the families of these staff deserve recognition for what they had to put up with throughout the years. As long as the remaining buildings are still standing, people will try to use them as shrines. I would like a record of the prison officers' and governors' story, but not there [at a Maze peace centre]. There are better places than that.

The history of Maze/Long Kesh will always be argued and contested; there will always be different stories and different perspectives; different ways of seeing – and not seeing – things. Today's battle is about what is left of the jail and whether it should stand or fall. Again, such decisions need to be taken by people who can stand back from what happened there, from their own experiences and memories and their own script about the conflict years.

I have argued, and will argue in the coming chapters that any process for addressing the past should be shaped internationally. In the same way that in 1995 the Presbyterian Minister Roy Magee argued for a Commission to inform the debate on prisoner releases – a Commission that would not be politically-led – so a similar approach is now needed in relation to the key decisions on Maze/Long Kesh and the possible establishment of a peace and reconciliation centre at this site. The prisoner story and the story of the prison is yet another element of the ongoing picture here which, post-conflict, remains unfinished and incomplete, and needs to be addressed.

"Eventually [the leadership's] patience snapped." Republican Danny Morrison, thinking back to the bomb and statement that ended the IRA ceasefire, February 1996. *(Elle Rowan)*

10 February 1996

STATEMENT BY THE PRIME MINISTER

The evil act at Docklands struck at the heart of 17 months of peace in Northern Ireland. Innocent people had their lives shattered in a most violent and shocking way. My heart goes out to them and their families. We all owe a debt, too, to the emergency services who coped so magnificently.

Where there was optimism, a dark shadow of doubt has now been cast. The IRA once again callously threaten the desire for peace. They will not be allowed to prevail. Too many lives have already been saved, too much good has come out of the ceasefire, to allow that to happen.

I intend to carry on the search for peace with the Irish Government and the democratic political parties. The IRA and Sinn Fein must say now that their campaign of violence has stopped, and they will never resume it again.

We will be vigilant about security both on the mainland and in Northern Ireland. We will assess carefully and coolly this challenge to the peace process and the way ahead. The prize of peace is too precious to be squandered.

I have visited Northern Ireland many times. I have seen the changes that the ceasefire has brought: the lightness of mood among the people, the increasing prosperity, the happiness, the freedom to walk down a street without fear. I am determined to entrench their freedom as a permanent part of peace in the life of Northern Ireland. Nothing less will do.

Above: "The evil act at Docklands struck at the heart of 17 months of peace." Then Prime Minister John Major, commenting on the IRA bomb in London in February 1996. *(Elle Rowan)*

Opposite: "His eyes still haunt me." Veteran journalist Eamonn Mallie, thinking back to a meeting with Bobby Sands in 1979. *(Elle Rowan)*

Above: "It was a horrible, horrible time." Former Press Association Ireland Editor Deric Henderson, on reporting the hunger-strike period. *(Elle Rowan)*

Opposite: Block, number, name – from hunger strike to death. *(Elle Rowan)*

Block No.	Prisoner Number + Name	Hunger Strikers Date On	Date in Hospital	Remark	
H3	950/79 SANDS	1·3·81	23·3·81	DIED 01·17 TUE 5·5·81	66
H5	391/80 HUGHES	15·3·81	10·4·81	DIED 17·40 TUE 12·5·81	58
H5	354/77 McCREESH	22·3·81	14·4·81	DIED 02·15 THUR 21·5·81	60
H5	18/80 O'HARA	22·3·81	15·4·81	DIED 23·29 THUR 21·5·81	61
H5	9521/77 McDONNELL	+3 11·5·81	29·5·81	DIED 05·11 WED 8·7·81	5
H5	✳ 141/77 McLAUGHLIN	14·5·81		OFF HUNGER STRIKE ON WED 27·5·81 AT M.P.H.	
H6	177/78 DOHERTY	23·5·81	11·6·81	DIED 19·15 SUN 2·8·81	72
H3	1404/77 LYNCH	24·5·81	11·6·81	DIED 0100 SAT 1·8·81	70
H5	278/79 HURSON	29·5·81	22·6·81	DIED 0430 MON 13·7·81	45
H3	985/77 McILWEE	9·6·81	3·7·81	DIED 11·27 SAT 8·8·81	60
H3	✳ 364/77 QUINN ✗	15·6·81	3·7·81	OFF HUNGER STRIKE ON FRI 31·7·81 TRANS To RVH 18·45HRS.	
H6	376/77 DEVINE	22·6·81	16·7·81	DIED THUR 20·8·81	
H3	454/77 McKEOWN	29·6·81	23·7·81		
H3	✳ 533/76 McGEOWN	10·7·81	5·8·81	OFF HUNGER STRIKE ON THR 20·8·81 RVH	41
H3	1052/77 DEVLIN	15·7·81	10·8·81	OFF HUNGER STRIKE FRI 4·9·81 To RVH	51
H3	1403/77 McCLOSKEY	4·8·81	28·8·88		
H3	135/79 SHEEHAN	11·8·81			
H6	1065/76 McMULLEN	18·8·81			
H5	881/77 B FOX	25·8·81			
H3	661/76 CARVILLE HJ	1·9·81			
H6	179/78 PICKERING JH	8·9·81			

Block No.	Prisoner Number + Name	Hunger Strikers Date On	Date in Hospital	Remark	
H3	950/79 SANDS	1·3·81	23·3·81	DIED 01·17 TUE 5·5·81	66
H5	391/80 HUGHES	15·3·81	10·4·81	DIED 17·40 TUE 12·5·81	58
H5	354/77 McCREESH	22·3·81	14·4·81	DIED 02·15 THUR 21·5·81	60

EDITORIAL

PROPERLY CONVICTED

If there is an issue which unites loyalist and republican terrorists and their supporters it is their campaign for the early release of prisoners. Their view is that their release, indeed the granting of amnesty is the logical result of the peace process and would actually advance it.

One has only to inspect the violent and murderous history against the community by the prisoners - every one of them convicted after the due process of the law - to conclude it is inconceivable that public opinion would be ready to accept early release of those responsible for such atrocious crimes.

It is not just that this premature release makes a nonsense of the seriousness of their crimes and atrocities it also insults the feelings and undiminished grief of the families of the victims. The ceasefire is barely six months old. Talk and especially any move to release these prisoners, is irresponsible and undermines the rule of law.

The irony, of course, is whatever its other merits, if selective internment had been introduced some years ago, as this Federation argued, then there would not be this current debate about the release of convicted criminals. If they had been interned on suspicion and without trial the Government could legitimately and morally have opened the gates and let the suspects go.

Response to Editorial in "Police Beat" from Pat McGeown Sinn Fein Prisons Spokesperson.

If anything this editorial shows just how reactionary and backward looking the Police Federation is. Not only do they come out against releases in the current climate but they actually hark back to the bad old days trying to justify internment. One wonders what planet these people are on. Of course it also demonstrates that had anyone listened to them before it is highly unlikely that we would have had any peace process.

If they cannot recognise that the releases of political prisoners are an integral part of building peace and reconciliation then perhaps they would be as well keeping their mouths shut as they are adding little to the positive dynamic for peace in this editorial.

For them to use the logic that political prisoners have been convicted by some fair and just due process of law is a nonsense and ignores reality. Political prisoners have been convicted using special draconian laws, special inhuman interrogation centres, and special no-jury courts.

They don't have to take my word for this just read the many human rights reports from the European Court, the British Government's Bennett Inquiry, Amnesty ~International, Heksinki Watch and many others.

As for hiding behind the feelings and grief of the families of the victims. The RUC would do well to look at their own record. The families of Sam Deveney, Patrick Rooney, Nora McCabe, and many others are still waiting for an acknowledgement of their feelings and grief.

If the Police Federation concentrate on re-opening old sores rather than looking forward that in itself this is a clear indictment of their incapacity to play a positive role in the peace process.

Above: "It was not possible to have a successful peace process without such releases."
Queen's University Law Professor Kieran McEvoy. *(Elle Rowan)*

Opposite top: "Properly Convicted" – *Police Beat* Editorial February 1995. *(Elle Rowan)*

Left: Sinn Fein spokesman Pat McGeown responds. *(Elle Rowan)*

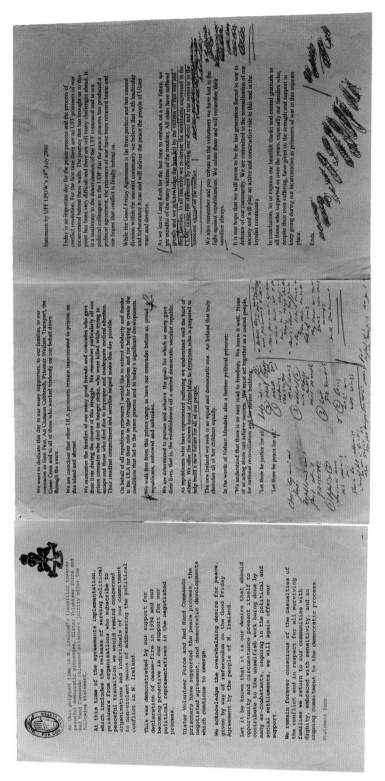

Above: Loyalist and republican release statements, July 2000. *(Elle Rowan)*

Opposite: "I told her not to piss up their legs." Loyalist Jackie McDonald's advice for then Secretary of State, Mo Mowlam, before her meeting with prisoners in 1998. *(Elle Rowan)*

Above: Jim McVeigh, the last IRA "OC" Long Kesh. *(Elle Rowan)*

Opposite: William "Plum" Smith, spokesman for UVF/Red Hand Commando prisoners at the time of the releases. *(Elle Rowan)*

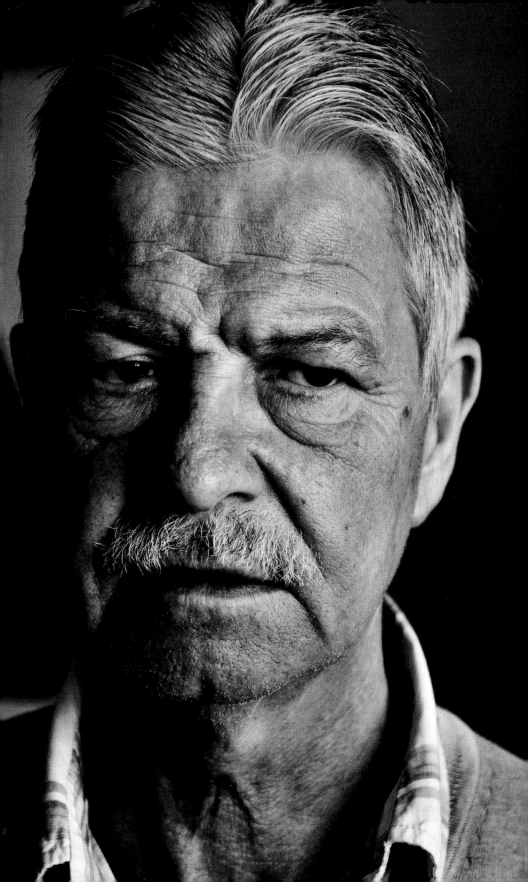

Above: "Anything you were taught, forget about it. You are now in the Maze."
Retired prison officer Dessie Waterworth, remembering the advice he was given on
his first day in the job. *(Elle Rowan)*

Top: Dessie Waterworth in his prison officer uniform. *(Dessie Waterworth)*

interpreted as a vindication of their years of terrorism, which has further enhanced their ability to avoid acceptance of any responsibility.

Deals have been done with, to quote, "OTR's" argued to be and portrayed as an element of the prisoner release scheme, but nonetheless another indication to the terrorists that the slate has been wiped clean.

I think we could be forgiven for asking what have they given in return? We see no evidence of a will to move forward on the policing issue. We believe that the increasing calls for inquiries, into historical events is not founded in any righteous intention of finding the truth, but with the aim of further undermining the police service and bringing about its liquidation. We predict that this strategy will continue unabated.

Above: Extract from a speech given to Police Superintendents' Conference in 2001. *(Elle Rowan)*

Top and left: "As part of this investigation we also endeavoured to locate the burial site of British SAS operative Robert Nairac. We were unable to do so." Author's notes of IRA briefings in March and June 1999. *(Elle Rowan)*

Opposite: "As a child I watched my grandmother cry every day." Eimear McVeigh, niece of Columba McVeigh. *(Elle Rowan)*

Above: "The whole sordid business was literally hidden." Sandra Peake of the WAVE Trauma Centre, on the IRA practice of "disappearing" bodies. *(Elle Rowan)*

CHAPTER FIVE

Dissident Wars: Keeping the Candle Lit

"The political response must go beyond condemnation. It is imperative that everyone makes clear their opposition to the murder of Constable Kerr. Every citizen must defend the [peace] process . . . those involved do not represent republicanism."
Gerry Adams, April 2011.

"There's a degree of paranoia with them that we are trying to feed."
A senior police officer, speaking to the author about the dissident republican threat, February 2015.

When we look back at certain seismic events in our recent past, with the benefit of hindsight we realise how much of the picture we could not see, or have guessed at, at the time. A case in point is the Docklands bomb in February 1996. For all the concerns about the stability of the ceasefire, that explosion still arrived as a sudden and shocking development. People had become used to the peace, however imperfect. Now, in the news and headlines of that bomb and more deaths, they watched how the ceasefire simply disintegrated and saw how fragile peace really is. For so many people, this was an incomprehensible return to the darkest days of violence.

As however we have noted in Chapter Three, what has become clear with the passage of time is that at this particular period, the IRA was managing internal discontent and dissent, and doing so out of range of our seeing and hearing. In these behind-the-scenes machinations and manoeuvres, a significant number of the organisation's members were questioning the direction which had been taken and the decisions linked to the Adams/McGuinness peace strategy, including the ceasefire. This would lead to cracks within the organisation, a failed attempt to overthrow Adams and McGuinness, and, ultimately, the emergence of violent dissident republican groups. While so many of us now regard the days of the conflict as being far behind us, the continuing existence of these dissident elements means that even today, violence is ongoing. Although this is not happening at anything like the previous levels at the height of the conflict, there is still a danger posed by these splinter organisations. Like the IRA before them, they will not be condemned off the stage, and how to engage them, and include them in a meaningful dialogue is something which urgently needs to be addressed. For the republican community, in particular, this is unfinished business – part of the unfinished peace.

The dissidents were undoubtedly at their most dangerous, potentially posing the biggest threat to the political and peace processes, in the periods just before and immediately after the Good Friday Agreement of 1998. It all came to a head in late 1997, with a challenge inside what the IRA calls a "General Army Convention". This is a set-piece and secret IRA gathering with delegates chosen to represent the entire organisation. The larger plan was to destabilise the republican peace strategy, undermine Adams and McGuinness, and pave the way for a new leadership to take control of the IRA. Ultimately, the move failed – but there were resignations, including from senior figures who knew the ways of "war": people who were better armed and had better access to expertise than those who are today's dissidents. In the early months of 1998, this new threat materialised and corresponding violence erupted.

To begin with, there was confusion. Was this violence the IRA indicating that it was unhappy with the direction and design of the political talks in that period and, in the words of unionist leader, David Trimble, "venting its spleen"? While it took some time to work out, what would later become clear is that we were witnessing the first actions of those who in October 1997 had attempted that coup inside the IRA. In late February 1998, within just a few days, Moira was bombed and then Portadown. This was a deliberate targeting of the constituencies of unionist politicians, Jeffrey Donaldson and David Trimble. Months later, there was another bomb in Banbridge and, this time, more than 30 people were injured. The operational tempo, the bombing expertise and the know-how in all of this have not been matched by today's dissident organisations – the IRA coalition, Óglaigh na hÉireann or the Continuity IRA.

What stopped the 1998 dissidents was in fact one of their own bombs, in August 1998 – the Omagh bomb, and the screaming headlines of the highest ever body count in a single incident in the entire period of the conflict. The Good Friday of the Belfast Agreement had been followed by that Black Saturday, and the darkness and ugliness of this atrocity in Omagh.

The IRA moved to apply pressure on those responsible for the bomb, telling them they should disband "sooner rather than later". In an interview at the time, the IRA clearly dissociated themselves from this element: "Arguably, actions that this grouping have carried out have been designed and timed, not only to derail the peace process, but also specifically to damage our struggle. It is ridiculous for anyone to suggest we would assist them in that." The dissidents were forced into retreat at that time – and, in terms of the expertise and operational capability they had to begin with, they have never recovered.

However, while there are not today the same threats to politics and peace as during that very volatile period in 1997–1998, there are still dangers that cannot be ignored. The scattered remnants of these organisations under their many different titles and guises are still out there. In the bigger scheme of things, they cannot and will not change anything in terms of politics and security but, unless they are stopped, they could well take more lives in a futile fight that they refuse to give up.

* * * *

Fast forward to the autumn of 2010. The page in my diary for Thursday, 28 October was blank, except for the pencilled circling of a time that evening – 19.00 hrs. I had been contacted several days earlier, and given this date and time. I had also been given a set of instructions: on the evening in question, I was to go to the front of Clonard Monastery in west Belfast, where I would be picked up; I was not to bring my mobile phone; the people I was due to meet would supply me with a pen and paper. Additionally, I was asked to ensure that there would be a delay of several days between the meeting I would be attending and anything I published as a journalist as a result.

All of this was preparation for an interview I was to do with leadership representatives of the dissident republican faction, Óglaigh na hÉireann (ONH), for publication in the *Belfast Telegraph*. In the days prior to the meeting, I was given a few more details. From Clonard, a driver would take me to the meeting place, where there would be one person on "security"; the interview would be with two representatives of the dissident organisation – one representing the "Army Council", the other from its "General Headquarters Staff". It was also agreed that I could bring my own paper and a pencil or clear biro pen after all.

This would be a very timely – if, for some, controversial – interview. It was coming just weeks after the then Director General of MI5, Jonathan Evans, had highlighted the "real and rising security challenge" posed by dissident groups in Northern Ireland, in explanation of the decision by the security services to raise the threat level in Britain to "substantial". Some months before, in April

2010, Óglaigh na hÉireann had targeted, in a bomb attack, the military base at Palace Barracks in Holywood, which houses the MI5 Northern Ireland Headquarters. Before that, in January 2010, the organisation had been linked to an under-car booby trap bomb attack, in which Police Constable Peadar Heffron had been critically injured. Other incidents around that time had included the targeting of a police dog handler in east Belfast and an Army Major in Bangor.

Before that meeting on 28 October, I had written an outline of what I wanted to discuss with the Óglaigh na hÉireann representatives. I wanted to know about the roots of the organisation, its size, its immediate aims and its relationship with other dissident organisations, its strategy and what it thought was achievable. I also had questions on specific attacks, including the bomb at Palace Barracks. I wanted to ask about ONH's attitude to Sinn Féin, and what ONH considered its mandate to be. How did it justify this continuing violence? In conclusion, I wrote the following general observations, also as questions I hoped to broach during the exchange: "Sucking another generation in? A war which can't be won; a war with no winners? Killing for sake of killing?"

On 28 October, just before 6.00 p.m., I took the train from my home into Great Victoria Street station in Belfast, and then walked from there to the front gates at Clonard. Inside a bag, I had a notepad and three pencils. People were leaving the church and, from inside the grounds, a man called my name. I followed him to a car. He opened the back door and I got in . . .

* * * *

Sometime later, along with the driver who had collected me at Clonard, I left the house I had been taken to, with almost 20 pages of notes. Three men, not the two I had been expecting, were present for the interview, and introduced themselves as representatives of the General Headquarters Staff and Army Council. Before leaving the house where the interview was conducted, I had made it clear that I did not want to be driven all the way back to Clonard, and I told the driver that, if there was any sign of police, he should stop the car and I would get out and walk.

There was another twist to come, however. As I was getting out of the car, the driver gave me a bag. Inside was a religious candle. It was the strangest, most bizarre of offerings on a night when this man had brought me to a house where men had talked "war". I walked to where I could use a phone, and called my wife and then the news editor at the *Belfast Telegraph*, Jonny

McCambridge, to tell him the interview had been completed. It was published five days later.

So, what was I told by the men in the upstairs bedroom of that house? At times it was chilling, callous, frightening: a cold conversation about war and terror, about attempts to kill and a clear determination to try again. It was a journey into the past – except that it was in the present. There will be those who will dismiss what was said as dogma, delivered with a mixture of arrogance and naivety – sheer bloody-mindedness.

ONH: "Our fundamentals are about securing the organisation, about credible recruitment and carrying out high-grade operations . . . Every time we are not involved in the execution of an operation, we are recruiting, developing expertise, gathering intelligence and planning the next operation. All of that is made easier on the back of some of our operations. The Provisional IRA took approximately 15 years to wind down. There is no ready-made pack IRA that can be assembled in a short period of time.

"An ONH capable of having a sustained campaign will take time to develop. It will take time to develop the structures, personnel, finance and weaponry . . . Inside the organisation, successful operations increase morale. [This] also gives republicans increased confidence to carry out more daring attacks. Republicans who acknowledge that ONH are doing the right things offer their services. That, in turn, increases ONH capabilities even further."

When I asked whether they presently had what previously would have been Provisional IRA bomb-making expertise, they replied that this was the case. They refused however to elaborate on this issue or provide any further details.

Regarding the recent spate of incidents which had prompted the MI5 comments about the current threat level, the ONH leadership stated: "We deliberately picked areas that were seen as safe zones for security forces. It was to send a direct message that nowhere is safe." On that MI5 assessment, the men in the room commented: "It says that they are acknowledging a growing threat, which they admit they played down and ignored; played down and underestimated. ONH will decide when and where it attacks. Sceptics will say, 'They would say that, because they don't have the capabilities.' [But] eighteen months ago they told us we couldn't even detonate a bomb. Nothing is beyond our reach."

I then spoke to them about their attempt in January of that year to kill the police officer, Peadar Heffron, a Gaelic footballer and Irish speaker, asking: "Is he not as Irish – more Irish – than those who make up your organisation?"

"Absolutely not," was the terse reply. "Irish history is littered with mercenaries, who have worked for and implemented British laws."

I then addressed those observations I had scribbled in preparation for the interview, suggesting that this was a war that could not be won, and that killing had become the cause. "As far as we are concerned, we are not engaged in killing for killing's sake. We are engaged in a war against the illegal occupation of our country and usurpation of Irish sovereignty . . . We think that a war will create the conditions for credible dialogue aimed at British withdrawal. Internal settlements are not what Irish republicans fought, died and went to jail for." In a different phase of this conflict, we had of course heard these words spoken by others – better armed, better organised others.

The interview was published in the *Belfast Telegraph* some days after the meeting, on 3 November 2010. It would be the subject of criticism in some quarters. Jimmy Spratt, a former Chairman of the Police Federation, who became a Democratic Unionist Party (DUP) MLA at Stormont (a post from which he has recently retired), commented: "There is a very serious dissident threat. These organisations are intent on murder and mayhem, and the platform given to them in this type of interview does not help our present situation. I think it could drive people into the arms of the organisation." Brian Ervine, then leader of the Progressive Unionist Party had similar objections: "It is all free publicity for them. There is no such thing as good or bad publicity. This is a very small organisation being larged [sic] up, and maybe being given a lot more news than they deserve. I also would have concerns that this type of publicity will help them recruit."

These are the old, tired, "oxygen of publicity" arguments: "Don't let them breathe in the newspapers or on television or on radio; don't let anyone hear them", and so on. Of course, I expected criticism. These are not easy decisions, but to comment meaningfully on such organisations, you need to have some understanding of their thinking. So, you need to meet them and speak with them – this is an essential part of reporting conflict. The former Controller of the BBC in Belfast, Robin Walsh was supportive: "The *Belfast Telegraph's* journalism was both courageous and proper. Warnings by various authorities of escalating violence served to increase public curiosity about those responsible, and the *Telegraph* interview quite rightly sought to satisfy that curiosity – and succeeded."

Within days of that interview being published, Óglaigh na hÉireann was back in contact – not face-to-face this time, but via a phone call to me. There had been a grenade attack on police in west Belfast, and ONH wanted to confirm that they had been behind it. I summed up the exchange in another piece for the *Belfast Telegraph*:

A sinister call on a shopping trip (*Belfast Telegraph*, 8 November 2010)
It was a call but not a conversation – a voice, but no name or number at the other end of the line.

Just days after this newspaper published a face-to-face interview with the dissident republican organisation, Óglaigh na hÉireann, this was them back in contact, in a coded call to my mobile phone.

On Friday night the armed faction had tried to kill police officers in a grenade explosion in west Belfast – and this was the statement on that attack: what, in the jargon of conflict, is called the "claim of responsibility".

. . . The caller just started speaking – this was the Belfast Brigade of Óglaigh na hÉireann. He [then] spoke of an ambush on police and said a Russian-style grenade had been used. Before hanging up, he gave a codeword to authenticate the call, a call that ended seconds after it began.

The dissidents don't recognise what we call "new policing": the era of the PSNI after the RUC . . . "Policing in the North is still controlled by National Security MI5," the dissident group said in that recent interview with this newspaper. "Everything that the RUC did – the abuse, harassment and frame-ups – still continues today."

Attacks like the one on Friday night are about trying to push the police out of the community, away from the community. The Chief Constable, Matt Baggott is determined not to allow that to happen.

Those I met on 28 October 2010 talked about building an organisation, and about credible recruitment and operations. The pattern since has been a familiar one – irregular appearances and attempts to mount attacks, the vast bulk of which fail. All of which suggests that we are not witnessing a re-run of the IRA campaign, or some new beginning but rather, the slow end of something. However, while there has been nothing to suggest that a sustained campaign is possible, there have been killings that are a reminder of the danger. In March 2009, Constable Stephen Carroll was killed, as were soldiers Patrick Azimkar and Mark Quinsey, in a separate incident that same month. In April 2011, Police Constable Ronan Kerr was killed in an under-car bomb attack, and in November 2012, Prison Officer David Black was shot dead while driving to work.

The killing of 25-year-old PC Ronan Kerr near his home in Omagh sparked huge public outrage and an outpouring of grief. The response of the Sinn Féin leadership was particularly telling, as I pointed out in an article for the *Belfast Telegraph* just a few days after the young policeman's death. The gulf between these dissident groups and the mainstream republican leadership could not have been made any plainer.

Persuasion, not coercion, is how to deal with dissidents
(*Belfast Telegraph*, 4 April 2011)

The language used by Gerry Adams yesterday is highly significant. Commenting on Saturday's bomb attack in Omagh, he spoke of "murder" – a word that speaks loudly to confirm the republican journey away from war. That is the journey of mainstream republicans – including the IRA. Mr Adams would never have described as "murder" an action by that organisation that claimed the life of a member of the security forces.

But mainstream republicans no longer see the police as an enemy – things have changed. When they endorsed the new policing arrangements in 2006, that move, more than any other, said their war was over.

"The political response must go beyond condemnation," Mr Adams said yesterday. "It is imperative that everyone makes clear their opposition to the murder of Constable Kerr. Every citizen must defend the [peace] process . . . those involved do not represent republicanism."

Gerry Adams and Sinn Féin are very precise in their language, so the word "murder" has been deliberately chosen by the Sinn Féin President. While his words are carefully chosen, so too is the targeting of police officers by dissident groups.

Two officers were seriously injured in under-car explosions in May 2008 and January 2010. A female officer was also targeted last August, the device falling from her car. And, now, the killing of Ronan Kerr.

The dissidents don't, won't, listen to Messrs Adams and McGuinness. Groups such as Óglaigh na hÉireann (ONH) and the Real and Continuity IRAs see the peace process as a betrayal; a sell-out. And, in the thinking of these factions, there is still a war, still an enemy.

Policing has changed and is changing. The reforms recommended in the Patten Report have made it different, made it easier for Catholics to join. But those Catholics are stand-out targets in their communities. Constable Peadar Heffron was easily found. So, too, Ronan Kerr.

Martin McGuinness described those responsible for killing Constable Kerr as "enemies of the peace process; enemies of the people of Ireland". He said their motivation was "to destroy the peace" – but that they would fail.

In their thinking, the dissidents will consider what happened at the weekend as a success. This is what they have been trying for since they killed two soldiers and a police officer in March 2009. There is no security or intelligence answer to this – no initiative that will stop them. Sinn Féin Junior Minister Gerry Kelly accepted this last week, when commenting on a security alert in north Belfast.

And if there is no security or intelligence answer, then there is an onus to try to talk, to get through to the dissidents, to try to persuade them to end these attacks. Some argue that there is no point, because they are "fanatics and murderers". But the point in trying is found in what happened at the weekend.

Already, the dissidents will be looking for, and thinking about, the next target. Gerry Adams said they "should stop, and stop now". But that won't happen. There is no easy answer. This latest attack is about creating fear and about getting inside the heads of those the dissidents still consider to be their enemy. They don't want Catholics in the police service; don't want anything that suggests progress.

In the background, some people are speaking to the different armed factions, talking and trying to get them to stop. Mr Adams, Mr McGuinness and Mr Kelly have all said they, too, are prepared to talk to the dissident groups.

If that happens, the argument of the Sinn Féin leadership will be that these armed actions won't work. But can they get through?

After this latest killing, they have to keep trying.

A newly-formed faction claiming the IRA title eventually admitted placing the bomb that killed Ronan Kerr. But what was the purpose, the point? What was this killing going to achieve or change? Within that dissident world, this new faction was seen as something of a last chance – a final attempt to bring arms, expertise and personnel under the umbrella and organisational control of a coalition. Police intelligence assessments suggested a "winnowing process" – meaning the weeding out and dumping of those within the dissident ranks who were under suspicion of being informers. That police assessment, given in late 2012, also suggested this dissident IRA coalition was plotting "multiple casualty attacks" – yet there has not been a step change that has taken their activity from sporadic to something more sustained. The words, the talk, the plots have not materialised into anything significantly different. Rather, as a result of the ongoing efforts of the intelligence and security services, there has been constant disruption and interruption of their plans and then a dismantling of the leadership in arrests linked to covert listening and watching.

I am conscious as I write that this mishmash of dissident groupings is probably planning at this moment to kill someone – but the question remains, for what purpose? What will that achieve in political or security terms? These are questions that have to be asked, and that cannot be avoided. A better armed and resourced IRA stopped when it knew there was a military stalemate and that it could not win. Yet these dissident organisations in their many guises continue, trying to "keep the candle lit". They will not force changes to political agreements, will not bring about British withdrawal and will not become an equivalent IRA. Those days are gone. Too much has changed. Nor have they been able to match the level of threat posed by those dissidents who first emerged from the IRA organisation in late 1997/early 1998.

On 18 March 2014, I met two representatives of this "IRA coalition" in a cemetery in west Belfast. I was told to be there at 7.30 p.m., to stand at the gates and that "we'll get you sorted out from there". I stood on the opposite side of the road and crossed when I heard a whistle from inside the gates. Then, I walked a short distance inside: there were two men waiting for me. One of them took a statement from inside his shoe, and the other shone a small torch and read out the statement, as I copied it down. This was a briefing about an ambush on police not far from the cemetery, several days earlier.

Dissident IRA Statement, 18 March 2014

On Friday, 14 March at 10.30 p.m., an active service unit of the IRA embarked on an operation against British State Forces, namely a PSNI patrol. This attack involved the IRA striking the PSNI landrover as it passed the City Cemetery on Belfast's Falls Road. The IRA had a second active service unit with automatic weapons close by, with the intention of engaging personnel who exited the vehicles. The device used in this offensive action was an explosively formed projectile (EFP), detonated by command wire. These devices form a major part of the IRA's already substantial weapons inventory. Our development of this type of device is further evidence of the increasing expertise and ingenuity of our engineering department. The precision of the device is evidenced by the fact that it struck its intended target.

The PSNI are the vanguard of the British occupation and oppression in Ireland. They are the heavily armed protectors of the State, enforcing British law in Ireland. They engage in harassment of Irish citizens on a daily basis, arrest republicans and facilitate the work of MI5, with the full knowledge and backing of the British Government. For these reasons the PSNI are legitimate targets for the IRA. The IRA has demonstrated its ability to execute PSNI personnel in the past, and will continue to do so in the future.

It was a statement that sounded big and yet it left so much unsaid. Minimal damage was caused to the police vehicle by shrapnel. There was no way of proving that an armed active service unit was present and waiting to open fire, nor any way of verifying any of what was said, such as the claim by this IRA coalition that it had new supplies of Semtex explosives and detonators.

What we do know is that a previous IRA organisation, armed by Libya, recognised that there was no military solution, no way of winning the war and of forcing the "Brits" out. At this time too, British politicians and generals also recognised that it was difficult to envisage a military defeat of the IRA. There was a stalemate, and therefore a moral obligation to explore an alternative, which meant there had to be talking and negotiations in an effort to bring about change and compromise. As a result, politics and policing and security in Northern Ireland would look different. These are the things of the real world. Today's dissident IRA has nothing like the same wherewithal in terms of weaponry, expertise, personnel, finance and support. It is floundering and faltering on a battlefield that many and most have long since abandoned. The threat cannot be dismissed, because within it there is a potential for lives to be lost, but nor should it be overstated or dressed up as something more or bigger than it actually is.

For the present, the security and intelligence services will continue to disrupt the activities of these dissident groups, arresting them, neutralising their bombs and, on occasions, frightening them to the point where they dare not move. This is something I explored in another recent piece for the *Belfast Telegraph*.

Covert methods fuel paranoia of the dissidents
(*Belfast Telegraph*, 19 August 2014)

Almost four years ago, in an interview with this newspaper, the leadership of Óglaigh na hÉireann boasted: "Nothing is beyond our reach."

. . . Yesterday, I saw a leader of the Óglaigh na hÉireann faction walking and talking [with someone] on the Falls Road. He would regard it as safer to do his talking outside and on the move, rather than meet on the same street corner or in the same house or office.

For the dissidents, the challenge is to operate outside the listening circle, while the job for MI5 and police intelligence is to ensure that doesn't happen. They achieve this through the gadgetry and methods that have become part and parcel of the intelligence war.

Just look at how many dissident operations have been interrupted, how many arrests have been made, and how many bombs have failed to explode or only partially detonate. These are not chance happenings but, often, the end product of intelligence gathered. We know that explosives have been removed from bombs, that weapons have been bugged, that there are those inside the dissident organisations – so-called covert human intelligence sources – who are also working for the forces of law and order. But there is no such thing as 100 per cent intelligence. In this murky world, the pendulum swings back and forth – success for police, then a setback from the dissidents.

There are times when groups such as Óglaigh na hÉireann are afraid to move, afraid to talk. They will always be asking themselves: who might be watching, who might be listening and who among them might be talking? What was that conversation I witnessed on the Falls Road about yesterday? Was it about trying to avoid those who might be listening?

The dissidents must know that much of their talking and planning is within the earshot of MI5 and police intelligence. It is why so much of what they do fails.

Sometime after the publication of this article, a senior police officer told me: "There's a degree of paranoia with them that we are trying to feed." So much of this is psychological – that deliberate play inside heads. The threat, however it is described and assessed, is being and will be contained by police and intelligence. Yet there is never absolute knowledge, and no such thing as perfect security or protection.

In that interview I conducted with Óglaigh na hÉireann in 2010, the continuing MI5 presence in Northern Ireland was cited as evidence that policing has not changed. The 2014 statement above, from representatives of the dissident IRA coalition, makes the same argument. This is an issue which needs to be addressed. In a later chapter of this book, I will argue that policing needs to be done by the police, and that things need to happen without MI5 and all the jargon and gadgetry linked to National Security. But how do you stop the next killing? This remains today's challenge – how to establish a dialogue with the dissidents that attempts to talk them into a different approach, a different way of being heard. And within this is a clear challenge for the Catholic, nationalist, republican community: to engage with the dissidents in a non-confrontational way, and to close down the space for violent actions, by making absolutely clear that there is no support for their activities.

Of course, the dissidents can disagree with Sinn Féin, with Adams and McGuinness and, of course, a different argument can be listened to – but it is lost altogether when guns are fired and bombs are set off. Church, community, political leaders and the Irish Government and political parties need to go face-to-face with the dissidents, because this is an approach – *the* approach, in fact – that might just begin to change things. Part of that discussion has to focus on why people are still going to jail for their part in something that cannot succeed; something so obviously futile and fruitless. Any such discussion also has to be about the next generation and what they could be sucked into.

We could become complacent about the dissidents – about those attacks that rarely succeed; about how amateurish much of this looks; about how infiltrated and compromised these organisations have become. And then there is the shock of another killing, which shakes us out of that complacency, but when it is too late. Before the ceasefires, when John Hume engaged in a difficult dialogue with Gerry Adams, people suggested he was wasting his time and was being used. Now, it is someone else's turn to start a similar conversation and see what is achievable; to do something that might just save a life. A community cannot support young men and women in joining a police service, and then leave them vulnerable to dissident attack. That dialogue – however uncomfortable or unpalatable – needs to happen. This too is part of the unfinished business of the peace process: addressing a threat that first showed itself in 1998, and that has never quite gone away.

CHAPTER SIX
Tears for a Lost Son: The "Disappeared"

"Republicans did a terrible thing whenever they buried the people that are called 'the Disappeared'. It was a very cruel thing to do, and it caused immense hurt to many families throughout our society."
Martin McGuinness, speaking at Féile an Phobail, August 2015.

"He was the uncle I never knew, and the uncle I will never forget."
Eimear McVeigh, niece of Columba McVeigh, writing for this book.

"There were multiple levels of silence . . . Silence compounded by an underlying fear, which stopped families speaking out."
Sandra Peake, WAVE Trauma Centre, writing for this book.

Among the many unanswered questions of the conflict years are those surrounding the highly emotive issue of the IRA's practice of "disappearing" the bodies of those within their communities, whom they had secretly abducted and murdered – leaving their families utterly in the dark about what had happened, and thus unable to grieve. This had first started in 1972 and, for years, there was silence within these communities; a quiet fear; an incomprehension on the part of the victims' relatives, who did not know whether their loved ones were alive or dead. Within the so-called Long War, there was this long, agonising wait for some news; for some development that would at last begin to answer the questions.

Then, in the early part of 1999, there was an important development. On the evening of 29 March, I took a call from "Peter", asking for a meeting with me. "Peter" was once "P. O'Neill" – the spokesman authorised to deliver statements and briefings on behalf of the republican organisation to members of the press like myself. For a period extending from late 1997 to early 2000, he would call me when the IRA leadership wanted to speak. A quietly spoken man, today, he has melted into the peace – as anonymous now as he was in the war.

As I made my way to the meeting in west Belfast on that March evening, I was expecting to hear something about the ongoing political talks of the period. Yet more negotiations were happening at Hillsborough Castle, this time around the implementation of the political structures of the Good Friday Agreement. The weapons issue had still not been resolved and politics had become trapped in a few words: "no guns – no government" – one of those phrases that puts all sides into their different corners.

However, the lengthy briefing Peter delivered that evening was on another matter entirely – the Disappeared. The statement was about nine killings and the nine people who had been "executed". Their names were read out, one by one: Seamus Wright; Kevin McKee; Eamon Molloy; Jean McConville; Columba McVeigh; Brendan Megraw; John McClory; Brian McKinney; Danny McIlhone. With each name, a reason for the "execution" was given. Jean McConville "admitted being a British Army informer"; Columba McVeigh "admitted being a British Army agent, directed to infiltrate the IRA"; Danny McIlhone "admitted stealing weapons from an Óglaigh na hÉireann dump and using the weapons in armed robberies". In that same briefing, a tenth name was added to the list: "As part of this investigation, we also endeavoured to locate the burial site of British SAS operative, Robert Nairac. We were unable to do so."

It was all matter-of-fact – as cold as the secret graves in which these Disappeared had been silenced. "This issue has caused incalculable pain and distress to a number of families over a period of many years," the statement acknowledged. It was also clear however that the IRA were not apologising for these killings – its regret was related to the "disappearing" of the bodies.

The IRA briefing spoke of a "special unit" under the command of one of its "most senior officers", and an 18-month investigation. This "unit" had first been mentioned in an IRA interview in August 1998. These seven months later, in this statement, came the breakthrough news – that the organisation believed it had established the whereabouts of the graves of the nine people it had "executed and buried". It was a message offering hope to those families who still waited to be able to bury and properly mourn their lost loved ones. They had become known as the Disappeared – but this term does not adequately convey what really happened: the abductions, the interrogations, the executions, the secret graves, the wilderness of bog land, the prolonged agony of the families waiting for news, the lies and the clear intention that the remains of these dead would never be found.

A few short weeks later, on 16 April 1999, the IRA had to issue another statement: "We repudiate media reports that the IRA has set conditions for the families around funeral arrangements or post-mortems. These are matters entirely for the families themselves. Speculative media reports around this issue only add to the anguish of the families." On 28 May, the IRA returned the remains of the first of the nine – Eamon Molloy. A coffin was left in a graveyard. Several days later, on Tuesday, 1 June, Peter was in contact again to deliver another briefing.

IRA Briefing, 1 June 1999

Had we been able to recover all the bodies, we would have done so. In the one circumstance in which we could establish the exact location, we recovered the body. We attempted to recover other bodies and have been unable to do so. In these instances, it has proven impossible to establish exact locations.

The IRA leadership has approached this issue in good faith. We organised an extensive and thorough investigation into the whereabouts of the bodies. A number of factors, including lapse of time, changes in leadership and the deaths of both members and former members of Óglaigh na hÉireann, who were involved, both hampered and protracted this investigation. We concluded this inquiry when we were satisfied we had gathered all available information. We are well aware of the importance of detailed information in expediting the recovery of the bodies.

All the information in our possession, which could assist in their location, was passed on. As we have previously stated, we are not responsible for all those who have gone missing in the last 25 years. In our approach to this investigation, we set ourselves towards doing all within our power to rectify this injustice, and to alleviate the suffering of the families. We are conscious that the nature of the terrain in which some of the graves are located and geological change over the years will render difficult the recovery of the bodies. However, it remains our hope that this can be carried out as quickly as possible, and the prolonged anguish of the families brought to an end.

In a speaking note to guide me during BBC interviews that day, I wrote: "There was never going to be any good publicity for the IRA in this . . . but there could be a lot more bad publicity . . . These families have been waiting, some close to 30 years, for bodies to be returned . . . and they've had their expectations raised by the IRA statement in March . . . If nothing is found during these searches, then it will be the IRA who will take the blame for that."

By 2003, there was confirmation that Jean McConville's remains had been found. In October that year, the IRA updated its initial briefing of March 1999. By now, there was a new "P. O'Neill" – a man I knew as "Tomas". There had been a reappraisal of the information available to the IRA.

From IRA Leadership Statement of 24 October 2003

. . . We are sorry that the suffering of those families has continued for so long. We wish to apologise for the grief caused. We believe that the sites identified are the locations where those killed by the IRA are buried . . . Some months ago we undertook a detailed re-examination of all of the available information, including revisiting each site. As a result, we passed on information regarding two sites, where the bodies of Jean McConville and Columba McVeigh had been buried.

We have acted in good faith in regard to this issue, and continue to do so. Our intention in initiating our investigation has been to rectify this injustice, for which we accept full responsibility. During the course of all of these searches, we have continued to process all information that might assist in any way. So far, the remains of four people have been recovered. We will do all that we can to bring closure for the other families. If further information comes to light, we will assess and process that information.

Over the following years, the republican leadership contacted me on two other occasions to speak about two other cases. In November 2009, a statement was issued, denying IRA involvement in the disappearance of Peter Wilson, who had been missing since 1973. His remains were found in November 2010. In February 2010, there was a further briefing, in which it was disclosed that in 1972 the IRA had "executed and buried" another man – Joe Lynskey.

Grim history that echoed down the telephone line
(*Belfast Telegraph*, **9 February 2010**)

The voice on the other end of my phone was one I hadn't heard for a while – for a number of years now. That was the last time the IRA's "P. O'Neill" called. When that organisation left its war stage in 2005, its leadership spokesman went quiet . . . The man I met yesterday no longer functions as "P. O'Neill", but he still speaks with all the authority of the republican leadership.

The purpose of this meeting was very specific . . . It was about the disappearance of Joe Lynskey in 1972 – "executed and buried" by the IRA.

. . . The Disappeared still haunt that organisation. They are a reminder of an ugly, ruthless and violent past. This particular story goes back almost four decades, when the many different wars were at their height; when one killing was followed by another, and people got lost as statistics in a mounting death toll. Those wars may well now be over, but there are questions that relate to the past that still demand answers. Some of those questions were answered in that briefing yesterday – others were not.

We now know the IRA killed Joe Lynskey and "disappeared" his body – as other bodies were "disappeared" in that period. But we don't know anything about the unmarked grave in which he was buried . . .

The story of the Disappeared will not go away.

Columba McVeigh was one of those named in that first IRA briefing of March 1999, and now, in 2015, he is one of those whose remains have not yet been found. While writing this book, I asked his niece, Eimear, for her words and her thoughts about their family's experience. Only when I read them, did I really begin to properly understand what this term "disappeared" actually means in real, human terms. The IRA statements and briefings were unemotional, matter-of-fact, and methodical; and so much of what we as journalists report on in Northern Ireland is couched and communicated in words that have become a kind of "conflict lexicon". Such terms, for example, as "the Disappeared" or "The Troubles" have become the understood way of referring to certain things – a kind of shorthand. Yet, through overuse and our habits of thinking, these phrases say nothing: they have become meaningless.

Eimear's words however are not about politics, but about people and their suffering: her family; her experience; the heartbreaking story she tells of what happened to them. How, as a child, she watched her grandmother cry, not understanding why and then coming to understand as she got older. "He was the uncle I never knew and the uncle I will never forget," Eimear wrote. "Columba McVeigh disappeared in 1975 – 12 years before I even existed. Unknown to me and beyond my own control, he was destined to factor hugely in my life."

Her words take us beyond the blunt, factual terms of that IRA briefing 15 years earlier, away from that political battleground, and inside her family's torment. This is what "the Past" represents for them; this is what the term "disappeared" really means. And this is when I was made to think and understand beyond that conflict lexicon.

Eimear McVeigh, niece of Columba McVeigh, one of the Disappeared
As a child, I watched my grandmother cry every day, calling out his name; a sight that haunts me now. His photograph hung on her kitchen wall, and

meant nothing to me. As kids, we knew something wasn't right, but could never pinpoint it; deep down we knew it was something to do with the young man in the photograph. My parents sheltered me for as long as they could. However after my grandmother's death, I felt a deep obligation to support my father in finding his older brother, and so I began to find out what had actually happened to Columba. Suddenly everything made sense.

I try my best not to dwell on the past, as hard as it is sometimes; I hope to one day make peace with it. But when I look back and see my grandmother's face, as she cried out for her lost son, a part of me can't help but feel angry. As well as having grieved her death, I now grieve for her all over again, but in a different way. When I have kids of my own someday, I fear the grief will only deepen further. Why was my grandmother allowed to live in limbo like that for so long? Why was her son not returned to her? What kind of society lets their citizens painfully wilt away like that? And why, after 40 years, does the torment still continue for Columba's siblings?

Maybe if our political leaders had been subjected to my grandmother's suffering every day like we were, Columba's case, like many others, would have been taken more seriously, instead of just being tossed around every now and again for political gain. I find our political landscape frustrating; I find most of our politicians' behaviour in their work embarrassing. If we all treated our work colleagues with such disdain, chaos would ensue: nothing would get done. Negativity and lack of empathy are easy options.

Thankfully, from my own experiences, the people of Northern Ireland aren't taking this easy option: we make a genuine effort to get along, be amicable towards one another, and even become friends, despite what our backgrounds may dictate. At present, I feel we are leaps and bounds ahead of our political leaders, who I fear will only continue to hold us back from making any more real progress.

Eimear tells a story of human suffering; the story of what this practice did to people. Had there not been ceasefires, not been a peace process, then they would have been left in that limbo she described, left to "wilt away".

So, for a number of families, the waiting continues – waiting that goes back into the 1970s and the darkest decade of the conflict years, and waiting that prolongs their suffering into the here and now. In the garden of the WAVE Trauma Centre in north Belfast, there are two sets of roses – one representing those of the Disappeared who have been found, and the other, those who have not. It is one way of never forgetting and of always remembering. One of the gardeners there is Jean McConville's son, Thomas, and there is a tree in memory of his mother. The WAVE Centre helped to break the silence, and to make the stories of the Disappeared an important part of the past – part of what had to – and still has to – be answered.

Sandra Peake, WAVE Trauma Centre

The story of the WAVE Trauma Centre's involvement with the Disappeared goes back to 1995, when I was asked to meet Margaret McKinney. She was searching for her son Brian, who had disappeared in 1978. When I met Mags, I was struck by her tremendous courage, given all that she had faced, and also her sense of longing for the opportunity to bring Brian home for Christian burial. When we started, we did not know that we would be joined by others who became "the Families of the Disappeared". Many of them did not know that their loved ones had been "disappeared" until the late 1990s, because the whole sordid business was literally hidden.

There were multiple levels of silence . . . then. Silence within the community. Silence sometimes within the family; silence within the neighbourhood; silence within the church; silence at work; silence at a government level . . . This silence [was] compounded by an underlying fear, which stopped families speaking out. Indeed, while Joe Lynskey had been the first of the Disappeared, in 1972, it was not until 2010 that it was confirmed that he had been murdered and secretly buried. The family believed, and were encouraged to believe, that he had gone to America to seek a better life. This kind of cruel deception was part of the process of silencing the families.

The British and Irish Governments and the republican movement want to resolve this issue and the families want to ensure that the silence does not descend again in the public mind. That is why the families speak out today. That is why those who have had loved ones returned to them continue to speak out – on behalf of those who still wait. The significance of being able at last to have a wake, a coffin to carry and a grave to tend, following a Christian burial, cannot be overestimated.

In 1998, Mags met President Clinton with a group from WAVE. She told her story, and there were tears in the White House that day. In 2014, she met Bill Clinton again in Belfast. Mags was more frail [by then], but less haunted by the past. She thanked him for his support and showed him a photograph that is very dear to her. It is a photograph of Brian's grave. "That's what you did for me. Thank you," she said. There were more tears that day.

The stories of the Disappeared went untold, unheard and unnoticed for so long – frozen in the silence and the fear described earlier. But those IRA statements and briefings that began in March 1999 opened this chapter of conflict killings to the type of scrutiny the IRA and its leadership had managed to avoid for several decades.

In April 2014, Gerry Adams was arrested in connection with the abduction and murder of Jean McConville in December 1972 and, for several days and nights, that arrest became news and headlines across the world. Part of that police investigation which prompted the detention of the Sinn Féin leader relied on tapes recorded by former members of the IRA for the Boston College oral history project. The idea and undertaking was that the tapes would remain private until those who participated had died. Brendan Hughes, a former senior IRA leader and once a close associate of the Sinn Féin President, was one of those who participated in the project, and what he said on his tapes was part of what led to the Adams arrest. In his recordings, Hughes alleged it was Adams who gave the order to "disappear" the widowed mother-of-ten, Jean McConville – something the Sinn Féin leader has repeatedly denied. Once the transcript of the Hughes interview became public, and once other information became available from the Boston project, graffiti appeared on the Falls Road. The words "touts" and "informers" were written – clearly meant for those who had cooperated with the Boston project. The graffiti was there to intimidate and to speak of betrayal. It was a reminder that the past is still not answered; a reminder of the unfinished business.

Every minute of Adams' detention in April 2014 was being watched and reported upon by the national and international press. What would happen, what were the implications for the peace process? Jean McConville, a widow, had been taken from her children and driven away. Accused of being an informer, she was shot in the head and secretly buried. Only those who did it and who were part of it knew where her body had been left. Jean McConville disappeared in a year when almost 500 people in Northern Ireland lost their lives in the conflict; while her case has since become one of the headlines of a dark past, back then the grim story of what happened to her was buried along with so many others.

Ghosts of Disappeared haunt IRA (*Belfast Telegraph*, 2 May 2014)
It's not every day that you arrest such a high-profile political and public figure. So, every hour that Gerry Adams is held will be scrutinised – and with each of those passing hours, the republican mood is becoming more angry.

You could hear it in the commentary that stretched from questions about the timing of this arrest, to the charge of political policing, right through to the accusation of involvement by the "Dark Side". And this is a reminder of the days when "spookery" and references to the "securocrats" were all part and parcel of the republican vocabulary.

To arrest Adams as part of the McConville murder investigation was always going to be a big decision and a dramatic headline. And it was always going to bring that charge of political policing. But what if the PSNI had not arrested him? Then, from another direction, the police would have faced the same criticism.

For some time now, this investigation has been moving towards this arrest. Indeed, in recent weeks the word "inevitable" was used – the only real questions being how and when it would be done.

We know that police contacted Adams' solicitor earlier this week and from then, the arrangements were made for the Sinn Féin president to present himself at Antrim.

And then came the emerging and breaking news that a 65-year-old man had been arrested in connection with the abduction and murder of Jean McConville in December 1972.

About five hours later a republican told me that Adams would be "there for the night" . . . And, as yesterday morning arrived, a range of sources were putting a longer timescale on his likely stay in the Antrim Serious Crime Suite.

"I don't think he'll be out today," one source told me, adding, "He could be there for a while." But the Adams line hasn't changed. He continues to deny any involvement in the abduction, murder and disappearing of Jean McConville. But, like ghosts, the Disappeared hang round the necks of the IRA and the republican leadership – their voices speaking from the graves. Indeed, the questions that relate to this ugly chapter from the conflict years are becoming louder.

Interviews recorded by former IRA figures for the Boston College oral history project have become "a substantial part" of this investigation, but not the only part. Late yesterday, as the Sinn Féin leader's time in custody stretched into another long night, what was not clear was where all of this was leading.

The day after that report, republicans staged a protest rally on the Falls Road in west Belfast, with Martin McGuinness on stage with MEP Martina Anderson and Bobby Storey. Although this has never been publicly confirmed, Storey is believed to have been the senior republican leader in command of the "special unit" that was established to ascertain the whereabouts of those who had been disappeared by the IRA. On the Falls Road, McGuinness pointed to the timing of the Adams arrest – with local government and EU elections imminent. What follows is an edited version of his comments.

Martin McGuinness, speaking at arrest protest rally, 3 May 2014

I have consistently said in recent days that the timing of the arrest of Gerry Adams was politically motivated. The decision to extend his detention is part of this. Does anyone here doubt that the arrest of Gerry Adams is inextricably linked to the local government and EU Elections that will take place across this island in three weeks? . . . Does anyone here doubt Gerry's arrest at this time is not intended to disrupt that election campaign? The PSNI has had the Boston tapes for a year.

The allegations contained in books and newspaper articles, which the PSNI are presenting to Gerry as evidence that he was in the IRA in the 1970s, have been around for 40 years. But they are only now trying to use these. Is that not political policing? This is a replay of the failed effort in 1978 to charge Gerry with [IRA] membership. That case was based on hearsay, gossip and newspaper articles, and it failed. Thirty-six years later, those within the PSNI who are hostile to the peace process, are using the same old dirty tricks. They are deliberately and cynically exploiting the awful killing of Jean McConville and the grief and hurt of her family. Our sympathy is with the McConville family.

Let me be very clear about Sinn Féin's approach to policing and to the PSNI. We worked very hard to reform policing. Sinn Féin's negotiations strategy succeeded in achieving new policing arrangements, but we always knew that there remained within the PSNI an embittered rump of the old RUC. These people want to settle old scores, whatever the political cost . . . The arrest of Gerry Adams is evidence that there is an element within the PSNI who are against the peace process, and who hate Gerry Adams and Sinn Féin. They are what the reformers within the PSNI have described to us as "the Dark Side". They are small in number but very influential. This group is working to a negative and anti-peace process agenda, and [is] actively involved in political policing . . . Gerry Adams is committed to moving this [peace] process forward. He will not be deterred or deflected, and neither will we. The Dark Side fear him. That's why they are doing what they do.

The timing of the Adams arrest, so close to elections, was always going to leave it open to criticism, and put the police on some sort of back foot. His detention would extend from Wednesday, 30 April to Sunday, 4 May. During the questioning process, it became clear that this investigation was not just about the McConville killing, but that there was also an attempt to construct an IRA membership charge against the Sinn Féin President. This was a reminder that investigation is still a part of the past and the present; a reminder too that no one is excluded from investigation. This time it was the most senior of republican leaders. Who will it be the next time? This is the unpredictable nature of our past, of what has happened and what will happen again.

On Sunday, 4 May, as events developed, Twitter delivered the updates on what was happening, and not happening – stories of a political and policing clash in a storm of angry words and accusations. It was eventually confirmed that the Sinn Féin leader would be released, with a report being submitted to the PPS. (In due course, the PPS would announce that Adams and others would not face charges.) The Adams IRA question is one that will never be answered during police interrogation, and this was and is the challenge beyond this arrest: what is the process that will deliver frankness, honesty, information and explanation? The Sinn Féin leader emerged from custody, talking about a "malicious, untruthful, sinister" campaign against him and behind the headlines and the news, nothing really changed. Were we any closer to knowing the truth about the McConville killing; about who gave the orders and carried out the actions; about who fired the gun and dug the grave? Does this type of investigation and questioning discourage – rather than encourage – the openness that is being sought? These are questions that demand and need proper consideration. And there has notably not been the same scrutiny or spotlight on specific individuals in the high places of government, the military, intelligence or policing; not that same fine-detail inspection and constant examination. Perhaps it is Adams' denial of IRA membership that brings so much attention to him: perhaps this is the reason why he has never been able to escape that spotlight.

In this period, the story of the Disappeared became the story of the Adams arrest within that frame of high-level politics and policing. It was another of those times when others – those remaining families still waiting in agony for the truth about their lost loved ones – were forgotten. In 2015, there was an outpouring of public anger when Gerry Adams, in response to specific questions about Jean McConville, told the CBS *60 Minutes* programme:

"That's what happens in wars." It is difficult to imagine how unthinking and hurtful those words would have sounded to her family, listening to the interview.

The "war" language needs to be replaced with something more thoughtful; something that fits a post-conflict or peace process context; something that at least tries harder to address the suffering and questions and needs of the families. In the same way, how we address "the Past" – which we must address – should not be reduced to political decisions or failures to decide; or to narrow, self-serving party-political interests. Politics was part of the problem; at times – then and still – part of the poison; part of what is still wrong today. So, we need a process that thinks outside all of the usual boxes, and that genuinely seeks to ask and find the answers to the questions of what happened, and why. It seems clear that such a process should be conceived with external, international input.

In the tone and methodology of the various IRA briefings relating to the matter of the Disappeared over the years, it can be seen how republican cooperation with any proposed Information Retrieval Commission might work. It would have to happen off-stage and be conducted privately, with any information being delivered in a very controlled and managed way. We could expect the approach to be business-like, unvarnished, and not addressing the actions of specific individuals but, at all times, presenting things in terms of a corporate or organisational IRA stance. On the issue of the Disappeared, there has been no naming of those responsible for orders, or of those directly involved in the killings and burials – nor will there be, unless the individuals themselves decide to come forward. The "P. O'Neill" statements to the media were limited or edited disclosures – never full disclosures – and it is important that this is understood. In the frame of the briefings outlined in this chapter, we can see how information or truth recovery could work – and not work – in terms of the much more detailed responses that are being sought and demanded by some.

For a number of reasons, that initial IRA statement of March 1999 remains a constant reference point in terms of the Disappeared – not only because it was the first detailed information to emerge from the IRA on this series of killings, but also because of what remains unresolved, and those who are still missing.

Almost a decade after that first briefing, I wrote again on the subject of the Disappeared, not long after the remains of Danny McIlhone were found. This *Belfast Telegraph* article was published just a few days before Christmas 2008.

These deaths still haunt the Provos
(*Belfast Telegraph*, **22 December 2008**)

. . . In its own way and in its own words, that organisation will justify the killings – the "executions" – but it cannot defend the practice that opened out the story of the Disappeared.

It is a chapter from the past that still reads into the present – stories of killing, of secret burial, of hidden and lost graves, of tortured, traumatised families and it is an episode that still haunts the IRA itself.

It is something in the war that just won't go away – and it is something that has been described as "a dark and disturbing period for many republicans". You do not hear the word "shame" – but disappearing bodies is something I have heard described as falling outside the IRA's own "moral framework"; what it would consider as the rights and wrongs of war.

Republicans don't want to talk about it.

Others use it as a political beating stick – to remind everyone of the IRA's ugly past.

But for those, such as the McIlhone family, who have waited so long for some news, for information that might lead to the discovery of the remains of a loved one – there is no need for such reminders.

For many years, grieving families have lived in the reality of this horror . . . That distress continues. Some of the bodies have still to be found . . .

There are those who have disputed the IRA's allegations. In July 2006 the Police Ombudsman made a statement on one of the cases of the Disappeared, saying there was no evidence that Jean McConville, "gave information to the police, the military or the Security Service. She was not an informant."

But, within 24 hours, the IRA responded – in another meeting with another "P. O'Neill", and in another statement read to me. An IRA "investigation" had confirmed that Jean McConville "was working as an informer for the British Army". This is the IRA in its own words, continuing to justify the killings.

But the story of the Disappeared is not over. There are bodies still to be found, and until all are returned, that war of decades and that war of words will not end.

Joe Lynskey is still missing. Eimear's uncle, Columba – that young man in the photograph in the kitchen of the family home – is still missing. Robert Nairac is still missing. Seamus Ruddy is still missing. As I was writing this book, the remains of Seamus Wright and Kevin McKee were found, more than 16 years after "Peter" had read their names to me in an IRA briefing.

In August 2015, at a Festival event in west Belfast, Martin McGuinness shared a stage with PSNI Chief Constable George Hamilton to talk about the questions of the past and whether they will ever be answered. When McGuinness was asked if the IRA would assist a truth process, he brought the Disappeared into the conversation, pointing to republican co-operation with the Independent Commission for the Location of Victims' Remains as proof that they would engage with a wider process to address the past. The deputy First Minister also described the disappearing of bodies as "a very cruel thing to do", adding, "because of appeals from within the leadership of republicanism, we now find that there are four cases to be resolved out of many, many more that have been resolved. They have only been resolved because republicans were prepared to come forward and contribute."

These stories, like many others, rewind into the past and then fast forward into the present, and they are an indication of how long it will take to address the unanswered questions of the conflict years. When we think about the time it has taken to get answers about some of the relatively small number of Disappeared cases, then we can only imagine how much longer it will take to get to the truth of – or at least to achieve more information on – the almost 4,000 deaths. In our unfinished peace, the task and challenges ahead are huge.

CHAPTER SEVEN

Endgames: "They will no longer train for war . . ."

"People across all communities are now beginning to live again. And it is against this backdrop that unanswered questions remain about the origins, legacy and aftermath of our recent conflict."

Eibhlin Glenholmes, Belfast republican, writing for this book.

"Everyone was focused on a positive end to Operation Banner. In moments of reflection, the sense of history was palpable: after 38 years of bloodshed, during which 763 forces personnel had been killed and more than 6,000 injured, here was an end."

Mervyn Wynne Jones, former MoD Chief Press Officer at Thiepval Barracks, writing for this book.

"It was very moving for me – no tears, I confess, but a huge lump in my throat – as I looked back at 40 years of hell, pain and immense trauma for this island,"

Methodist Minister, Dr Gary Mason, writing for this book, reflecting on the day in June 2009 when loyalists confirmed the decommissioning of arms.

The opening thoughts above are all framed in a post-conflict context: a context where there is a sense of people beginning to live again; where there has been history in the making, with an end to the wars and an opportunity to reflect on the hell and trauma that this place lived through. Eibhlin Glenholmes, Mervyn Wynne Jones and the Reverend Gary Mason all write from very different viewpoints. However, each of them has been close enough to what has happened to have witnessed some of those big moments of change in "the North" – the ceasefires, the ending of the longest operation in British military history and the confirmation of the decommissioning of loyalist arms. They were each here, albeit in different places and in different roles when, after years of conflict, things moved in another direction.

I remember the Methodist Minister, Gary Mason, standing at the hospital bedside of David Ervine in January 2007. David's family were there with a few friends, as a prayer was said. Death can arrive so suddenly, so unexpectedly, so cruelly. Ervine, who had become the loyalist voice of the peace process, was just 53 when he died. His funeral was a sad day, but also a remarkable occasion that had something important to say about where we were on the long road to peace. It was, in many senses, a day of hope – hope generated by simply observing those who had gathered together to celebrate Ervine's life: the former Irish Taoiseach, Albert Reynolds, Sinn Féin President, Gerry Adams, the then Chief Constable, Hugh Orde, Secretary of State, Peter Hain, the UVF leadership, the UDA leader, Jackie McDonald and Peter Robinson.

At the time, Robinson's party – the DUP – were just months away from an historic political agreement with Sinn Féin that would lead to the government of Paisley and McGuinness; and in a last piece of writing, Ervine had urged them to finish the job. The day of the loyalist's funeral was one that spoke loudly of the general respect for him and for his contribution to the peace process. In the conflict period, Ervine had been to jail after being caught with a bomb; after the Good Friday Agreement however, he was twice elected to Stormont. On this January day in 2007, the coming together of those who packed the Reverend Mason's church in east Belfast said something about a conflict that was ending and that was over, in terms of the almost daily incidence of bombing and shootings which had dominated our lives for so many years previously. On this day, we could see how things had changed.

Writing for this book, Gary Mason thinks back to the day of Ervine's funeral, and then he thinks forward, to another moment in his church in June 2009, and describes what he witnessed and what, for him, that particular day meant.

Dr Gary Mason, Methodist Minister

Let me tell you a story of three boys, all born in the late 1950s and early 1960s, in [the] sectarian hotbed of Northern Irish society. They were normal kids, whose lives were to be shaped by a conflict not of their making. Two of the boys attended Sunday school together. One boy's mother was a faithful teacher in that Sunday school. Two of the boys also attended the same primary school, from the ages of four to eleven. They were best friends, accompanying each other on the walk to school and on the return journey. One of the boys is now dead – a casualty of the conflict. The second boy was sentenced to life imprisonment. I am the third boy – [now] a Methodist clergyperson.

I have now spent 28 years of my ministry in the inner city of Belfast, never more than 200 metres from an interface or "peace line": the barriers that separate Protestant and Catholic communities. A sizeable proportion of my work and ministry has been to act as a critical friend to those who have used violence to pursue their political ends.

The last Saturday in June 2009 – known in loyalism as the day of the Whiterock Parade in west Belfast – became the day the UVF and the Red Hand Commando said the guns were gone. I remember going down to the church I served that Saturday morning: the Methodist church at East Belfast Mission – the church, where in January 2007 I conducted the service of the late David Ervine, the UVF bomb-maker turned peacemaker. On that Saturday in June 2009, the world's press were there to get the decommissioning statement. The front of the church hall, where the statement was read, saw no flags, no weapons on display, no masks, no men behind tables covered with a flag, separating them from the press.

The statement was read from the church lectern. Yes, let me just repeat that, the church lectern. The backdrop to the [delivery of the] statement was a display of church flowers to be used in the church service the next day, Sunday. Emotional day, yes, so let me do a healthy bit of what we in the church call confession: it was very moving for me – no tears I confess, but a huge lump in my throat – as I looked back at 40 years of hell, pain and immense trauma for this island. And yet, what else could I do as a clergyperson, but think of that wonderful text in Isaiah: "They will beat their swords into ploughshares, and their spears into pruning hooks. Nations will not take up the sword against other nations, and they will no longer train for war."

"They will no longer train for war" – the gun [is] finally out of Irish politics, yes, I believe so, and I am immensely grateful.

In May 2012 I took the most senior leadership of the UVF and the Red Hand Commando on a "conflict transformation" educational trip to the Middle East. One evening, as we were walking through Jerusalem on the way to a drinks reception, I was slightly lagging behind that UVF/RHC leadership, with a number of friends from the Middle East. I turned to those friends and said, "The men in front of you have been involved in a military campaign for almost 30 years and I know the war is finally over, when we see that leadership walking through Arab East Jerusalem on their way to a drinks reception at the British Consul in Jerusalem." My Israeli and Palestinian friends turned to me and said, "[We] hope someday we can say the same – the war is over."

This is how our story is told internationally, but it is not quite that straightforward or uncomplicated. I agree with Mason that the wars are over but it took time, and is still taking time, to complete the long, seemingly endless transition to something more stable and authentic. This issue – the continuing existence of parts of the loyalist and IRA structures – became a big part of the most recent crisis talks at Stormont. Today, the peace does not seem as convincing or as clear as it was on that day in January 2007, when Gerry Adams was able to walk on the Newtownards Road in east Belfast, and sit in the same church as the loyalist leadership. That is a part of the city, where people are still identified by what side of the road they walk on, and where they can't or won't walk. A new hostility and anger has grown out of what has been termed a "cultural war" – bitter disputes over flags and marching. Some of the "combatant" organisations have been more convincing and credible than others in their exit. We should not pretend that the leaderships – loyalist and republican – have just vanished. They have not. Not all of the organisational structures have yet been dismantled. In the concluding chapter of this book, you will read how this issue became part of those crisis talks in the months towards the end of 2015.

Some parts of these groups continue to linger and loiter and live on in some shape, as if still waiting for something to happen, and as if not able or willing to complete their final exit. So, there are understandable doubts about the reality of this withdrawal, or retirement – call it what you will. In the eyes of some, for all the significant progress that has been made, the existence of such doubts makes the transition less convincing, the past more current and the peace less believable. I will write later about the need for a final confirmation that all the wars are over.

In the effort of tracking the transitions, we can see what has been achieved and done, but think about how others might see this – the many others who might not have such an overview, those with a multitude of questions about what happened to them and their families. They see prisoner releases, the so-called on-the-run (OTR) cases settled, with suspects being allowed to return home; they see how some of those who were part of the conflict still continue to function with their war titles and rank – and they set all of that against an unanswered past.

From the original IRA ceasefire of August 1994, it took until July 2005 for the statement that formally ended the armed campaign to finally materialise, and until September 2005 for the most significant acts of arms decommissioning to happen and to be witnessed by local churchmen. Meanwhile, the UVF, Red Hand Commando and UDA were all part of that composite Combined Loyalist Military Command (CLMC) cessation, which was announced in October 1994. The statements confirming the end of their operations however did not come until May and November 2007, with arms decommissioning only beginning in 2009 and continuing into 2010. None of the organisations decommissioned all of their weapons. After all that had happened, these processes of transition were always going to take time – but there is such a thing as too much time and too much delay.

Significantly, all of those "war-ending" statements were scripted in the language of war. In July 2005, the declaration from the IRA leadership included this sentence: "We reiterate our view that the armed struggle was entirely legitimate." In May 2007, announcing a move to "a non-military, civilianised role", the UVF and Red Hand Commando contextualised their decisions in a couple of short sentences, as follows: "We have taken the above measures in an earnest attempt to augment the return of accountable democracy to the people of Northern Ireland and as such, to engender confidence that the constitutional question has now been firmly settled. In doing so, we reaffirm the legitimacy of our tactical response to violent nationalism, yet reiterate the sincere expression of abject and true remorse to all innocent victims of the conflict." On Remembrance Sunday in 2007, the UDA said, in a lengthy and rambling statement, that it was "committed to achieving a society where violence and weaponry are ghosts of the past". The military wing of that organisation – the Ulster Freedom Fighters – was to be stood down at midnight that day. "It was these Freedom Fighters who brought the enemy to the peace table and established the first ceasefires in 1994," this endgame statement read.

A new beginning will not be made out of the stale or worn-out words of war, or out of old assertions or justifications. Those statements announcing the end of military operations, which in some cases stretched back a decade, should now be revisited, rethought and reworked. New statements should be issued in their place. How often did loyalists target the IRA? In the overall context of a 30-year conflict, the answer is, not very often. How many Protestants did the IRA kill in attacks, in which they were deliberately singled out – such as at Kingsmill, or in numerous other incidents in which they were clearly deemed affordable casualties in the pursuit of other targets? This is what happened in Enniskillen in 1987, on the Shankill Road in October 1993 and on numerous other occasions.

Back in November 1987, today's Fermanagh and South Tyrone MP, Tom Elliott, was a soldier in the Ulster Defence Regiment, and was meant to be on parade at the War Memorial in Enniskillen on the day of the Remembrance Day bombing. His mother, returning from church just after noon that Sunday, broke the news to him – there had been "a massive bomb", in which a lot of people had been killed.

Top: Members of Jean McConville's family – Jim, Nathan and Thomas – photographed in the garden at the WAVE Trauma Centre. *(Elle Rowan)*

Above: Republican protest in 2014 after Gerry Adams was arrested and questioned about the abduction and murder of Jean McConville. Adams was released and will not face charges. *(Brian Rowan)*

Top: Senior Sinn Féin members, Carál Ní Chuilín and Martina Anderson at the Gerry Adams arrest protest, 2014. *(Brian Rowan)*

Right: The author records events at the same protest. *(Photograph courtesy of @Bronac7)*

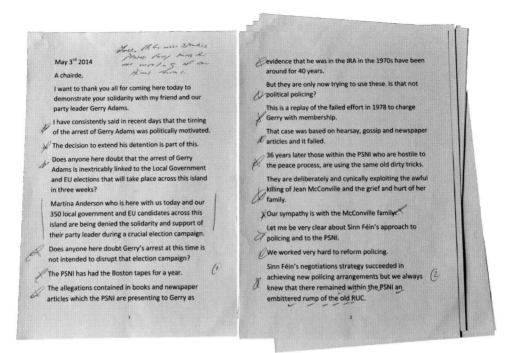

May 3rd 2014

A chairde,

I want to thank you all for coming here today to demonstrate your solidarity with my friend and our party leader Gerry Adams.

I have consistently said in recent days that the timing of the arrest of Gerry Adams was politically motivated.

The decision to extend his detention is part of this.

Does anyone here doubt that the arrest of Gerry Adams is inextricably linked to the Local Government and EU elections that will take place across this island in three weeks?

Martina Anderson who is here with us today and our 350 local government and EU candidates across this island are being denied the solidarity and support of their party leader during a crucial election campaign.

Does anyone here doubt Gerry's arrest at this time is not intended to disrupt that election campaign?

The PSNI has had the Boston tapes for a year.

The allegations contained in books and newspaper articles which the PSNI are presenting to Gerry as

evidence that he was in the IRA in the 1970s have been around for 40 years.

But they are only now trying to use these. Is that not political policing?

This is a replay of the failed effort in 1978 to charge Gerry with membership.

That case was based on hearsay, gossip and newspaper articles and it failed.

36 years later those within the PSNI who are hostile to the peace process, are using the same old dirty tricks.

They are deliberately and cynically exploiting the awful killing of Jean McConville and the grief and hurt of her family.

Our sympathy is with the McConville family.

Let me be very clear about Sinn Féin's approach to policing and to the PSNI.

We worked very hard to reform policing.

Sinn Féin's negotiations strategy succeeded in achieving new policing arrangements but we always knew that there remained within the PSNI an embittered rump of the old RUC.

Top: Angry words – Martin McGuinness' speech after Adams' arrest. *(Elle Rowan)*

Above: Sinn Féin press conference after Adams was released without charge. *(Brian Rowan)*

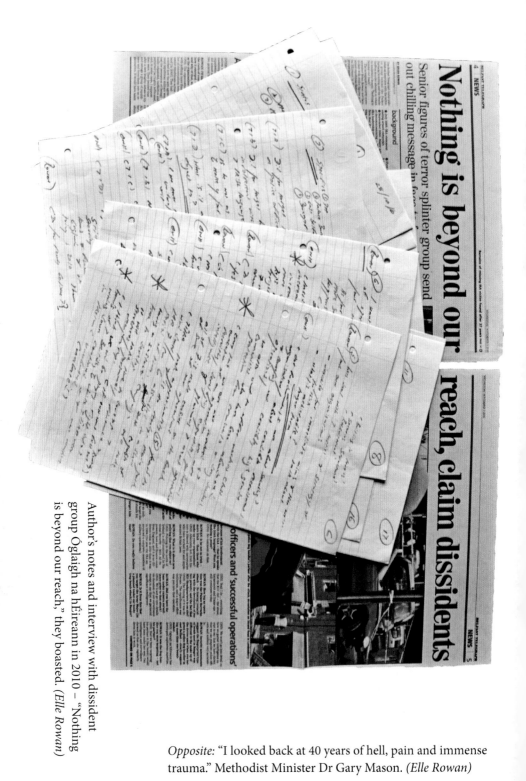

Author's notes and interview with dissident group Óglaigh na hÉireann in 2010 – "Nothing is beyond our reach," they boasted. (*Elle Rowan*)

Opposite: "I looked back at 40 years of hell, pain and immense trauma." Methodist Minister Dr Gary Mason. (*Elle Rowan*)

AN *IRELAND'S BIGGEST SELLING POLITICAL WEEKLY*

PHOBLACHT
Republican News

Sraith Nua Imi 9 Uimhir 44   12 Samhain   Thursday 12th November 1987   (Britain 35p) Price 30p

> *Republicans will never forget it and in the ongoing struggle to end injustice and bring about a free, peaceful Ireland will carry it in their hearts and minds forever.*

SEE OPINION – PAGE 2

ENNISKILLEN TRAGEDY

WHAT THE I.R.A. SAID

THE following statement was issued by the IRA on Monday, November 9th, the day after the bomb explosion in Enniskillen, in which 11 people were killed:

❝The Irish Republican Army admits responsibility for planting the bomb in Enniskillen yesterday which exploded with such catastrophic consequences. We deeply regret what occurred.

GHQ has now established that one of our units placed a remote-controlled bomb in St Michael's aimed at catching crown forces personnel on patrol in connection with the Remembrance Day service but not during it. The bomb blew up without being triggered by our radio signal.

There has been an ongoing battle for supremacy between the IRA and British army electronic engineers over the use of remote-control bombs. In the past, some of our landmines have been triggered by the British army scanning high frequencies and other devices have been jammed and neutralised. On each occasion we overcame the problem and recently believed that we were in advance of British counter-measures.

In the present climate nothing we can say in explanation can be given the attention which the truth deserves, nor will it compensate the feelings of the injured or bereaved.

Signed: P. O'Neill,
Irish Republican Publicity Bureau, Dublin.❞

Republicans do not attempt to justify or explain away what happened in Enniskillen last Sunday. There is no way that what the IRA has called the "catastrophic consequences" can be reversed or minimised. It was an appalling tragedy that should never have happened. But what is clear is that the IRA had no intention of injuring civilians, and did not themselves detonate the remote-control bomb. They did not anticipate the tragic results of the premature detonation of the bomb. That was a monumental error for which republicans have paid, and will continue to pay, dearly.

In the aftermath of Enniskillen, everything that republicans have said has been distorted where it has not been censored. This is to be expected but what cannot be denied is that the IRA has been consistent in claiming responsibility for an action so damaging to the Republican Movement and so useful to the enemy. Nor can it be denied that the war in the Six Counties which has claimed so many lives is not now and never has been the fault of the Irish people — nationalist, loyalist or republican — but that ultimately Britain is to blame.

"What the IRA said": *An Phoblacht* report on the Enniskillen bomb in 1987. *(Elle Rowan)*

"The IRA knew it would murder many innocent civilians." Fermanagh and South Tyrone MP Tom Elliott thinks back to the day of the Enniskillen bomb. *(Elle Rowan)*

Above: A question for the Chief Constable – Katherine Finucane and Eibhlin Glenholmes at the West Belfast Festival 2015. *(Photograph courtesy of Antrim Lens)*

Opposite: "A conflict that ruined childhoods, claimed lives and ended dreams." Belfast republican Eibhlin Glenholmes. *(Elle Rowan)*

Top: "In moments of reflection, the sense of history was palpable." Former MOD chief press officer Mervyn Wynne Jones (pictured with former Prime Minister Tony Blair), on the ending of the Army's Operation Banner.

Below: Images from the 38-year long Operation Banner.

Top: "Much needs to be done if we are to avoid being betrayed again by our 'poisoned memory'." David Porter of the Eames/Bradley Consultative Group on the past 2007–09. *(Photograph courtesy of RTE* Collusion *documentary, 2015)*

Above: "War and conflict tend to dehumanise us and make us look at our fellow man as a thing, a number, a reprisal, a message, a lesson, a reminder . . ." Jarlath Burns of the Eames/Bradley Consultative Group on the past, 2007–09. *(Photograph courtesy of Irish TV series* Mallie Meets*)*

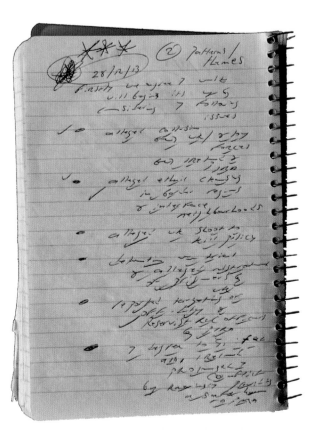

Top: Author's notes during the Haass/O'Sullivan talks. *(Elle Rowan)*

Above: The author (centre) chairs the 2015 West Belfast Festival event, "Will the questions of the past ever be answered?" with Martin McGuinness and George Hamilton. *(Photograph courtesy of Antrim Lens)*

Truth mission: Kathryn Stone and author David Park
BRIAN THOMPSON PRESEYE

EXORCISING THE GHOSTS OF THE PAST

As One City One Book author David Park, whose novels include The Truth Commissioner, takes part in a round-table discussion with real-life Victims Commissioner Kathryn Stone at the Belfast Telegraph tomorrow, **Brian Rowan** says listening is part of the solution

Top: "Exorcising the ghosts of the past": Author David Park reads from his novel *The Truth Commissioner* at an event held the offices of the *Belfast Telegraph* in 2014.

Left: Part of the audience at the David Park event. *(Brian Rowan)*

Above: "The powerful paradox of theatre is that it can be most real when it is most imagined." Lyric Theatre Trustee Stephen Douds. *(Elle Rowan)*

Opposite: "The past is the present for those who suffered pain, loss and grief as a result of our dark and grievous history." Chief Constable George Hamilton. *(Elle Rowan)*

"The answers to how we deal with these issues have been there for quite a while."
Ulster University academic Dr Jonny Byrne. *(Elle Rowan)*

Tom Elliott, Fermanagh and South Tyrone MP, writing for this book

I hadn't heard the news at that time, as there were no mobile phones, no social media, and news took a little longer then to reach the public than it now would. I was due to take part at the annual Act of Remembrance in Enniskillen for those from the area killed in the two World Wars. During the week prior to Remembrance Day, I had a farm accident, which resulted in me being unable to attend Enniskillen on that day. So I was housebound when my mother passed on to me the news that would affect many people and the community for years to come.

Immediately on hearing the news, we put on the TV and radio, listening intently for any snippet of information that we could glean from either. Phone calls commenced, back and forward between friends and family, trying to gain information, assessing what information was accurate or not, and piecing it together. [Everything] was describing a picture of sheer devastation for the community, but more importantly for a number of families. Relatives living outside Northern Ireland were also very concerned. Being far away often creates a sense of uncertainty and insecurity. When speaking to those people, there was a clear sense of desperation.

At the same time, news was emerging that another bomb – outside the small Fermanagh village of Tullyhommon – had failed to explode that day. This was where a group of youth organisations were due to commence their Remembrance Day parade. There could have been an even greater loss of life, in particular [of] young civilian life. The hours and days that followed were a huge mix of grief, bewilderment, despair, and following Gordon Wilson's intervention, there was [also] confusion. At a time when so many innocent people were murdered, some people were seeking revenge. Here was a man, who had lost his daughter through this atrocious act of terrorism, promoting forgiveness to those who had carried out these murders of the innocent.

The greatest source of anger around this atrocity is that the IRA knew it would murder many innocent victims.

Others of course will remember those shot down by soldiers in Derry and in Ballymurphy, on other days that live in the minds and memories of other communities; or remember also those gun attacks and the multiple deaths in bookmakers' shops and pubs, when loyalist gunmen opened fire. So there will always be arguments about who started, and what started, this conflict; different narratives and different beliefs, which are all parts of the same story on the same stage, seen through different eyes and experiences. Acknowledging the past fully is not about picking one of these experiences, and ignoring others. They all have their place in any complete retrospective of those decades of the 1970s, 1980s and 1990s. The different narratives will never be reconciled, but must all be included in any review of the past.

There was a time, dating back to the 1980s, when Eibhlin Glenholmes' name appeared under the banner headline "Most Wanted". The Belfast republican, wanted in Britain for questioning about IRA attacks, went on the run, and only returned to her home city in the period after the Good Friday Agreement. In 2002, while still at the BBC, I reported that her case, and those of some dozens of others, had been settled. Yet, over a decade later, and after the publication of more detailed information, a row developed, with many politicians claiming that nothing was known about these on-the-run, or OTR, cases. That position is just not credible. Yes, it is true there was no knowledge about so-called "comfort letters" being issued to suspects, but there is a huge difference between fine detail and no detail. There was enough information in the public domain to provide leads, and yet, apparently, none of these leads were seen or followed. Today, Eibhlin Glenholmes, who was shot and wounded as a teenager, is a member of the Victims' Forum.

Eibhlin Glenholmes, Belfast republican writing for this book
Engaging with the legacy of the past is now the unfinished aspect of the peace process. In this post-Good Friday Agreement period, questions continue to emerge based on the differing perspectives on the causes of the conflict, what happened and who was responsible. It is my belief that, if we are serious about healing and learning the lessons from the past, then we must hold that [the] roles and actions of all combatant organisations must be fully considered, including governments, state agencies and the legal and judicial system. I say this to illustrate that the British state strategy has been to create a narrative that presents them as independent neutral arbiters in a war among warring tribes. In my experience and that of my community, this analysis does not stand up to any reasonable investigation. I recall the many dark days of conflict as the northern state sought to silence basic civil rights demands. As basic demands for respect and inclusion intensified, my experience was that state practices became more repressive and more draconian.

The 1969 pogroms, the state's rejection of the demands for basic civil rights, the excessive use of state force [and] the deployment of the British army brought state conflict and violence to me, my family and my community. In my thinking, both the Orange and British states were the aggressors. It was they who created and sustained by fear and coercion their policies and practices of exclusion and discrimination against the Catholic minority population. It was this mix of exclusion – underpinned by coercion and threats of violence – that created the conditions of conflict. This also created a counter-context, in which oppression was resisted and challenged.

I am also extremely proud of the efforts of the generation of Irish republicans who resisted oppression, exclusion and injustice. They refused to be criminalised. Loss of liberty and their lives was the personal cost of their resistance. Yet it was this generation of Irish Republicans, in the midst of conflict, who were a critical dynamic in shaping an alternative to armed conflict, and which was later to become known as the peace process. This peace process was designed to end a conflict that was forced on them and their community by the British state: a conflict that was not of their making.

Thankfully, the days of conflict and political exclusion are now nearly over. We have functioning (albeit fragile), inclusive political institutions. The Orange State has been deconstructed. The Royal Ulster Constabulary has gone. The sectarian Ulster Defence Regiment has gone. The northern state is governed through the power-sharing Executive. Future constitutional arrangements will be based on the principle of consent. We now have in place a civic-based policing service that is accountable, and the British army has left our streets. People across all communities are now beginning to live again.

And it is against this backdrop that unanswered questions remain about the origins, legacy and aftermath of our recent conflict. This is evidenced in the volume of daily battles, led by families bereaved through state killings in courts; revelations around the use of state agents; the insurmountable evidence around the practice and policy of collusion, shoot-to-kill and torture. All these conflict practices raise fundamental questions about the British state's policy intentions in Ireland. To my mind, no longer can the British state deny its combatant status in the conflict in Ireland over the last forty years: a conflict that ruined childhoods, claimed lives and ended dreams. I am also acutely aware that state oppression was met with defiance and resistance. Ordinary men and women stood firm to confront the "living nightmare" of the Orange state and the indignity of the British military occupation. Defiance and resistance was a response to state oppression.

In this context, and as a last resort, many Irish republicans confronted force with force and were involved in a military campaign against the British state and unionist paramilitaries. Our conflict had a huge human cost, in terms of lives lost and people injured. Regrettably, this conflict impacted on so many families. We must all wish that our context and our lived experiences could have been so different, but I know that I and my community did not go to war – war came to us. I am acutely aware of the pain and loss endured by all sides during the conflict. Each and every death must be regretted at a human level, and as such every family, without any qualification, has a fundamental right to truth.

Significantly, it is a source of quiet comfort for me that republicans have made a huge contribution to the legacy debate at different stages of the peace process. In my opinion, such statements of acknowledgement signal intent and should be built upon, as this society faces into the final phase of legacy negotiations. In summary, as I reflect on the progress made over the past 20 years of the peace process, I do so with a heavy heart associated with the lives lost, and yet a sense of hope and optimism for the future. While there may never be an agreed narrative of the past, it is vital for future stability that we learn the consequences of the politics of oppression and exclusion. So that never again may our past be repeated, and generations of young men and women make choices that they otherwise would never have to make, to defend their people and confront oppression.

What does that phrase "the final phase of legacy negotiations" actually mean? It is about finally agreeing the methods or structures within which answers will be delivered; some process which will necessitate cooperation from the many participants and players. The final shape of such a process will determine how much truth or information will emerge. In one of his brilliant turns of phrase, Seamus Heaney once said, "If you have the words, there's always a chance that you'll find the way". In that thought rests the challenge for the legacy negotiations and the "past process" which must be undertaken: firstly, that we find the right words, and then, that we identify the right time and place in which to use them. Better words will be required than those used in the various endgame statements of some years ago. What will be needed are words that properly acknowledge "the pain and loss endured by all sides" and the "huge human cost" that Glenholmes touched upon in her testimony above.

In this "final phase", the language in which we frame things will have to chime with the mood of reconciliation, and with the new beginnings and sense of hope that came with the political agreement of 1998. This is not just about the IRA and the loyalists. It is about everyone. In the next chapter, we will look at how the Haass/O'Sullivan talks set us the challenge of securing agreed statements of acknowledgement from the many sides, including national governments. We will also see how the word "sorry" was incorporated as a crucial element in an initiative titled "Uncomfortable Conversations". These are the next steps, the challenges of today and tomorrow.

Several years ago, the British Army responded to the IRA's 2005 statement confirming the ending of their armed campaign, by signalling a phased end to "Operation Banner" – a move that would close down routine military support for policing, and reduce the army presence here to that of a peacetime garrison. In an article for the *Belfast Telegraph* in July 2007 on the subject of this initiative, I interviewed Lieutenant General Nicholas Parker, at the time the most senior Army officer in Northern Ireland.

After 38 years of action, Operation Banner is finally wound down (*Belfast Telegraph*, 16 July 2007)

Picture a general in his army boots, trying to tiptoe over the eggshell that is the Northern Ireland story of the past 38 years, and the military's part in all of that.

At the end of that very long war, which Nick Parker prefers to call a "campaign" or a "mission" or a "challenge" or a "fight", or really anything but a war, the Army is getting ready to switch the lights out on Operation Banner. It's the longest running operation in British military history, and it is how [the Army] describes all those years in a support role to the police here.

There is a symbolic significance to all of this, of course there is. It is a further clearing of the battlefield, and it means an entirely different role for the Army in Northern Ireland and for the 5,000 soldiers who will remain in a peacetime garrison. This has been a learning ground for the British Army – and also a playground for the war games that were part and parcel of a 38-year fight.

Lieutenant General Nicholas Parker is the most senior Army officer in Northern Ireland today – the GOC or General Officer Commanding. My interview with him was a kind of sword fence, in which I sensed he was always on his guard. It was a military interview, with an eye to the political picture.

So, there was no straying into the language of war, no verdict on winners or losers, no detailed description of the IRA as an enemy, other than a comment: "Well, it's taken 38 years. So, it would be totally wrong for me to sit here and somehow say, 'Oh no, they were irrelevant'. Of course that's not the case."

On all of this, he knew those army boots could, with one wrong step, crush the eggshell.

Rather he chose to put the Army's role in the context of helping to create an enabling security environment that allowed for political progress. That stable security situation was the "carpet" on which others could arrange the political furniture.

"I think at the highest level we've learned that security is simply an enabler," the General told the *Belfast Telegraph*. "You have to work as part of a general consensus. You need to support the police. You produce a carpet, which other people can then move the furniture around on," he continued. "And it's that, it's the social, political, economic programmes that need to be woven into what you are doing, which will eventually bring you to a conclusion – whatever that conclusion is. I think we've learned that, and I think that is the sort of lesson that we should be taking to other places, because it seems to apply wherever you go."

The General believes that the argument or debate about winners and losers here is used to "aggravate" and is "not a responsible way of looking at what's been going on, which has been a highly complex process".

So, I try again – would it be better described as "a war with no winners"? He's not going there – well, trying not to go there; not wanting to get involved in this "war" discussion, always wanting to get away from that word as quickly as possible, and to set a different context, and a different tone.

He is more comfortable with his [own] words – his description of events. "To a section commander on Leeson Street in 1972 with a sniper firing at him, he is, as far as he is concerned, in a war," the Army's most senior officer in Northern Ireland responds. "So, in those terms, yes, it's a fight, but if you take it to the bigger stage, it's not a war. It is a challenge of some sort that you've got to build the jigsaw round. And if you treat it as a war, some of the pieces of the jigsaw won't fit, because there will be this sense of conflict."

That's the jigsaw in which the creation of a stable security environment is the "enabler" – the piece that allows the picture to develop. But there are many pieces missing – Army pieces, police pieces, IRA and loyalist pieces – [in] that off-stage scene that is the "dirty war".

I then quoted to the General a document – an "analysis of military operations in Northern Ireland" – written last year, and which says the British Government's main military objective in the 1980s was "the destruction of PIRA rather than resolving the conflict". My argument was that it sounded like the language of war – that it had the ring of winning and losing – and was the stuff of victory and defeat.

"Your point is an entirely fair one," the General accepts, on the basis of what I read to him, but then he goes on to offer further explanation. "If you look at the campaign – if I may call it a campaign. In the seventies, there was a lot of action, reaction, trying to establish the carpet. The eighties, I think, was the laying of the carpet, and in that sense it is entirely legitimate that somebody says: 'My priority at the moment is to achieve a level of security which will then allow me to shift the furniture.' But if you read it as defeat, then you are slightly missing the point. That's the way that they were expressing the need to provide a security environment that would let their other programmes progress."

So, was the IRA "destroyed" when it left the stage in that statement of 2005 that ended the armed campaign? "I don't think that's a helpful interpretation," is the soldier's response. "Because you are going back to the winning and losing, you're going back to the war. What has happened is that we have created a security environment where now the PSNI are able to do this on their own."

It was obvious that the war – the "dirty war" – was not what the General wanted to talk about. He wanted to look forward – to the significance of 31 July, and the ending of Operation Banner.

The Army's role now – in its peacetime garrison – will be very different, set in a context that looks outside Northern Ireland and to other missions in "some pretty challenging areas". After nearly 40 years, Banner is ending – the war is over – or is it the "challenge", or the "fight", or the "mission" or the "campaign"?

Those army boots are going elsewhere – and all sides have brushed much under that "carpet" that the General talked about so many times. There will be other questions on another day.

The venue for that interview with the General was at Thiepval Barracks in Lisburn. It was the morning of 12 July 2007 – Ulster's big marching day – and here was a discussion about another military march, away from one battlefield and towards other challenging arenas. Also in the room that day was Mervyn Wynne Jones, then the MoD's Chief Press Officer for Northern Ireland. The ending of Operation Banner was a carefully choreographed process, within which there were inevitably decisions that at times played into politics.

One instance of this was a briefing on the intention to disband the Home

Service battalions of The Royal Irish Regiment, which had grown out of the UDR. The expectation was that this announcement would trigger an "earthquake" response inside the unionist community. That plan for disbandment was signalled just days after the IRA endgame statement in July 2005. The Parker interview two years later was clearly intended to represent the drawing of some military line – the turning of a page into another place. When I was writing this book, I was sent a photograph from a military briefing in October 2006 at Bessbrook Mill. In this photograph, there is a board detailing the levels of threat prevailing at the time in Northern Ireland. The highest level of threat was identified as the danger of soldiers walking into a PR trap. This gives some insight into how things were changing, as the military prepared its exit.

Mervyn Wynne Jones, MoD Chief Press Officer Northern Ireland, 2001–2007

I remember a sense of resolve throughout the Headquarters. Everyone was focused on a positive end to Operation Banner. In moments of reflection, the sense of history was palpable: after 38 years of bloodshed, during which 763 forces personnel had been killed and more than 6,000 injured, here was an end. [For me] six long, challenging years as Chief Press Officer HQNI – by degree both exacting and immensely rewarding – were concluding. I felt some relief to be going home, but knew instinctively that nothing professionally could ever again match the experience I'd had in that turbulent place.

The mob violence long associated with the "parades season" had seemed more muted that summer. I had no desire to witness again the tinderbox violence at Drumcree church, and the provocative and ugly behaviours of marchers and marched-past alike in the Ardoyne. The white-hot heat of a riot and the instantaneousness of its combustion had been a revelation, and yet I had a sense of such events already belonging to the past. That mindset for me had begun with the hugely dignified and rain-soaked parade in Belfast on 6 October 2006, marking the disbandment of the Home Service battalions of The Royal Irish Regiment. It had not been easy for them in those final months, but the Queen was there to award them all collectively, both past and present, the Conspicuous Gallantry Cross. Tears were shed, but heads [were] held high that day. There was a very real sense of moving on.

Pressed to recall one event that seemed to me to foretell this new era, I return to Crossmaglen on the morning of 7 March 2007, when the last of the protective sangars – the metal-clad observation towers that had been a feature of the south Armagh landscape for decades – was being dismantled atop the village police station. Dressed incongruously in a suit, I walked into Crossmaglen square – scene of the killing of many of the more than 20 police and soldiers murdered in the village by the IRA – to talk to the media. I scanned the pre-Assembly election Sinn Féin posters, cynically but cleverly placed to maximise the occasion, and then a well-known Sinn Féin politician walked past. Catching each other's eye, we shook hands. A small gesture in the wider picture, but not lost on a seasoned journalist watching the encounter. "I don't believe what I've just seen," he said.

These transitions are not just about the IRA and the loyalists and the Army – and what they have done and have yet to do. To borrow an image from that interview with General Parker back in 2007, there is much furniture that now needs to be rearranged on that metaphorical carpet he described. Within that room and those arrangements, there is a newish fixture that looks out of place. For many, the MI5 Headquarters at Palace Barracks in Holywood contradicts the idea that we are now in peacetime. The Security Service will always be identified with the old ways, the stuff in the shadows. There will always be suspicion about what they are up to; why they are here; and what are they protecting and hiding.

Does the dissident republican threat – those sporadic and occasional attacks – really justify such a presence? The answer, surely, is no. New policing has to mean just that – policing without MI5, and police officers replacing Security Service officers in intelligence tasks. If there is the will, then all of this is possible and doable. There have been sweeping reforms and changes, but our progress risks being constantly pulled back into the past and into the actions and the protected and redacted files of the 1970s, 1980s and 1990s. As long as the presence of MI5 continues, a chunk of new policing will always look like old-style policing, and will always be open to that criticism and charge. In a later chapter, you will read how today's Chief Constable, George Hamilton wants all conflict-period documentation of this kind moved into a structured process on the past, by being handed over to the planned new Historical Investigations Unit (HIU). This is something else which has to be worked out as part of that "final phase of legacy negotiations". We are not yet at that point.

Since 2007, there have been consultations and negotiations about the past, and a succession of reports and proposals about what still needs to be done in this regard. It began with the work of Eames/Bradley, followed by Haass/ O'Sullivan, and after that came negotiations between the political parties and governments themselves. As a result, a paper agreement began to take shape, which still has to be built into a recognisable structure, leading on to a place where things begin to get done in an organised, and formal and joined-up way. The next chapters of this book will look at what has been proposed in this regard, but what is already clear is that there is no bridge that simply takes us out of the past and into the present. For many, those two places in time – the past and the present – are the same, and nothing has changed. It is about what has been taken away, and what will always be present.

No process can fix all that was broken. This is something that Lord John Alderdice – a politician and consultant psychiatrist – touched upon in an interview in 2008:

> It is like the war poets in the First World War: when you really look at what happened, there's nothing glorious about it. It's horrible and inhuman and destructive, and that's the reality. Now, what is the implication of that? It is this: that the awful pain and damage and scars [are] not necessarily repairable . . . Some of it cannot be fixed, whatever you do. There are people there who are massively damaged. I don't mean that you can't be helpful or supportive . . . but the horrible thing that has to be faced, in my view, is that this is not all repairable . . . The damage that was done to people, not just physically – that's obvious – but emotionally and in social terms, within their families and within their communities – it cannot all simply be fixed and put back together again.
>
> And part of the wish to deal with the legacy of the Troubles is not simply a perfectly understandable and appropriate wish to move on and make a better future and all those kinds of things, but part of it [also] is a wish to be able to resolve and heal and take away the horribleness of what happened on all sides. And it isn't possible. It [cannot] be done.

These were important words, for their honesty and for the warning that they contain. You can clear a battlefield, but not its ghosts. You can end a war, but you cannot hide its scars and, whatever is done, there will still be broken people, hurt forever and not able to be fixed. This, for many, is life after the war – the jigsaw piece that will not fit easily or sit comfortably in any new picture.

These few thoughts set a context for the next chapters of this book. There is a need for a process on the past, a need for questions to be answered, a need to help people. Yet there must be at all times too an understanding that there is much that cannot be fixed and that, in many cases, the truth will not come with an apology. The past is the uncertain future: the next steps, and not knowing where they will lead or what they will achieve. The legacy negotiations – in whatever phase – will leave much unresolved. Later, I will quote from David Park's novel, *The Truth Commissioner* – namely, his description of the bereaved families who leave a "process on the past", not quite grasping that it is over, and who then realise that what they have been given is not simply enough.

CHAPTER EIGHT
Trying to Bleed the Anger: Eames/Bradley; Haass/O'Sullivan

"War and conflict tend to dehumanise us, and make us look at our fellow man as a thing, a number, a reprisal, a message, a lesson, a reminder, but all we saw were people: mothers, fathers, families, each of them broken and each of them looking towards us to help to fix them."
Jarlath Burns of the Eames/Bradley Consultative Group, writing for this book.

"Much needs to be done if we are to avoid being betrayed again by our 'poisoned memory'. There are those who were directly culpable for the violence. However, many are complicit in keeping alive the animosity of bitter disputes that inflamed our past and continue to threaten our future."
David Porter of the Eames/Bradley Consultative Group, writing for this book.

"In any post-conflict society, the legacy of the past is the last issue that comes to be resolved."
David Park, author of the novel, *The Truth Commissioner,* speaking to the author in May 2014.

Belfast, 11.00 am, 28 January 2009

It was the first time we got some proper insight into what would open up and pour out if there was to be some process on the past here. After many months of talking and thinking, a Consultative Group was bringing forward its report and recommendations, but much of that got lost in the anger of this occasion. The headline in the *Belfast Telegraph* the following morning was: "Old wounds reopen". Yet, those present in the Europa Hotel those 24 hours earlier had seen that those wounds were not old. There was an explosion of emotions which was harrowing for those who witnessed it, and of course even more harrowing for those who directly experienced it.

The Consultative Group on the Past had been headed by the retired Church of Ireland Primate, Lord Robin Eames, who played a quiet but an important role in the moves towards the Combined Loyalist Military Command ceasefire of 1994; and Denis Bradley, a former Vice-Chairman of the Northern Ireland Policing Board, and a man who, years previously, had been one of those who helped facilitate so-called "backchannel" contacts between the British Government and the republican leadership. Those contacts were secret – out of sight – but what played out inside this famous city-centre hotel was very visible and needed little explanation or interpretation. It was an occasion when the pictures and the angry words exchanged spoke for themselves.

The image that accompanied many of the next day's headlines was of Michelle Williamson confronting Gerry Adams. Michelle's parents – George and Gillian – were both killed in the IRA Shankill bomb in October 1993, and now, almost 16 years later, there was nothing old about this daughter's hurt and suffering as a result of that day of death and destruction. It was there inside the room, along with the trauma of other bereaved relatives, as Eames and Bradley struggled to be heard, as they tried to explain their proposals in an atmosphere that was not conducive to listening. And it was there in that angry moment when Michelle Williamson stood within touching distance of the Sinn Féin President and shouted at the man who carried the coffin of the bomber Thomas Begley. This is how personal, and how fraught and tense things were that day. As the event ended, there were some quieter conversations and observations in that room too – about the fact that, while people could work some of this out in their heads, perhaps they could not deal with it in their hearts; that perhaps they had been hurt too much, and this was too much to ask of them.

It had all taken place very openly – on a very public stage. Television cameras, press photographers, radio microphones, reporters and correspondents had been there to record and report on it all. "Will the past ever be forgotten in this country?" was the conversational opener of the taxi driver who picked me up outside the Europa Hotel to take me out of the city. The answer, of course, is no – but, then, forgetting the past is not the purpose of any process that will re-visit and examine those conflict years. Answering questions; trying to address the damage and the suffering caused; providing care; remembering those killed and injured; thinking about and trying to help their families; providing a means for everyone to record their story – these are some of the things that can be done, but there is no such thing as forgetting or blocking out the suffering of those days that stretch through decades into the here and now.

Canon David Porter was part of the Eames/Bradley Consultative Group, and is now Director of Reconciliation at Lambeth Palace. He recalls his experience of watching that day unfold – and then explode. . .

David Porter, Member of Consultative Group on the Past, 2007–2009, writing for this book

Completing the work of the Consultative Group on the Past was always going to be a compromise. We heard stories and read analysis from such a wide range of people and perspectives. As group members, we brought different experiences and backgrounds to our task. Long discussion and argument produced a report to which we could each give assent. In publishing our report when we did, we compromised.

It would have been better if we had been given the time to work across the parties, to build some consensus for our recommendations. Yet how difficult that task still remains six years later. There was and remains an urgent need for financial help for those who lost a loved one in the early days of the conflict. The headlines were dominated by the recommendation addressing this. Sitting on the platform in a packed room with tensions high, it was clear that the one thing that could not be compromised on was the pain. The controversy exposed a fundamental fracture in our community around the events of the previous 40 years. A fissure that runs through us, all about how we talk with each other about the harm done in our times. What do we do with the pain?

There will always be the demand of justice for the violent actions of some. Yet we should also acknowledge that the conflict belongs to us all, drawing its energy from an inter-generational fear and hostility. We are a people who, through our learnt hate, have created victims in this and previous generations. Much needs to be done if we are to avoid being betrayed again by our "poisoned memory". There are those who were directly culpable for the violence. However many are complicit in keeping alive the animosity of bitter disputes that inflamed our past and continue to threaten our future.

The core recommendations of the Consultative Group's report are as valid today as when they were published. To recover truth and acknowledge wrong will come with a cost. We will struggle to forgive those who have hurt us. Any progress towards reconciliation will require great courage. Twenty-one years on from the ceasefires, and sixteen years since the Belfast Agreement, it is for this new generation that we must draw out our poison, in order to give them their future.

Perhaps the confrontations of that day inside the Europa Hotel were needed – to help bleed some of the anger – just as the Eames/Bradley process was also needed, to sketch out for the first time the possible shape of a process for dealing with the past. Those outlines have since been adjusted by others, but not abandoned or erased. The Eames/Bradley report, for all the controversy of that January day back in 2009, has been developed by others and used, not as some starting point, but rather as something closer to a finished design.

The Consultative Group on the Past began its work in 2007 and, when it was briefed by former Metropolitan Police Commissioner, Lord Stevens and his team on their collusion investigations and the extent of agent-running in Northern Ireland, they got a glimpse of what is sometimes described as "the Dark Side". We know something of the agent stories – "Stakeknife" within the IRA, Haddock within the UVF and Nelson within the UDA, but those stories, and what has been made public, merely scratch the surface. There is now to be a deeper examination of Stakeknife – his actions and what was known across the intelligence agencies. That investigation will look at 20-plus killings.

"It did make you think about the seriousness of what we were embarking on," David Porter said as he recalled that visit to the Stevens Investigation. "It brought us face-to-face with the reality of what had been going on in Northern Ireland, and the consequences of having had over 30 years of violent conflict with terrorist organisations and counterterrorist operations, and the complexity of that was made very evident to us . . . It opened my mind to the reality that counterterrorism and counterinsurgency is always morally ambiguous. There are no clear lines and boundaries." When eventually all of this is examined, how those lines and boundaries became blurred and were crossed and criss-crossed will disturb the narrative of the past for many people.

However in 2009, the Eames/Bradley report did not get out of the room. It was delivered against the background of the premature revelation of one of its recommendations: that a "recognition payment" of £12,000 should be made to all families – security force, republican, loyalist and other – who had lost a loved one in the conflict. This information emerged in a pre-arranged briefing with journalists on the morning of Friday, 23 January – just a few days before full details of the report were to be released – and, in no time, it became the stuff of screaming headlines. That information spilled out like a poison, resulting in those scenes inside the Europa Hotel on Wednesday, 28 January.

The safe pair of hands who didn't play it safe
(*Belfast Telegraph*, 28 January 2009)

Nineteen months ago, they were handed a poisoned chalice.

Two men from very different backgrounds – ex-Church of Ireland Primate, Lord Robin Eames and former Vice-Chairman of the Policing

Board, Denis Bradley – were sent to pick over the conflict and to consult on the best way to deal with the legacy of the past.

Now, there is a report and recommendations – and the inevitable fallout, the beginning of what someone recently described as the "big, bloody debate".

Part of the work of the Consultative Group was to find an alternative to deeply costly public inquiries.

. . . Politicians are too emotionally involved to decide on a process on the past, but there is a simple choice – to address the questions, or leave them unanswered. The job of trying to shape a process was given to Lord Eames and Denis Bradley, to Jarlath Burns and Willie John McBride, best known for their Gaelic football and rugby, and to a team that includes the Reverend Lesley Carroll, David Porter, James Mackey and Elaine Moore – all from different backgrounds and experiences.

. . . . But, for all that experience, it could be argued that in June 2007, then Secretary of State Peter Hain gave the Group an impossible task. It has left them open to all the criticism of recent days, and the Consultative Group will need the thickest of skins, as politicians and others bite at them over one proposal in particular. That is their recommendation to give the families of all who died in the conflict a "recognition payment" of £12,000.

There is criticism of how that news emerged last Friday. "I can't work out the thinking," one source commented. "It's going to distort the whole thing." Maybe the shock had to come before today's launch event – maybe people needed time to think about it, and then to read this report in its wider context. Perhaps it was, in the words of one source, an attempt "to bleed the anger".

There is no such thing as a consensus on dealing with the past. So, this almost needs to be dictated and directed by others. Eames/Bradley is not the truth process. Their job was to create a model in which the past could be explored and explained and, then, to give that work to others who can look at it through uninvolved eyes. That is the thinking behind the plan for a Legacy Commission, headed by an international chairman working alongside two others in the fields of investigations and information recovery.

People who have already been hurt could be hurt some more. That is the nature of these processes.

So, either you open the past to scrutiny, or you close it all down. Maybe some believed that Eames/Bradley – that safe pairs of hands – would do the latter. They have not. Instead, they have created a process for digging and uncovering. Buried secrets could emerge. Is that what Eames/Bradley was meant to deliver?

The problem with the timing of the revelations relating to the victims' payment proposal was that the media storm which ensued obscured much of the rest of what the Eames/Bradley consultation was proposing. I summed up my own take on the situation at the time in an article written for the February 2009 edition of the WAVE Trauma Centre's newsletter:

The recommendation that was leaked on the Friday before publication of the Eames/Bradley report was its big secret – the one big piece of information that had not yet emerged from the Consultative Group on the Past. It had been kept locked up in the thinking of that Group and only shared at the very last minute, and when it was too late. When the recommendation was spoken, the damage was done. Most of the rest was known – including the main proposal for a Legacy Commission with Investigations and Information Recovery Units. But the recommendation for a "recognition payment" of £12,000 to all families who had lost someone in the conflict was new – both new and contentious.

It was a shock to me when I heard it for the first time that Friday in the company of a number of other journalists – but there have been other shocks and surprises in the peace. It is the nature of conflict-transformation processes. There are unquestionably those who would now like to use this proposal as the flame to burn the Eames/Bradley report – to get rid of it. It would be the easy way out – a way of avoiding the hardest questions from the past.

. . . That controversial proposal is just one of 31 recommendations – one piece in a much bigger jigsaw: a piece that at this point will not fit the picture. It could have been left out. Others will say and have said it should have been left out, but once they decided to make the proposal, the Eames/Bradley Group had to make it across the board. They could not create their own league table of victims – and if they had, that too would have poisoned this debate.

Jarlath Burns describes his work with the Consultative Group as the most turbulent, traumatic and shocking period of his life – so much so, that he had decided he would never talk about it again. But, when I approached him about this book, he agreed to share some of his personal thoughts about the unanswered past and his learning from that process.

Jarlath Burns, Member of the Consultative Group on the Past, 2007–2009

I was a member of the Eames/Bradley Consultative Group on the Past. I always felt I was a strange appointment, because I had never really been involved in any political, religious or social capacity in the day-to-day public intercourse that is common in Northern Ireland, so I was puzzled as to my selection [for] the Group.

I never regretted the decision to accept the invitation. The Group very quickly developed a bond of trust that was reminiscent of those who dwelt in the trenches in another war – because in many respects, there were similarities between the two: we were bombarded from all sides, on occasion we felt battered, bruised, experienced harrowing stories and were in the middle of the political and societal firing line at all times.

I discovered many things during that time, and my own opinions, prejudices and preconceived notions were shattered routinely as we met the various victims, listened to their stories and heard of their expectations. I learnt that victims from the unionist side yearned for justice – that someone, somewhere would be accountable for their suffering – while on the nationalist side, there was a thirst for truth, to discover why their loved ones were selected to die. They were keen to find out, not so much who pulled the trigger, but who was pulling the strings.

War and conflict tend to dehumanise us and make us look at our fellow man as a thing, a number, a reprisal, a message, a lesson, a reminder – but all we saw were people: mothers, fathers, families, each of them broken and each of them looking towards us to help to fix them. At our very first meeting, one of our members, David Porter, remarked, "If we don't deal with the past, the past will deal with us." He was right. We haven't, and it is.

These are thoughtful words from Jarlath Burns, within which there is much for us all to think about. The consultative process of the Group brought its members face-to-face with those who have been hurt the most, and who now look to others for answers and help, and for some acknowledgement of what happened to them.

In an interview back in January 2009, both Eames and Bradley stressed the importance of cooperation in information or truth-recovery. "My feeling is that they won't do it because we said it, or we asked or we requested it," Bradley said at the time. "I think the UVF will do it because there will be a demand within their own community. I think the IRA will do it because there is a demand within their own community – because people are fair and they say, 'Well, you know, we've been looking for truth [and] if you boys don't step up to the mark, how can you expect other people to step up?' So there is going to be a playing off – one against the other – from here on in, and that is rightly so . . . We need them all on board, and the information recovery [process] will be as good as the participants who get involved." Lord Eames then picked up on Bradley's thought: "We have spread the net very wide in the State services – MoD, MI5, Special Branch – all of them would come under the umbrella that Denis has mentioned."

As their comments indicate, Bradley and Eames were creating the widest possible frame, and challenging everyone to step inside the proposed information process. My own belief is that levels of cooperation, and the terms and conditions of such, should be known before the doors of any commissions are opened. That would require a phase of research and consultations, to establish exactly what is achievable – probably involving international/ independent figures in conversations with all sides in the conflict. The bulk of information is likely to be delivered and framed in general terms from the standpoint of the various groupings or organisations involved, rather than from named individuals.

While Eames/Bradley set out their suggested model in that public forum of 28 January 2009, many questions were left hanging – all of which could still be asked today. I set out some of the most important of these in an article for the *Belfast Telegraph* at the time:

Many Questions Unanswered
(from *Belfast Telegraph*, 28 January 2009)

- Are the IRA, the loyalists, the security forces, the intelligence services and governments really ready for this – ready for an information-recovery process that will ask of them the most awkward of questions?
- Who on all sides were the directors of the war?
- What were the consequences of their strategies and orders?
- What was known about the murderous activities of informants?
- What was the extent of collusion?
- Who can explain the practice of "disappearing" bodies? Who allowed that to happen?
- Who was in the IRA, and who was not? When were they in it?

- Who believed it acceptable to employ the most senior leaders of the UVF and the UDA as agents, as they sat in rooms directing the killing of Catholics?
- How much were they paid? Was it more than the £12,000 that has caused so much controversy in recent days?
- How much was UVF man Mark Haddock paid?
- How much was the IRA agent "Stakeknife" paid while he was interrogating other informers and leaving them for execution?

It is too early to get angry – because there is the possibility of much more and worse to come if the questions are ever answered. But they may not be – by any of the sides . . .

Just a few weeks later, in my article in the newsletter of the WAVE Trauma Centre, I expanded on this thinking:

Eames/Bradley Report's Big Secret (*WAVE Newsletter*, February 2009)
The issue now is whether that one, hugely contentious proposal [the £12,000 payment to bereaved families] can be set aside, to allow for a more measured discussion on what else has been recommended – because in a blizzard of condemnation, some of the bigger questions have been lost. There is the issue of information or truth-recovery, and who will and who won't cooperate. And there is the question of continuing investigations and how much of an obstacle that particular proposal might be on the road to some better understanding of what happened here in Northern Ireland or the North, and elsewhere, over a period of some decades. The vast bulk of continuing investigations will go nowhere in terms of potential convictions.

That is a fact. Jail is no longer the type of justice that can be expected. Time and the peace process have moved beyond that. That is one of the hard truths after the war. Continuing [police] investigations are a way of saying "No Amnesty". But is it the right decision? . . . Whether it is called an amnesty or something less controversial, it is through a mechanism or process of that kind, that truth will best be achieved . . . Investigations will frighten off many of those who could assist a truth-recovery process.

The big goal in all of this is to get the [main] players in the conflict to some table of explanation, and at that table to hear the stories of their wars – what happened and why. And [this] needs all sides: republican, loyalist, security forces and intelligence services. This is the route to more information and more truth – and [police] investigations and the threat of jail, however slim, are obstacles in the way. The big question is whether all sides will talk, and that should be one of the first pieces of work for any new Legacy Commission – to determine who will cooperate and who won't . . . There is no point in a half-truth process. That gets us nowhere.

One of the most important decisions in this recommended process, if it is allowed to breathe, will be the appointment of the International Chairman of the Legacy Commission. That person needs to be of such standing and independence that it makes it, if not impossible, then very difficult for people not to cooperate.

It is too easy to dismiss the Eames/Bradley process as a waste of time, or to turn it into the next political football, or the next excuse for not shovelling up the past. The harder question is: what is the alternative? This debate got off to a bad start because of a shock proposal . . . The idea of a recognition payment did not need to be discussed and decided now. Indeed, it could be argued that it is something that is best left to be decided upon much further down the road – to be decided upon when the work and the conclusions of the Legacy Commission are known. At that point, we would have an international analysis of the conflict.

There are many ugly truths hidden in the war . . . The loyalist groups were responsible for the slaughter of many uninvolved Catholics, and some of those in the leadership of the UVF and the UDA were working for the State. They were informers, sitting in rooms where life and death were being decided. The IRA has the story of the "Disappeared" to explain, and the stories of Bloody Friday, La Mon, Enniskillen and the Shankill – all that slaughter and more. This is just some of what an exploration of the past will touch on: horrific events, the war games, the orders and the doing.

Eames/Bradley . . . have created a process that would allow for that digging . . . Since their report, we have heard the loudest voices of opposition, but what is the message in the quietness and the silence of others? What do they want; how are they heard; who is listening?

Within weeks of the report, then Secretary of State, Shaun Woodward brushed aside the proposal on recognition payments. He said there was "not remotely enough consensus" to proceed. His decision was explained in these terms: that this one suggestion meant the rest of the recommendations were not getting a fair hearing and, so, a decision was taken to "close that element down". It was about trying to open up the rest of the report for consideration.

However, an intervention by Gerry Adams around this time expressed a much wider concern. Adams presented his arguments in the frame of Sinn Féin's call for an Independent International Truth Commission, "established by a reputable international body like the UN": "Given that the British Government was the major protagonist in the conflict, how can bereaved families or those seeking truth and justice feel anything other than deep concern at the process that is being proposed by the Eames/Bradley Group? The British Government cannot be the objective facilitator of any truth-recovery process. It also cannot with any honesty write the remit of any group tasked with that role. Any truth process, which has the fingerprints of the 'securocrats' in Whitehall anywhere near it, simply will not work. . . The process unveiled by the Consultative Group on the Past is therefore deeply flawed and incapable of establishing the Independent International Truth Commission which we believe is necessary," Adams concluded.

We were watching an unpicking of Eames/Bradley – with slow responses, no responses and dismissive responses. Much further down the road, there would be other negotiations and attempts to establish a process. These would not bring forward an Independent International Truth Commission, but rather, further proposals for investigations and information-retrieval that have their roots in that report of the Consultative Group back in 2009. These several years later, many of the questions about final structure, participation/cooperation, and the terms and conditions for such, remain unanswered.

There was a long gap and a long wait between the Eames/Bradley process, which ended in 2009, and the beginning of the Haass/O'Sullivan talks in 2013. In the interim, Lord Eames had suggested that there should be "an international dimension" to decisions on the appointment of the Legacy Commission that his Consultative Group had proposed – and that international input should also be sought in relation to how any such Commission would operate. It was another attempt to bring this conversation on the past to the point where a process could be actively begun – but that wait continues and, indeed, extended beyond the Haass/O'Sullivan talks into yet more rounds of negotiations.

US Diplomat, Dr Richard Haass and Harvard Professor, Meghan O'Sullivan, came to these negotiations with deep knowledge of the peace process. This time, the approach was built around the participation of these international facilitators and the five parties in the Stormont Executive – the DUP, Sinn Féin, the Ulster Unionists, the SDLP and Alliance. The talks were aimed at achieving a five-party consensus, not just on the past, but on the toxic issues of flags and parades. The British and Irish Governments were not at the table. They remained in spectator roles. In other words, in the wrong place. Their absence as active participants asked – and still asks – the question: do they really want to deal with the past? It is a scary place in terms of where it could take people.

Haass and O'Sullivan wanted to move things along from the constructive ambiguity of the Good Friday Agreement period some 15 years earlier, to the point of specificity. In other words, to dig down into the fine print of what needed to be done. What this fine detail should entail would be a cause for concern both inside and outside these talks. The Haass/O'Sullivan process would span several months and extend beyond this, into Christmas and then New Year's Eve 2014 – but without finishing with a deal. In keeping track of the progress of these talks, I wrote many thousands of words detailing their many twists and turns, through one draft document and into the next.

On the issue of parading, the talks got nowhere. In a very real sense, they marched on the spot. On flags, a number of ideas – including the creation of a new, neutral Northern Ireland flag – were run up and run down the political poles. Nothing changed. On the past, Haass/O'Sullivan did make some progress: if not to the point of a deal, then much closer to an agreed structural design that borrowed from the themes of Eames/Bradley.

In one of his news conferences, Haass spoke of "ideas that ripen in the marketplace". He was right. This time, the plan was for a Historical Investigations Unit (HIU), an Independent Commission for Information Retrieval (ICIR), and an Implementation and Reconciliation Group (IRG), tasked with monitoring and overseeing the process of addressing the past. The proposed package also included acknowledgement of, and support for, victims and survivors, and, in a section on sharing experiences, plans for a storytelling archive.

The hope was to get somewhere before Christmas – which then became after Christmas and before the New Year. In particular sessions, the talking continued for hours and, at times, those taking part both looked and sounded tired. At 4.30 a.m. on Christmas Eve morning, inside the hotel venue, Haass said he was "not in the business of doing post-mortems, because the patient is still alive". On that theme too, the Alliance negotiator, Naomi Long talked of a process "on life support". There was a break for several days, then a last effort to get something over the line, in a final phase of negotiations that stretched from Saturday, 28 December to Tuesday, 31 December 2013. At this stage, the talks were attempting to drill down into more specifics – including what an examination of patterns and themes during the conflict period might entail. The proposal was that the past should be painted on the widest possible canvas. Drawing out these patterns and themes would require the tackling of certain crucial questions by republicans, loyalists and both the British and Irish Governments.

On 31 December and New Year's Day 2014, in a couple of analysis pieces for the *Belfast Telegraph*, I set out to sum up what this process had achieved, and failed to achieve. In the first of those articles, I described a process that was about getting the scaffolding in place, in order to leave the building work to be done by others. Where I saw the most potential to build on something meaningful was within the design of the process of addressing the past. A form of limited immunity had been built into the information or truth-recovery pillar – but of course, while you can build a structure, you cannot not force people through its doors.

(From *The Belfast Telegraph*, 31 December 2013)

All of this drafting and sketching is about bringing some order and structure to what, up to now, has been a piecemeal, fragmented and scattered approach to addressing the past. Other proposed strands will look at acknowledgement, reconciliation, a storytelling archive and the needs of victims and survivors. But it will only work – can only work – if those left with this project . . . want it to work. Haass and O'Sullivan have coaxed and urged and persuaded all they can – but this process needs political will and leadership.

Some victims' representatives gathered at the talks hotel yesterday evening, understandably anxious and concerned about the next steps, and about what all this writing and rewriting will add up to in the end. What will it mean for them? What will it really mean for truth and justice? It depends on the commitment to the proposals, on political will to do the building, and on leadership. These are the key ingredients.

If this Haass/O'Sullivan process is implemented as intended, then, five years after the Eames/Bradley report was shelved, there will be something that can be called a process on the past. [Something] different, a step change – something worth doing and having.

My own reporting watch in that final phase of the negotiations would continue until 7.00 a.m. on New Year's Eve morning. Hours before then, Sinn Féin confirmed, in the following statement, that it would recommend the Haass document to the party's leadership, the Ard Chomhairle: "Over a decade ago, Sinn Féin proposed the establishment of an Independent International Truth Commission. In our view, that remains the best option. But a basis for compromise on this issue has been proposed. That is what the majority of our people want. Closure for victims and survivors is the real benchmark against which this proposition will in time be judged." Also in those tired, early hours of 31 December, SDLP negotiators said that they would recommend a "general endorsement" of the paper, Alliance recognised the progress made on the past, but pointed to the non-deal on flags and the gaps in relation to parading, while the DUP and the UUP stated that they needed time for further discussions with their parties.

As Haass and O'Sullivan made their exit, this was the mixed bag of responses with which their proposals had been met. What time will judge, more than anything else, is who is really serious about doing the right things when it comes to answering the past and ensuring that there is no repeat in the future of the horrors of the conflict period. A possible structure on paper for this process is not the test of any of this. At some point, politicians need to let go, relinquish their control and let others take these things forward, as they step aside.

The Haass/O'Sullivan negotiations were never going to settle everything. They were never going to agree on how the conflict started; its context; what it should be called; what happened, and why. If part of the plan is for an independent information process, then that is what it should be – independent, and not shackled or controlled or manipulated in any way, particularly by the political script writers, with their inevitable attempts to predetermine the work and findings of any such Commission.

(From The *Belfast Telegraph*, 1 January 2014)

. . . One of the last battles in these talks was around a list of conflict-era themes and patterns, which should be examined as part of a detailed analysis within the information process. [Such a] list was part of a Draft Five document last weekend, which disappeared from the next draft. But, as a result of a unionist push, it was slightly altered and reinstated in the final text. Examples of the themes it could consider include:

- Alleged collusion between governments and paramilitaries;
- Alleged ethnic cleansing in border regions and in interface neighbourhoods;
- The alleged UK "shoot-to-kill" policy;
- The reported targeting of off-duty UDR soldiers, prison officers and reservist Royal Ulster Constabulary officers;
- The degree to which, if at all, the Republic provided a "safe haven" to republican paramilitaries;
- Intra-community violence by paramilitaries;

- The use of lethal force in public order situations;
- Detention without trial;
- Mistreatment of detainees and prisoners;
- Any policy behind the Disappeared;
- The sources of financing and arms for paramilitary groups.

. . . The reason this section of the final text was so important to unionists was because it took any examination of the conflict period into a much wider framework. But what that list also demonstrates is that any excavation of the past will not just be about republicans and loyalists, but will put a focus on governments, security and intelligence.

For some, this is the frightening aspect.

. . . This process won't be judged on what happened in the intense last week of negotiation – but on what happens next.

That's the real challenge.

When we look at the two processes together – Eames/Bradley and Haass/O'Sullivan – we will see many similarities. The titles and names used may be different, but the thinking and purpose are more or less the same. The Eames/Bradley recommendations included the following key proposals:

- An Independent Legacy Commission;
- A Reconciliation Forum;
- A Review and Investigations Unit;
- An Information-Recovery Process;
- A Unit to examine linked or thematic cases emerging from the conflict;
- No new public inquiries to be undertaken.

The 2009 Consultative Group did not propose an amnesty, but suggested that the Legacy Commission should make recommendations on how, "a line might be drawn at the end of its five-year mandate, so that Northern Ireland might best move to a shared future". Almost five years later in November 2013, at the same time as the Haass/O'Sullivan talks were ongoing, the Attorney General for Northern Ireland, John Larkin proposed the drawing of such a line – an end to all prosecutions, public inquiries and inquests into conflict-related killings. He suggested that this line should be drawn at Good Friday 1998. While the Attorney General did not frame his comments in terms of an amnesty, this is how they were widely interpreted. There was an angry reaction – but there have been equally angry reactions during other phases of the peace process, such as at the time of policing reform when the RUC title was lost, or when prisoners were released, or when it was first mooted that unionists should share government with republicans. This is the turbulence that comes with the transition from conflict into an evolving peace.

The issue of amnesty – however this is described – will eventually come to be addressed and will be resolved. However, there was already too much going on inside the Haass/O'Sullivan talks for such a contentious issue to be dealt with at this time. Larkin's suggestion may have been brushed aside and may have been considered as unhelpful in its timing, but a decade earlier, at a time when he was serving as PSNI Chief Constable, Sir Hugh Orde had also raised this issue of "closing the book". In relation to Larkin's position, the Dublin commentator and barrister Noel Whelan, observed: "Unlike the politicians, he [Larkin] does not have to pander to a constituency," and noted that there was nothing in legislation that restricted the Attorney General from talking publicly on issues with such implications for the criminal justice system. "Larkin did no more than offer a view," he said. This is a view and a position that others agree with – including some in political circles – but there is a reluctance, a political fear, to say it publicly.

As these Haass/O'Sullivan talks ended, the proposed structural frame for addressing the past included the following:

- An Historical Investigations Unit (HIU)
- An Independent Commission for Information Retrieval (ICIR)
- An Archive to record conflict-related experiences
- An Implementation and Reconciliation Group (IRG)

The final documents and the proposed agreement included the following formulation: "We encourage individuals, organisations and national governments to work together on specific statements of acknowledgement, including by discussing language, timing and other matters in private before public statements are made, to ensure that such acknowledgements are carried out in ways that contribute positively to healing and reconciliation." In other words, the statements would be choreographed, with each party knowing in advance what the other was going to say.

The Haass/O'Sullivan proposals would be carried forward into yet another round of negotiations, this time including the British and Irish Governments with the Executive parties, but with the US facilitators no longer involved. By now the wheel had been invented – the wheel being the structural mechanism emerging from this process, which was different in name but along the same lines of the Eames/Bradley design.

Before the next set of negotiations after Haass/O'Sullivan were launched into, a very timely event was hosted in the offices of the *Belfast Telegraph*, with the novel *The Truth Commissioner* by David Park as its focus. The then Victims' Commissioner, Kathryn Stone would also be in attendance.

Exorcising the Ghosts of the Past (*Belfast Telegraph*, 27 May 2014)

Even in fiction, there is little imagined about the past of this place that some call Ulster, the province, Northern Ireland, the Six Counties, or the North. What happened really happened. You can change names, dates and places, but the stories, even if told on the pages of a novel, chime with reality.

Yes, we now have this heralded "peace" that is held up to others as an example, but we still live in divided communities; in some places, separated by walls, and where words and descriptions come to identify or mark us out.

And the blood and the bodies and the brokenness of the conflict years are still with us and within us in the present – very much a part of the here and now. Twenty years after the ceasefires, much more than a decade after the Good Friday Agreement, there has been no thaw in which the killing acts have vanished, or disappeared.

The past is today's battlefield: contested, clashing, controversial and all part of [the] complex and competing narratives. There is no one truth, no one story, or book – and there never will be. We know that in the hidden corners of that past and present, there are many ghosts.

And, six years ago, in his highly acclaimed novel, *The Truth Commissioner*, author David Park took us into those still haunted – and haunting – places of secrets and fears. "I found it emotionally draining to write," he told me. "It punched a hole in me, but at the same time, there was something cathartic as well. It's a book about what it is to be human; politics is secondary."

The novel won the Christopher Ewart-Biggs Memorial Prize – an award that recognises work which promotes peace and reconciliation.

Park is of this place, writes with the authority of that closeness to events, and knows that truth doesn't exist in pure light: that it can be "murky and dark". And, in that truth commission he created and structured inside his book those several years ago, he wrote: "Day after day, it's as if the dam is breached and out pours a torrent of rising levels of hurt that have been stored over long winters of grief."

Tomorrow evening, as part of the One City, One Book 2014 series of events, the creator of that fictional commission will engage with an audience that will include the real life Victims' Commissioner, Kathryn Stone. "You absolutely can't run away from the past. It catches up with you," she says. "It's impossible to move on, when you've no legs, or an empty space in the bed where your husband used to be." The Commissioner has been in those meetings and homes and conversations when the anger, emotion and hurt identified by Park has spilled out – when the dam has been breached.

So it happens, both in the pages of his novel and in the day-to-day reality of the Victims Commissioner's engagement with those who have been hurt and traumatised and bereaved. "There is a wound there that has not been healed," David Park tells me. "So, that wound needs to be salved.

Both Park and Stone understand that you cannot outlive the past, that you can't wait for it to go away in the natural cycles of life. They know that what happened won't die with the conflict generation; that others will remember. So, something needs to happen. And Park's book – and his reading from it at the event tomorrow evening – will open up and open out yet another conversation.

Alan McBride, whose wife and father-in-law were killed in the IRA Shankill bombing, will be in the audience. So, too, will Jude Whyte, whose mother, along with a young police officer, was killed by a UVF bomb on another Belfast street in 1984. Their names, along with thousands of others, are found on the pages of *Lost Lives,* that log of deaths stretching over decades from the 1960s through to now. It, too, is only part of the story. There are thousands more who have been hurt physically and psychologically.

"So many of the people I have met here have very real needs as a consequence of trauma," Ms Stone says. "And that trauma can be from what they have experienced themselves through bereavement, injury, or what they have witnessed, or what has happened to someone close to them." Those stories of sleeplessness, self-harming, anxiety and dependence on prescription medication or alcohol, are often buried under the conflict headlines of the high body counts, in those shootings and bombings that are on the tips of our tongues. But the Commissioner reminds us: "All of those things are the very real consequences of what happened to people."

And David Park understands how all of that cries out for practical help as one of the challenges of addressing the past. "Don't ask me what that looks like," he adds, accepting this is for others with that expertise. But the past has many layers. "We cannot have a process that's built on reconciliation unless we have a reconciled political leadership," he tells me. And, in that comment, Park is identifying and describing an unfinished and incomplete peace. "In any post-conflict society, the legacy of the past is the last issue that comes to be resolved," he adds.

Here, in Northern Ireland, that challenge to find the right process, the right design and architecture, remains a work-in-progress. This is about seeing what can be salvaged from the Haass/O'Sullivan talks. Looking at what might work in that collection of ideas and recommendations stretching across information or truth recovery; an examination of conflict themes and patterns; investigation; acknowledgement and an archive for all stories.

[While] the US team of Haass and O'Sullivan borrowed from the report of Eames/Bradley, Kathryn Stone recently borrowed from both in a set of proposals designed to make something happen. She leaves the post of Victims' Commissioner in just a couple of weeks' time, but wants to see a victims' pension introduced, a beginning to the information retrieval process, and acknowledgement that includes official letters of apology. All of that has now been poured into the political mix.

But, whatever happens, "truth" will not emerge as some magic wand, or fix. It didn't in Park's novel. Nor will it in reality ... Whatever is decided and whenever it is decided, we will see that tug-of-war between those who, in Park's novel, will try to preserve their truth while wanting everyone else's. This is all part of the battlefield, the win and lose, part of a process that could hurt as much as it heals. There will be no absolute truth, not from any side, never mind all the sides.

And Park captured those potential limitations and flaws in his book six years ago; that truth is not everything, but rather can come as "some formulaic, pre-learned response that expresses a vague regret for the pain caused". In the pages of *The Truth Commissioner*, he explained what this means for the bereaved families: "Often at the end they have to be helped from the chamber, as if they haven't grasped that it's all over, that their time has finished, and then they shuffle towards the exits, their confused, white-salted faces glancing back over their shoulders." These are the moments when the families understand, "that this is all they are to be given – and they realise it's not enough".

In those words of fiction, there is both a reality and a warning: that the past cannot be fixed in some process of questions and answers. Speaking about today's reality, Park tells me: "A lot of people are talking about truth and justice. Truth and justice is different from truth and reconciliation."

Queen's Law Professor, Kieran McEvoy, who has travelled the world looking at processes for addressing the past, will also attend tomorrow's One City, One Book event. He has just returned from Israel and Palestine, as part of research also looking at Cambodia, Chile, Tunisia and South Africa . . . He spoke to me of his learning from Park's writing: "I have been working on an academic book for a number of years on dealing with the past in Northern Ireland. And, when I read *The Truth Commissioner,* I thought: why bother? Park captured in fiction much more eloquently the difficulties associated with truth recovery – much better than the thousands of academic texts I've read."

And, on that specific point made by Park – on the difference between truth and justice, and truth and reconciliation – McEvoy says, "If you equate justice with jail time, the reality is that for a lot of unsolved murders, justice will not be achieved."

This is another reality of any exploration, examination or excavation of the past: that justice in many cases (indeed in most cases), will not mean court and jail. For many there will be a sense of betrayal, of let-down and the reality of more hurt. Whether addressed in fiction, or in academic studies, the past is not simple, not easily answered. . . This has to be part of the truth: that understanding of what a process, however [is] shaped, cannot deliver. And Park captured all of that in *The Truth Commissioner,* [showing] how the stories weave through many different lives; the fears about the past, how secrets might be exposed; the plots to keep them hidden.

The book finishes with a fire, but also with the thought that you can't destroy memory and knowledge: "The fire makes no difference in one sense – all the files have been scanned and their contents now sleep in the hard drives of computers, out there in cyberspace, beyond the reach of destruction." "A part of me as a writer was gone with that fire," the author tells me.

He means that, in the emotionally draining experience of this writing project, he, too, was letting something go in the smoke and the flames of his novel. But Park knows, as Kathryn Stone knows, there is no such thing as drawing a line. Somehow, [in] some way, something has to be tried to at least salve some of the wounds.

Talking is part of that; being heard is part of that. The conversation will resume tomorrow evening.

In the room at the event that night, and in similar gatherings and conversations, we heard truth, honesty, explanation – and we witnessed a willingness to engage and to listen. These are informal gatherings or meetings within which storytelling grows; one experience shared, and another offered. They are not cosy or comfortable or easy conversations, and they are a part of what could happen in a more structured process – if the right forum, the right rules and the right circumstances can be created, and if the talking is for the right reasons. Difficult, uncomfortable, painful conversations don't have to be confrontational. Indeed, when they are not, more is shared and more is achieved, and there is more understanding and learning.

CHAPTER NINE
April 2014: The "Troubles" with Truth

"The powerful paradox of theatre is that it can be most real when it is most imagined."

Lyric Trustee, Stephen Douds, writing for this book.

"We've seen what we shouldn't have."

(From Owen McCafferty's *Quietly*)

"The past is the present for those who suffered pain, loss and grief as a result of our dark and grievous history."

PSNI Chief Constable, George Hamilton, writing for this book.

"While the vacuum continues, those that have been most affected by the conflict lose hope for some form of redress, and societal reconciliation seems a distant dream."

Ulster University academic, Dr Jonny Byrne, writing for this book.

The play on stage in the Lyric Theatre was called *Quietly*. Its storyline involved a pub bombing and then, many years later, a first meeting. At times you could have heard a pin drop in the silence of the audience. But it was not quiet on stage. There was a tension and a rawness to the conversation. It was confrontational, and at times, chilling. The anger was easily understandable. Three actors played the roles of a barman, a bomber and the son of one of the men who died. This was their meeting, their conversation and the playing out of all that had been stored up over many years. It all poured out.

Unknown to me, Paul Doherty was also in the theatre that night. We have seen in an earlier chapter how Paul's father, Jim was killed, along with five others, in a pub bombing in Belfast in 1974. In April 2014, Paul was no doubt thinking about the then imminent 40th anniversary commemoration of that real-life bombing, at the Rose and Crown pub on the Ormeau Road in May 1974.

During that run at the Lyric theatre of Owen McCafferty's *Quietly*, there was a different post-show speaker each night. I had been asked to speak one evening on the theme of "truth" and, I began by telling McCafferty that there was nothing imagined about *Quietly*, and said the play, "had called me back to different scenes and places – to the rubble of the Shankill bomb, to a body lying almost naked on the road in south Armagh, to a pub that had been shot up, to cemeteries and places of tears and anger, and not knowing what to say or do. So, to borrow from tonight's script, 'We've seen what we shouldn't have.'"

The play gave vent to much of what has been unsaid about what happened here. It was, I suppose, a smaller version of that day several years earlier, when the proposals of the Eames/Bradley project played out in all the anger of those scenes inside the Europa Hotel. One was a play, the other was real – but both had been equally powerful in conveying the underlying and buried pain. For years, the theatre provided a safer space to express and explore what had happened. Lyric Trustee Stephen Douds reflects on some of this in a piece he wrote for this book.

Stephen Douds, Trustee, Lyric Theatre Belfast

Inside a terraced house are four friends and a ghost; outside, the collapse of law and order. Add in an extract of Harold Wilson's famous "spongers" speech: "Who do these people think they are?" That's the setting for Stewart Parker's play, *Pentecost*, set during the Ulster Workers' Council Strike of 1974. The play itself was written in the late 1980s and was Parker's last, before his early death. Revived a number of times since, the Lyric staged it in September 2014, not so much to mark the 40th anniversary of the strike, as to complete the trilogy of Belfast plays (which also included Owen McCafferty's *Quietly*) directed by the Lyric's Executive Producer, Jimmy Fay.

Though Parker may have had an eye on history when he wrote *Pentecost*, with one character observing laconically, "Sure, every week is historic in this place." *Pentecost's* last scene sees Marion, a woman in her early thirties, make an astonishing plea for reconciliation and wholeness. Although I'd seen the play several times before, I was especially moved by this production, in which Marion speaks of the debt the living owe to the dead of the Troubles. Committing herself – and by implication, the audience – to a better future, she says, "We don't just owe it to ourselves, we owe it to our dead too . . . our innocent dead. They're not our masters, they're only our creditors for the life they never knew. We owe them at least that – the fullest life for which they could ever have hoped."

In 2001, Mark Carruthers and I edited a collection of essays about how different art forms fared during the Troubles. The book, *Stepping Stones*, recorded the highs and lows of drama, fiction, music, film and so on, when there was an impressive (if much less reported) flourishing of creative energy. In the introduction we wrote: "In the context of Northern Ireland and the past 30 years, that is perhaps what artists have contributed most – they have chronicled the individual stories. Their work has been a crucial counterpart to the notion that society here has constituted nothing more than a collection of warring tribes, hell-bent on mutual destruction." Plays, poems, song lyrics, and films don't work when they are the voice of a community or a power bloc – or even a political party. Seeing *Pentecost* again reminded me that the real power in any art form is that it releases the voice of the individual. And the individuals don't have to be real. The powerful paradox of theatre is that it can be most real when it is most imagined – as true today as it was in 1974.

That night at the Lyric, the audience included BBC colleagues, the Senior Coroner, John Leckey (now retired), Stormont MLA, Michelle McIlveen, (now a minister in the Executive), and, of course Paul Doherty. Wherever and whenever we speak about the happenings of past decades, we are close to someone who really knows the hurts and the horrors of that.

The Troubles with Truth (address to the Lyric Theatre audience after the performance of *Quietly*, 10 April 2014)

. . . Listen to the wordplay . . . on this stage this evening – the argument that the facts are the truth, and the response that there's more to the truth than facts.

We all know the real-life experience of this place as a book of many chapters that compete with each other, fight with each other, for one to be heard and read over the other, in what is sometimes described as a hierarchy of hurt and victimhood.

So, the past is not the past – and in the storyline this evening, we see and hear how the shrapnel continues to spit out and spread long after the explosion. For many, what happened is the here and now, and there are those who want to make it today's battlefield. It's political and, for some, it is a play thing – still a game of winners and losers, and right and wrong. This ignores the complex puzzle of conflict within which truth is often lost or buried. There is nothing simple about war and about what happens afterwards.

From my own reporting experience, I will always remember an interview with a former loyalist life sentence prisoner. I remember it because of the words spoken and what they meant – and because of what happened next.

It was at the time of the debate about prisoner releases versus victims' rights – and I interviewed this man, as we edged away from conflict and began that journey towards peace.

He spoke to me about prisoners "sleeping with the victims". "That's the only way I can put it," he said. "They sleep with the victims." Just think of those words – "sleep with the victims" – meaning, of course, that they couldn't sleep with their consciences; that he couldn't sleep with his conscience.

The prisoners, he told me, "have to live with what's happened in the past". Billy Giles spent long years in jail and, six months after that interview, he took his own life – no longer able himself to "sleep with the victims".

... Truth, if that's what we choose to call it, has to be about something more than blame and fault. It can't be confined to what happened, but why it happened; can't be as narrow as who did what, but why they did it.. . Those many who spent long years in jail did not emerge from the ground one day as part of some bad crop. Something happened. And what is our challenge? That it should never happen again ...

So, let us with cool heads look at some of what Richard Haass and Meghan O'Sullivan recommended.

Let us explore what is meant by Acknowledgement.

Let us look at how an Archive might allow everyone to tell their story and their truth – an Archive that won't just remember the headlines of conflict, but everyone's experience; an Archive that remembers people and their names, not that they were the 100th person or the 1000th person, but that they were mothers, fathers, sons, daughters, aunts, uncles, nephews and nieces, husbands, wives, partners, grandparents and grandchildren. That they were real people.

And let us examine how an Independent Commission for Information Retrieval or Truth Recovery might work.

... For years we lived in a place in which we were afraid to talk in our sleep. But now, at least we feel safer – more able to express ourselves and our feelings, in books such as Park's *The Truth Commissioner,* and in plays such as Owen McCafferty's *Quietly,* here on this stage this evening – a performance that brought the ghosts and trauma of a dark period back into play and back into our thinking.

Across many media outlets – every day – we are reading a deeper exploration, not just of what happened, but why ... The truth of our Troubles, or the conflict, or the wars, is that there is more than one truth –

and that there will never be an agreed narrative. And my question is: Can we live in peace with that truth?

I'll finish with this thought – Yeats told us that peace is something that comes "dropping slow".

And, today, there is something else that we must accept: that there may be a longer wait for answers and information and explanations – because truth, to borrow Yeats' thought, will drop even more slowly.

Several months later, in September 2014, new Chief Constable George Hamilton used his speech at the British/Irish Association in Oxford to address many of these vexed questions. Hamilton – the sixth Chief Constable in the period of the peace process – knows there is a choice between policing the past and policing the present. You cannot do both, and this speech became part of an effort to urge new thinking – new thinking beyond comfort zones and into a process that will eventually take the millions of documents the police have retained, and use them in some kind of answering of the past. Hamilton wants to open the police "vault", and knows that, when that happens, the debate and discussion on the past will extend beyond the focus on collusion, and ask questions of others, including the IRA and the loyalists.

George Hamilton, PSNI Chief Constable, writing for this book

None of us should underestimate the extent to which the legacy of the past has implications for our present or our future. The past is the present for those who suffered pain, loss and grief as a result of our dark and grievous history. When [in September 2014] I gave the speech, "Dealing with the past in ways that will secure the future", PSNI was almost 13 years in existence. But the past stretches back far beyond those 13 years. The past has been, and continues to be, a constant issue for policing.

It had often seemed to me that policing was being left to bear the brunt of a broader failure to deal with the past. As the newly appointed Chief Constable, the speech [I gave] presented an opportunity to call for change to this "status quo". This opportunity took on even more urgency, given the rapidly reducing public finances – an issue which had come to the fore as I was appointed Chief Constable. I could see that huge budget cuts would force me to an invidious position, making decisions which would prioritise public safety today over the investigation of violence in the past. It was important for me, as the new Chief Constable, to be open and honest about this difficult and deeply unfair situation. In my concluding comments, I speculated that the next steps in dealing with the past would require selfless, challenging conversations.

With the publication of the Stormont House Agreement [in December 2014], it seemed that some of these conversations had taken place. In particular, the proposal for the Historical Investigations Unit (HIU) would remove the responsibilities for the review and investigation of acts of violence during the Troubles from the PSNI, allowing us to concentrate on Keeping People Safe in the present and the future.

Establishing and implementing the HIU will require yet further challenging conversations. It is a massive project, entailing changes in legislation, so that I can give full ownership of all the material for which I have responsibility as Chief Constable, to the future Director of the HIU. The words I used in September were designed to call for change – not only for the better of policing, but for the better of our society. Change does not belong to one moment, one individual, or one organisation. Change is a shared and constant responsibility upon all of us who care about delivering a safe, confident and peaceful society. The PSNI remain committed to continuing to play our part in delivering [on] that change. Others must do the same.

The Stormont House talks referred to by Hamilton were a spillover from the Haass/O'Sullivan negotiations the previous year. Inside these follow-up talks, the latest draft paper read back to the earlier proposals, suggesting some variant of the Historical Investigations Unit would appear to present a good basis for a way forward, as well as an Information Commission:

Richard Haass proposed a new Independent Commission for Information Retrieval (ICIR) to facilitate the families' desire to obtain information. If it is accepted that a new mechanism for accessing information should be made available to victims and their families, then something along the lines of the ICIR would appear to provide the basis for a way forward. While the Assembly could legislate to implement the ICIR, legislation might also be needed from the UK and Irish Governments. If research on themes/patterns is to be included in an agreed solution, there would need to be some consideration about whether the content of those themes could be resolved before the ICIR is set up. Consideration needs to be given to the relationship with existing processes and to setting a time limit for this work.

In these latest talks, the key discussions happened in the period leading up to Christmas 2014. These negotiations were not just about the past, but many other unresolved matters, including parades and flags, and with a specific focus on finance and welfare reform. What also became very obvious in this phase of negotiations was how little time the British and Irish Prime Ministers have for this type of talking these 15-plus years after the Good Friday Agreement.

The peace process is a Blair/Ahern trophy. So, in that sense, there is nothing left here for David Cameron and Enda Kenny. This is why they stepped in and stepped out of these talks; their arrival on Thursday, 11 December for just a one-night stay so different from the hot-house, long-running, never-ending engagement that was part of the process from 1997–1999 and into the decade that followed. This extract from an article I wrote for the *Belfast Telegraph* at the time describes the British Prime Minister's hasty exit from Stormont:

PM's early exit speaks volumes on the state of this process
(*Belfast Telegraph*, 13 December 2014)

. . . David Cameron has other things to worry about. But the speed with which he left told us something else. What it revealed is that, not just on the vexed questions of budget and welfare, but on a range of other matters as well, this negotiation process is still half-baked and perhaps even half-hearted.

The parading issue is marching on the spot, questions of identity are parked, and Mark Durkan of the SDLP suggested that parts of the Haass proposals of a year ago have not only been diluted, but in some cases tipped down the drain.

A comprehensive deal on the many items on this agenda was never going to be done in the course of a one-night stay at Stormont. And there was no big cheque to buy the necessary ingredients of momentum and will.

Instead, as Mr Cameron prepared to make his getaway, we got name-calling and blame game politics.

At a British and Irish Prime Ministerial level, there is no longer the day-to-day or week-to-week engagement with this place and its problems and its past. Northern Ireland or the North at peace is not as urgent a political issue as Northern Ireland or the North in conflict. Perhaps this was the message that was the starkest and the loudest in the course of this quick visit.

Remarkably, however, ten days later there was a deal of sorts. It brought all of the Haass furniture back into play, with the questions of how it is arranged and who will do the arranging still to be settled. The paper agreement means there will be a Historical Investigations Unit, an Independent Commission on Information Retrieval, an Implementation and Reconciliation Group, and an Oral History Archive, which would also include a research project led by academics to produce a factual historical timeline and statistical analysis of the conflict or Troubles period. The investigations and information-recovery elements would each span five years. An examination of themes and patterns to emerge from the conflict years will not be commissioned until after the investigations and information processes are complete. This again would involve "independent academic experts".

These themes and patterns were identified at the time of Haass/O'Sullivan, although not stipulated or specified in the final document of the Stormont House talks. However long it takes to begin this examination, the list of topics or headings will be the same: alleged collusion, British and Irish; alleged "ethnic cleansing" in border regions and interface neighbourhoods; the alleged UK shoot-to-kill policy; detention without trial and the alleged mistreatment of prisoners; the targeting of off-duty RUC reservist officers, UDR soldiers and prison officers; the degree to which, if at all, Ireland prolonged the conflict by knowingly providing a safe haven to the IRA; punishment and enforcement actions by paramilitaries – both republican and loyalist; the policy behind the Disappeared; sources of finance and arms for loyalists and the IRA. That long list does not include the political and social context in which the conflict occurred. It is a glaring omission: violence did not just happen; it grew out of something.

In paragraph 44, the Stormont House Agreement suggests a five-member Independent Commission on Information Retrieval, with an independent chair who may be of international standing and will be appointed by the UK and Irish Governments. The Implementation and Reconciliation Group will oversee themes, archives and information recovery. Paragraph 54 of the Agreement describes an 11-member Body, to be chaired by a person of independent and international standing and who will be nominated by the First Minister and deputy First Minister. The five Stormont Executive parties would nominate other members, as would the UK and Irish Governments. Investigation continues to be part of what is proposed and the question of amnesty is avoided or rejected. It means that a barrier still stands in the way of more information or explanation. Investigation means disclosure will be restricted, but these talks made some progress – and more progress than was anticipated when Cameron and Kenny left in such a hurry.

A chance to exorcise the ghost of Haass
(Belfast Telegraph, 23 December 2014)

Just a couple of weeks ago, these talks were being haunted by the ghost of Christmas past. As Prime Minister David Cameron and Taoiseach Enda Kenny departed the Stormont scene in a hurry, so the script once more seemed to be about fallout. It had all the feel of a Haass failure to it – another long negotiation with no end product.

But since then the mood has changed.

. . . Getting an agreement on budgets and welfare has been the top priority of these talks. But the past, parades, flags, institutional reform, Irish language and other outstanding issues have still to be addressed.

That was the cause of the talking into the night.

Within the tight timeframe stipulated by Secretary of State, Theresa Villiers in a weekend statement, no one was predicting agreement across each and every issue. But as the talks rumbled on, so there were hints of possibilities for resolving the past and perhaps some way out of the stand-off on inquests, which has been one of the high obstacles to climb.

Another talks battle is on a report on conflict themes and patterns: who should write it, who should decide on the headings to be included and when it should be written. On parades and flags, these negotiations have progressed no further down the road . . .

If these talks can make progress, perhaps even [result in] a deal, on budgets, welfare and the past, then that will represent significant steps out of the Stormont stalemate.

What happened in these negotiations will not be judged on what was written on paper, or said in the many news conferences in the Great Hall at Parliament Buildings, but on what happens next. Who will be given the big positions and tasks within the Investigations Unit, the Information Commission and the Implementation and Reconciliation Group? All of that will take some time to work out. Will those who are chosen be of such international standing that their presence will demand cooperation?

How much more information will be shared? What mechanism will be used for asking and answering questions? And when the process actually begins, will we, five years after that, be able to say that at last the past is being properly addressed and answered? There are political fears about a rewriting of history.

It could be that some politicians and governments fear being written into the chapters of that dark conflict period. If not completely rewritten, the prevailing narrative will be disturbed, as events are studied and inspected. It has been a slow process so far and those who have waited this long still wait to be convinced about the seriousness and the significance of this agreement.

As we have seen earlier, George Hamilton, who has followed in that peace process policing line of Sir Hugh Annesley, Sir Ronnie Flanagan, the late Colin Cramphorn, Sir Hugh Orde and Sir Matt Baggott, believes the Historical Investigations Unit presents an opportunity to change things; to take the millions of police documents out of the "vault" and into some process that will examine the past in its broadest meaning. Hamilton discussed this issue in more depth in an interview with me for the 2015 RTÉ documentary, *Collusion*.

Our own Pandora's Box of the Troubles
(*Belfast Telegraph*, 12 June 2015)

". . . It's a colourful metaphor, vault, but let's use that," [Hamilton] said. "If the vault was to be opened, I know there will be literally millions of documents." He means millions of documents that will begin to address the past in a much wider frame.

"I don't think we should be exempt from scrutiny from investigation in the police service, past or present. I think that's good . . . but I actually think other people have stories to tell and questions to answer, and I'm hoping [when] this metaphorical vault . . . is opened up . . . that out of that will pour material that will present challenges for other people in the system," the Chief Constable said. "What I'm saying is that I expect the Historical Investigations Unit to have a comprehensive look, a more generic look, a more proactive look at the material that the police have retained."

"And the other point to remember is that our record-keeping may not have been the best, but we did keep records and I'm not just talking about intelligence documents, I'm talking about plans for covert operations . . . about minutes of meetings. My understanding is that the IRA, the UVF and the other players in this didn't keep notes or minutes of meetings or records of decisions . . . We did. And I think all of that has left us somewhat exposed.

"I think it was the right thing to do. I don't regret it. But it has meant there has been a one-sided focus [on] the role of the police . . . and I think the Historical Investigations Unit going to look at all of the material that we are sitting on [is] bound to bring a more proactive, a more balanced perspective, to what actually happened during the period of the Troubles."

What he is saying is that opening the vault will pose challenges for republicans and loyalists. "Well, that's the common sense conclusion one can come to . . . One would expect that if we are sitting on millions of pages of intelligence documents from a very busy time, when there were killings happening almost on a daily basis and some sort of atrocity happening on a regular basis, you would expect that there will be material there that will present challenges for individuals and opportunities for investigators. That's the way it works."

". . . What we need is a legislative basis for information to be shared," the Chief Constable continues. "And when that happens, people who have a legitimate access to information also take on an onerous responsibility, around [the] protection of life and [the] protection of people's privacy."

All of this depends on implementing the paper agreement made in the Stormont House talks. Those are decisions for Government and parties currently stuck in a political logjam over welfare reform.

A major part of Monday's RTÉ documentary will be an examination of what has been described as the "wilful and abject failure" by successive governments to put in place a legal framework for agent handling. And one contributor makes the point that Whitehall cannot walk away from the conflict period leaving "Ulstermen" to carry the blame and the heavy weight of collusion.

The past cannot be outmanoeuvred. There is no easy way round it or away from it. It is in so many minds and memories: the heavy weight of what happened, and the long wait for explanations. That pouring out of information and documents that the Chief Constable described is what many people want – but not everyone. Those files, that material, will spread the questions, beyond what the State and its agents engaged in, to what others did and knew about. There will be intelligence information on the IRA and loyalist leaderships at particular and specific times and happenings. How that information is accessed and used becomes part of the next steps and decision-making. How does it fit within investigations, information-retrieval or recovery and that examination of the themes and patterns of the conflict years? How is it used and shared? How much of it is redacted or anonymised? How open or closed is this process? There is much working out to be done.

Agents will never, can never, be identified, but any process on the past that opens "vaults" will mean a clearer view. However, there is never full disclosure about war or conflict. Governments, the military, police, intelligence, republicans and loyalists will never tell the full story in all its ugly detail.

It is rather a case how much more will be told and how that telling will be managed in those multiple and varied strands of investigation, information-retrieval, archive, acknowledgement and reconciliation. Those are decisions for the independent and international appointees who will eventually take charge and control of these processes, but they will have to work within strict national security/disclosure boundaries.

The Ulster University academic, Dr Jonny Byrne read every word of the Haass/O'Sullivan proposals as those talks developed, and is equally well-versed in the Eames/Bradley consultations and the Stormont House Agreement. He sees the similarities in all these proposals, and knows that the challenge now is not so much about what to do, but when to do it; about having the commitment to see things through, about politicians being prepared to relinquish control.

Dr Jonny Byrne, University of Ulster, writing for this book

People often say that it takes a while for the proverbial penny to drop – never more so than with our political representatives and their attempts to deal with our troubled past. Over the past decade, we have seen four significant attempts – Eames/Bradley (2009), Haass/O'Sullivan (2013), All-Party Working Groups (2014), the Stormont House Agreement (2014) – to provide some form of acceptable resolution to the challenges of dealing with the legacy of the conflict. However, the old mantra, that "Nothing's agreed until everything is agreed", has meant that each time collective agreement seems possible, spoilers emerge, questioning the values which may or may not underpin a legacy process, which incorporates the ideals of Truth, Justice and Reconciliation. Or about whom it should encompass? Or what the intended outcomes would look like?

Instead, the public bear witness to silo-type perspectives of what a process should entail, which are clearly underpinned by their own ideological and political positions. Furthermore, while the vacuum continues, those that have been most affected by the conflict lose hope for some form of redress, and societal reconciliation seems a distant dream. Reflecting back upon the different processes, it becomes evident that there is very little "new material" since Eames/Bradley that underpins the thinking, and that common themes continue to define the conversations.

The recommendations consistently focus on the needs of victims; the importance of justice; an understanding around narratives of the conflict; and truth recovery. We see this clearly in the most recent initiative around dealing with the past, in the Stormont House Agreement, with recommendations that include the establishment of an Independent Historical Investigations Unit; a Commission on Information Retrieval; an Implementation and Reconciliation Group; an Oral History Archive; and mental trauma services to work with the Victims' and Survivors' Forum. With these frameworks in place, there is a possibility that we might begin the long and torturous process of dealing with the legacy of the conflict. Looking back, it's clear that the answers to how we deal with these issues have been there for quite a while – the same cannot be said for the willingness to implement them.

That issue of implementation, of finally giving this past process over to others, is now what this is all about. There has been enough delay, enough dithering. As Chief Constable George Hamilton warned, in his speech to the British/Irish Association, "to continue to ignore, hesitate or procrastinate on the past will have unpredictable and far-reaching consequences". The process, the questions, the answers will all be difficult. There was much muddle and confusion in actual-time reporting of the conflict period, and that too will come to be rearranged and rewritten. But it is about fixing and correcting, not distorting. Something has to be tried, and many now recognise that there is the scaffolding and structural design within which to build. Earlier, I wrote that more than 20 years ago, the ceasefires were the first bricks. This process on the past will provide the next bricks – as long as we have the courage to set them down and to see what can be built from those foundations.

CHAPTER TEN
Uncomfortable Conversations:
"Much Harder than the Previous Life"

"If we are not going to fight them, we have to talk with them – how else to bring about change, other than constant dialogue?"
Former IRA prisoner, Michael Culbert, writing for this book.

"At first I stood back and watched, but over time I began to feel that as a participant in the conflict, I have a responsibility to contribute to this transition."
Former Staffordshire Regiment soldier, Lee Lavis, writing for this book.

The people who have contributed to this book are from very diverse backgrounds and experiences. They are part of what the past is about – the co-existence of many different perspectives and opinions. Some of these contributions take us back to the 1970s, and then through to the present day. As we read and think, we all can learn something more about conflict and transitions, about the journeys of many different individuals towards something more peaceful and something better. We see what has been achieved and what still needs to be done, and we come to understand that all of this is a continuing process – protracted, painful and often plagued by setbacks.

We are also reminded by the contributors here how at times all of us can become conditioned to conflict, and habituated to its brutal consequences. This is highlighted in the considered and thought-provoking words of Jarlath Burns, a sportsman and school principal who was chosen to be part of the Eames/Bradley Consultative Group on the Past. He writes about how we can become "dehumanised", and how people become reduced to "a thing, a number, a reprisal, a message, a lesson, a reminder". Think about how we respond to the news of international conflicts; how we become accustomed to those reports of deaths, no matter how many have been killed; how we get used to the screaming, the bloodshed, the grief, whether in Afghanistan, Iraq, Syria, Egypt, Tunisia, Israel or Palestine. We hear but do not hear; listen but do not listen; see but do not see. It is all a blur and a distant noise from some place, somewhere, which somehow does not seem to have anything to do with us. Is that how the story of conflict here was heard elsewhere?

We are in a better place now. Yes, our evolving story is still that tug-of-war between past and present, but we have much more than others have. Judith Hill wrote about the "next phase of the peace journey", and about people feeling free to tell their very different stories from their many different vantage points. We have read some of those stories in the pages of this book – about what the 30-plus contributors saw or heard, what happened to them – and what they now think and feel. This is what a Historical Archive should be – a way of recording all of that, and including the many different perspectives. We know already that there is much that will not be disclosed; that there are doors in the corridors of the past that will always be bolted – but information is seeping out.

Many of the collusion stories fit around agents and agent-handling. To name but a few, the Nelson, Scappaticci, Haddock and Haggarty stories are horrendous examples of what this conflict became: agents involved in killing, and agents killing other agents. This is the tangled mess of collusion and conflict and war. The late David Ervine once said that to get to the whole story, you needed to look also at the handlers and those who managed them. You also have to look at political decisions and inaction. We now have a clearer view of what happened in circumstances in which there were no rules. The denials are no longer plausible, believable or credible. Former senior police officers, including Sir Hugh Orde and Peter Sheridan have likened collusion to "playing God" – deciding what intelligence to act on, who to protect, who to sacrifice. When I spoke to David Porter, who worked with the Consultative Group on the Past and who was interviewed for the 2015 RTÉ documentary, *Collusion*, he commented on the absence of a legal framework for agent-handling: "My sense is that there was an awareness that they [Governments] were leaving a vacuum, and that there was therefore ambiguity and a recognition that some of that space was useful. . . . I personally as an Ulsterman would be very concerned that Whitehall gets away with leaving the responsibility all in the hands of those who were risking their lives to protect me – to protect others."

In that same documentary, Daniel Holder of the Committee on the Administration of Justice (CAJ) made this observation: "There are some times, and this happens in many scenarios in the world, where shining a light on just one case can shine a light on how a system works . . . the Finucane case very much is that case." There has been an investigation and a review of papers but not the public inquiry that the family has long demanded, and Holder is right – that inside this story, there is a bigger story of dark practices.

The truth of what happened in the Finucane case will open up other ugly truths. Also interviewed for the RTÉ documentary, Pat Finucane's daughter, Katherine asserted: "We don't have the closure that we're seeking. We will keep going, in the name of my father and his legacy." Many, many families do not have the closure they are seeking – and these many cases remain part of that unanswered past.

Collusion is a significant part of what happened, but by no means all of the story. In his first year in office, PSNI Chief Constable George Hamilton has been trying to broaden the examination of the conflict period, and stresses the point that, "We cannot continue to sit on the past. We have to face it." He made that comment when he joined Martin McGuinness in that ground-breaking event and discussion as part of Féile an Phobail in August 2015. He wants everyone to turn the corner to the next phase of this process; his comments in west Belfast were about building on previous speeches: "We cannot leave dealing with the past to our children and young people. They are our future. It is the responsibility of those who lived through the past to find a way of addressing the past. Perhaps as a society we need to lose all our fears; we need to try to understand – not just our own story and experience of the past – but the story and experience of others. Fear gets us nowhere. Fear does not make peace. Courage, optimism and belief make peace." Think of that Festival event: a serving Chief Constable on the same stage as one of the most senior leaders in the period of the IRA's war. There is much that still needs to happen, but this is one indicator of the type of progress that is being made and where this long journey has reached.

In recent years, there have been many examples of efforts at reconciliation, happening at all sorts of levels and in all sorts of different places. The Hamilton/McGuinness event was but one example. There have been huge, unforgettable public gestures – such as, in June 2012, that moment when Queen Elizabeth met Martin McGuinness during a two-day royal visit to Northern Ireland; and, even more memorable perhaps, the historic moment in May 2015 when Prince Charles and Gerry Adams shook hands at a reception for the Prince in the town of Galway. It was the Prince's first official visit to Ireland in 13 years – a trip during which he visited the village where his great uncle Lord Mountbatten had been assassinated by the IRA in 1979. The acts of reconciliation we now witness were once unthinkable; unimaginable; undoable.

At another level too, there has been a dialogue developing in recent years between republicans and people from the Protestant/unionist community under the heading of "Uncomfortable Conversations". This initiative grew out

"We don't have the closure that we're seeking." John and Katherine Finucane. *(Elle Rowan)*

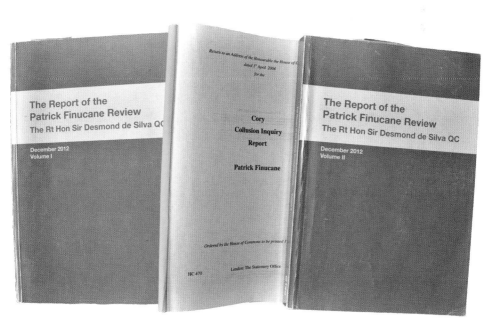

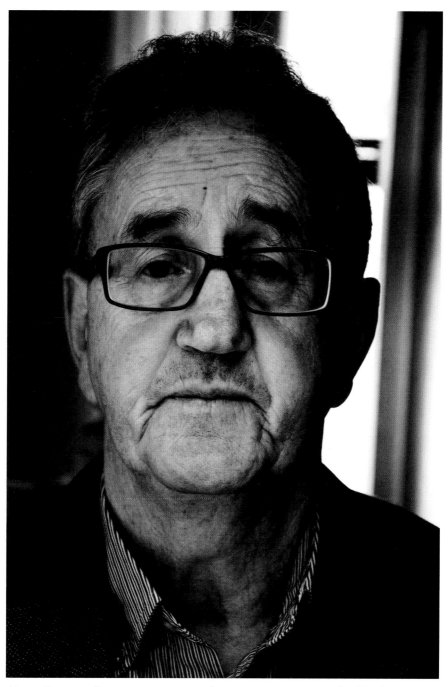

Above: From conflict to conversation – former IRA prisoner Michael Culbert. *(Elle Rowan)*

Opposite: From conflict to conversation – former Staffordshire Regiment soldier Lee Lavis. *(Elle Rowan)*

Top: Michael Culbert and Lee Lavis photographed at an old army sangar in west Belfast. *(Elle Rowan)*

Above: When one-time enemies meet – Lee Lavis, Seanna Walsh, Kieran Devlin and Pat Magee, photographed at the Veterans for Peace Conference 2015. *(Photograph courtesy of Veterans for Peace)*

"There was no rancour, no squealing or shouting, no finger-pointing." Belfast republican Seanna Walsh. *(Elle Rowan)*

Talks compilation – Crisis, the Stormont story of 2015.

In the political frames – Nigel Dodds, Peter Robinson, Martin McGuinness, Gerry Adams and Mike Nesbitt, with the media hanging on their every word. *(Brian Rowan)*

Top: For much of the talking, Ulster Unionist leader Mike Nesbitt was outside the political tent. *(Brian Rowan)*

Above: Irish Foreign Minister Charlie Flanagan and British Secretary of State Theresa Villiers on a day of fresh starts and false starts. *(Brian Rowan)*

Top: "Last best chance" to resolve loyalist issues – former Tony Blair Chief of Staff, Jonathan Powell, speaking in Belfast, October 2015. *(Elle Rowan)*

Above: Paying attention – the media presence at the Powell news conference. *(Elle Rowan)*

ULSTER VOLUNTEER FORCE   ULSTER DEFENCE ASSOCIATION

RED HAND COMMANDO

Joint Declaration of Intent, 13 October, 2015

UNFINISHED WORK

Twenty-one years on, since the 13th October 1994 CLMC ceasefire announcement, Northern Ireland is in a state of relative peace. The constitutional position of Northern Ireland as an integral part of the United Kingdom, for which many loyalists gave their lives and freedom, has been secured and recognised by republicans as well as unionists.

We recognise that the Northern Ireland Assembly, which we continue to support, is not inclusive of the loyalist community. We accept the democratically expressed will of the electorate however a vacuum in loyalist communities has been created which has led to significant disenchantment with politics, and to our communities being largely ignored and neglected. It is no coincidence that the attainment levels of working class loyalist young people are the lowest in the United Kingdom.

It is our desire to make a meaningful contribution to reversing this situation, to give our young people hope for the future, and to help build structures which will improve our communities and protect our culture.

1. We are re-committing to the principles of the Belfast Agreement. We eschew all violence and criminality. If there are those who attempt to use current or past associations with our organisations to further criminality they will be disowned and should be aware that they will not be permitted to use the cover of loyalism. We expect the authorities to take whatever steps are necessary to deal with any offenders. Anyone mis-using Loyalism for criminal purposes should be held accountable to the Criminal Justice System.

2. We recognise the relevance of this to recent events and the current political talks, and hope that this Declaration will encourage Loyalists to be included in the Legacy issues currently under discussion.

3. We will work to improve our communities and to encourage loyalists to engage fully with political parties that promote and preserve our heritage and culture.

4. To ensure the effective monitoring of Loyalist requirements we are forming a **Loyalist Communities Council** which will be independently chaired and supported by a secretariat. It is our hope that the Council will become a vehicle for attracting meaningful funding and initiatives to assist loyalist communities throughout Northern Ireland, enabling loyalism to play a full and active role in the community and wider remit and in constitutional politics.

4. The LCC will initially focus on three main areas of work:

- Addressing economic underachievement in Loyalist communities
- Law-abiding responses to criminality
- Loyalist disenfranchisement in the political process.

We trust that this Loyalist Communities Council will provide fresh hope to those who have become discouraged, and will be met with widespread support.

GOD SAVE THE QUEEN

A new set of loyalist words, October 2015.
(Elle Rowan)

NORTHERN IRELAND
Information Service

STRICT EMBARGO - NOT FOR RELEASE UNTIL 12.00 N

26 Augu

STATEMENT BY THE SECRETARY OF STATE

In the light of recent events, including the savage and disgrace
murder of Charles Bennett and the arrests in the United State
Ireland of people suspected of smuggling arms, I have reviewed
state of the IRA cease-fire with my security advisers. I have al
received information from the United States and Irish Govern
these cases.

Given the forthcoming court proceedings in both cases, it wou
wrong for me to comment in detail about allocation of respon
for these crimes.

There have been occasions in the past when I have been very
concerned about the status of the IRA's ceasefire, and indee
other paramilitary organisations. The available information
past has not been of sufficient strength to give me a full pict
in this case the information is already clear and indeed the C
Constable has said that there is no doubt that the IRA were
in the Bennett murder. Information is also clear in relation
arms importation. Both are utterly deplorable and incompa
the society that all are striving to develop under the Good Fr
Agreement.

I have left Sinn Fein in no doubt that all violence, for whatever reason
it is perpetrated, is unacceptable, and have called on them to use their
influence to ensure that there is no repetition.

At the same time, it should be remembered that the Sentences Act
requires me to reach an overall judgement about the status of any
organisation's cease-fire. I can and must take account of all the
factors specified in the Act in arriving at such a judgement. That is
what I have done, in accordance with the legislation, not in
accordance with anyone else's definition.

On that basis, although the situation in relation to the IRA is deeply
worrying, I do not believe that there is a sufficient basis to conclude
that the IRA ceasefire has broken down. Nor do I believe that it is
disintegrating, or that these recent events represent a decision by the
organisation to return to violence. I have therefore decided not to use
my powers under the Sentences Act at this time. But I want to make
entirely clear that I have come very close to judging that the IRA's
ceasefire is no longer for real. I will therefore be keeping their position
under close review, as required by the Act, and will not hesitate to act
decisively where I consider that their, or any other, ceasefire has
broken down.

The peace we have now is imperfect, but better than none. If violence
continues, the political process - which depends on confidence and
trust - will be increasingly at risk.

Author's notes of IRA statement and details of Secretary of State Mo Mowlam's 1999
IRA review. *(Elle Rowan)*

"All the main paramilitary groups operating during the period of the Troubles remain in existence." The *Assessment on Paramilitary Groups in Northern Ireland*, October 2015. *(Elle Rowan)*

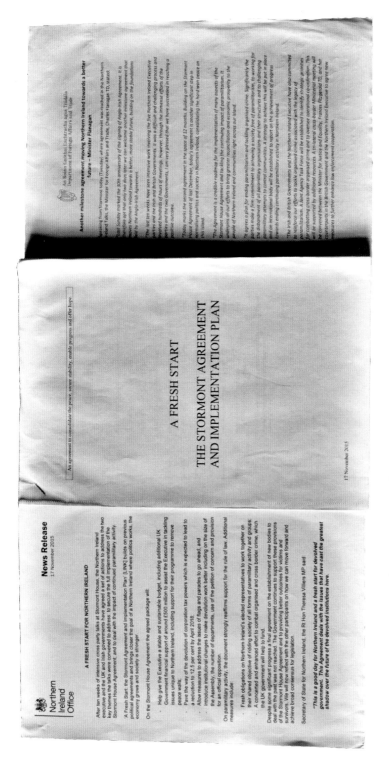

Past process mired in draft legislation. Stormont Talks 2015. *(Elle Rowan)*

Opposite: "Without commitment by the IRA to participate in a legacy process, there can be no loyalist involvement either." Winston Irvine, Progressive Unionist Party. *(Elle Rowan)*

Victims of bombs and bullets, Alex Bunting (top) and Peter Heathwood (below). *(Elle Rowan)*

Opposite: "Time doesn't always heal." Artist Colin Davidson who painted the *Silent Testimony* exhibition. *(Elle Rowan)*

"Thank you for shining so bright." Alice
Reid paying tribute tribute to her mum
Maureen. *(Elle Rowan)*

of an article written by Sinn Féin's National Chairperson, Declan Kearney, back in March 2012: a piece that attracted attention and generated controversy because it introduced the word "sorry" into the discourse. This first article, published in *An Phoblacht*, was written for the republican audience:

We should be prepared to go the extra mile. That means listening, which in turn means not only seeking to persuade, but also being willing to be persuaded...

Republicanism needs to become more intuitive about unionist apprehensions and objections, and sensitised in our response . . . We need to be open to using new language and consider making new compromises. Regardless of the stance of others, we should recognise the healing influence of being able to say sorry for the human effects of all actions caused during the armed struggle. All sensible people would wish it had been otherwise; that these events had never happened; that other conditions had prevailed. The political reality is those actions cannot be undone or disowned. It would be better they had never happened. Armed struggle is not a point of principle or an end in itself. It arose from political conditions, as a last resort, and those conditions no longer exist. Yet the consequences have to be dealt with. The legacy of our conflict – and the creation and perpetuation of the conditions which gave rise to it – need to be addressed.

Through meaningful dialogue, however, we can all seek to better understand the respective experiences of each other. Now the conflict is over, the imperative of creating a better society at ease with itself is a new challenge for us. And republicans should approach that laborious work with compassion and imagination. It requires bravery to take risks in struggle, but it takes exceptional moral leadership and self-belief to build a real reconciliation process, one with the ability to help overcome the hurt caused by armed struggle.

That's why we must ensure our engagement is based upon listening carefully to unionists and others and [we must] develop the capacity to explore what more can be done to help meaningfully heal our society's divisions. Dialogue using new language, and making new compromises to create trust, are the seeds of nation-building. Facing these issues and grasping their implications are fundamental to the process of uniting Ireland. The challenges arising for republicans are significant but the importance of taking forward this work is greater still.

Kearney's article was not just written from one day to the next, but was the result of long and careful deliberation. It was about trying to say something different; to move the process to the next phase, with reconciliation as the key theme. It is why the word "sorry" was introduced, and yet that very word caused confusion and, among some, concern. Unionists wanted to know, sorry for what? Republicans also wanted to know, sorry for what? This became the key focus of discussion in the immediate aftermath of the article's publication: the attempt to interpret the use of the word "sorry", and the frame and context in which it was meant. It was not a sorry for the IRA "war" – that much was made clear – but perhaps in this initiative, republicans were and are looking for the words that might help open up some new way.

Three months later that meeting took place between Martin McGuinness and the Queen, and then, there were further reports of a possible IRA apology being in the offing – something which I addressed in an online article, written on the back of these rumours:

IRA "historic apology" – what next after war?
(*www.eamonnmallie.com*, 1 July 2012)

It is one of those newspaper headlines that catches the eye: those words on the front page of the *Sunday Business Post* – "IRA prepares for historic apology to all its victims".

The context in which this news report is set is the Martin McGuinness handshake with the Queen, his follow-up speech at Westminster and the republican reconciliation initiative that is being developed by Declan Kearney.

How close are we to that predicted IRA apology – and would it be delivered in the name of that organisation? To answer those questions, we need to think in a much wider frame – and retrace the republican footsteps, not just of the past few months, but past few years.

It was Kearney, the Sinn Féin National Chair, who introduced the word "sorry" into this reconciliation discussion, not as an apology for the IRA war, but rather to acknowledge the human hurt caused by all armed actions . . . Since then, this new reconciliation discussion and debate has opened up and opened out. Kearney will tell you that it should not be reduced to one side's sorry, or to that one word – however important and however difficult it is to say.

In its endgame statement of July 2005, the IRA leadership spoke the following words: "We reiterate our view that the armed struggle was entirely legitimate." On the basis of that statement, we can understand that any use of the word "sorry" will not be a retreat from that sentence or that belief. Kearney is talking about "sorry" in a humanising context, to acknowledge hurt, not to de-legitimise the IRA campaign. This is not about sackcloth and ashes. Both Kearney and McGuinness, in interviews on Radio Ulster and on RTÉ television at the weekend, stressed what should be the collective nature of saying sorry; that it is about every side, and the many sides.

"Many people need to say sorry," Kearney said in a *Sunday Sequence* interview with presenter, Mike Philpott. "And that includes the British Government, other parties, as well as all the combatants who were involved in the war." Unionists would, of course, add the Irish Government to that list.

That republicans are discussing all of these matters is not surprising and not new. Back in March, the respected and influential Belfast republican Eibhlin Glenholmes [see her contribution to this book in Chapter Seven] told me she had "no qualms about apologising for any hurt". But she was not saying that the IRA was wrong. "Absolutely not," she told me. "We didn't go to war – war came to us."

Within those comments, and what is being said by Kearney and McGuinness, you get a sense of what is possible, and what is not. Others will have to speak – and not just loyalists, but those in governments/ politics and security/intelligence, who are trying to ignore the current conversations.

. . . Church figures such as Harold Good and Lesley Carroll are talking to Kearney and other republicans, as are Lord Alderdice, Alan McBride, Sir George Quigley, the loyalists Jackie McDonald and John Howcroft, and others. This is where the grown-up talking is happening. Another UDA figure, John Bunting, has indicated his willingness to join in and, a few days ago, acknowledged the McGuinness/Queen handshake as confirmation that the wars are over. Political unionists and the governments need to get involved and should not be allowed to hide behind the curtain, hoping to escape the stage and any blame for what happened here and elsewhere over a period of several decades. What republicans are prepared to say will depend on what others are prepared to say, and when/if they are prepared to say it. I have heard nothing to suggest any imminent development.

Whatever happens, there will not be a statement from the IRA leadership. Both Kearney and McGuinness made that clear in their weekend interviews. Referring to the *Sunday Post* report, Kearney said: "This is a story about which I know nothing . . . The IRA has left the stage.

The IRA no longer exists. In other words, the IRA can no longer speak." Those who were part of that organisation can.

But reconciliation, healing hurts, answering the questions about the wars, and trying to make sure these things never happen again, asks for an effort and an initiative that reaches out much wider than the republican community. If people want to hear a republican "sorry" that deals with the many hurts and armed actions, that speaks to combatants as well as non-combatants, then they are going to have to think and talk about how that can be made possible. This is not just about the IRA. It is about all the wars – seen and unseen – all the hurts, all the actors and all the sides. It is about big thinking, and different thinking . . . Remember this. The longer people hide from this conversation and its many challenges, then the longer all of this will take.

In 2015, some of the most important work of the Uncomfortable Conversations initiative was brought together in the publication of a book of the same title, which was launched on 16 April in Belfast's Linen Hall Library. The book – and indeed even the occasion of its launch – was another important indicator of how the discussion around reconciliation has been evolving.

Small step on road to true peace (*Belfast Telegraph*, 17 April 2015)
The lunchtime event in the Linen Hall Library yesterday spoke volumes about how this place has changed and is changing. Republicans Martin McGuinness, Michelle O'Neill and Declan Kearney shared the stage with former Methodist President, Dr Heather Morris.

The event was to mark the publication of a book, *Uncomfortable Conversations: an initiative for dialogue towards reconciliation*. It pulls together a series of articles . . . written not just by republicans, but others. Lord John Alderdice, Dawn Purvis, Dr Morris, Baroness May Blood, Dr David Latimer and a number of academics are among the contributors.

And yesterday, republicans spoke beyond their community on the need for reconciliation to become the next phase of the peace process. The room listened. A room that included the former loyalist prisoner and south Belfast UPRG [Ulster Political Research Group] representative, Colin Halliday. Alan McBride was also there. . . And in the rows of seats too sat former Presbyterian Moderator, John Dunlop, another former Methodist President, Harold Good, former Parades Commission Chairman, Peter Osborne, Kate Turner of the Healing Through Remembering project, and former NIO official, Chris McCabe.

> Dr Morris stressed that the book cannot be a full stop, but, rather, something that "sparks more conversations". The dream, she said, was about "a future that does not echo the past".
>
> . . . Speaking afterwards, Colin Halliday said loyalists had also been involved in similar, difficult dialogue. "What we need to do is somehow take this forward," he said.
>
> And that is the challenge: to take yesterday's event out of the room and onto a bigger stage.

Those uncomfortable conversations have continued; have drawn in others. Reconciliation, and all the right people being involved in such conversations, is essential in terms of what happens next. It is the point that David Porter made earlier in this book, in Chapter Eight, when he talked about drawing out our poison to give a new generation their future. In the main, this kind of crucial dialogue has thus far been with key figures in the churches, academia and wider civic society – and in this sense, without the participation of some of the crucial elements in the picture, it has limitations in terms of its potential to deliver. Perhaps the big reconciliation initiative will have to wait for that structured process on the past to both begin and develop. Then, we should see what the many sides are prepared to say by way of acknowledging past actions and hurts, and how all of that is choreographed, joined-up and presented for maximum impact.

This does not mean of course that everything and everyone has to wait for that structured process and that "big" moment. And not everyone is waiting. One striking instance of this is an initiative being undertaken by former British soldiers – now members of the group, Veterans for Peace – who, privately, quietly, are speaking to and engaging with former IRA prisoners. This is another once unthinkable dialogue taking place, and one which sets an example and shows the way to those in our political parties.

Lee Lavis, Veterans for Peace, writing for this book

As an infantry soldier in the Staffordshire Regiment, I completed a six-month tour of Fermanagh between April and November 1992, and a two-year period covering south Down and south Armagh from February 1994 to February 1996. My mindset for much of this period is demonstrated by an incident when I cheered while watching old footage of Michael Stone's attack on a republican funeral. In a wider sense, I also believed that all Irish nationalists were members – or imminently about to become members – or active supporters of the IRA, who in turn, I saw as criminals, psychopaths and terrorists. I would also highlight that this pattern of thinking was the dominant one amongst my fellow soldiers – which is pertinent, when you consider that non-locally recruited British soldiers were only deployed to overwhelmingly nationalist areas.

However, six months into my second tour, the IRA announced a ceasefire and the commencement of negotiations aimed at bringing an end to the euphemistically-named "Troubles". My reaction was one of disbelief, but as the weeks became months, I began to take an interest in reading books about the history of conflict in Ireland. Over time, the expansion of my contextual knowledge led me to see the conflict, and my own place within it, in far more nuanced terms than I had previously.

Then, in April 1995, I was sent on a PR trip to a Celtic football match with some disabled young people, their families and friends, and some local politicians from Newry. It was a revelation: outside of my uniform I had never previously met, let alone conversed with, people from a nationalist background. It was also the death knell for me as a soldier, because those at the other end of the gun had now taken human form.

Not surprisingly, just over a year later I left the Army, and settled in Belfast, which has enabled me to witness my adopted home's transformation from a place of perpetual conflict to one of relative peace. At first I stood back and watched, but over time I began to feel that as a participant in the conflict, I have a responsibility to contribute to this transition. As a result, in recent years, I have worked alongside other British Army veterans, former opposing combatants, and members of the wider nationalist community in the development of mechanisms for dialogue that promote understanding, while recognising differences in culture, lived experience and ideological beliefs.

In April 2015, I published an article on the *eamonnmallie.com* website, about Veterans for Peace and the ongoing dialogue between ex-British Army soldiers and former IRA prisoners, which gives more insight into the nature of their engagement with one another, and its value in terms of reconciliation.

It's not about sackcloth and ashes
(www.eamonnmallie.com, 27 April 2015)
Try to picture the scene. On stage, two former British soldiers sitting beside two men whose names will forever be identified with the IRA's "war and peace".

"There was no rancour, no squealing or shouting, no finger-pointing," Seanna Walsh said. Across several prison terms, the Belfast republican served over 20 years in jail. And, today, is remembered for the words he read to camera in 2005, declaring a formal end to the IRA's armed campaign.

Recently, in London, he was joined on stage by Pat Magee, whose bomb was intended to wipe out Margaret Thatcher and her Cabinet during the Conservative Party Conference in Brighton in 1984. The two republicans were invited to be part of a panel discussion and question-and-answer session at the annual conference of Veterans for Peace.

"I had nothing but thanks and good wishes for where we are today and hopes for the future," Walsh said. "It was difficult enough at times, some of the questions, but the way it was framed, it was meant to be an engagement, not an argument. You had people there who had obviously been hurt by the conflict, people who had been damaged by the conflict, and people in the audience who had lost loved ones."

These events, these engagements, just don't happen . . . This link – between former British soldiers under the umbrella of Veterans for Peace and former IRA prisoners – has been developing in the background in recent times. Eight veterans held a series of meetings here last year, a programme of events organised by Michael Culbert, the director of the project Coiste na nlarchimí, which works on behalf of republican ex-prisoners.

"At one stage the enemy was the British. They're now the opposition," Culbert said. "Our enemy was the British State. That is what has to be reconciled." And the developing conversations and contacts are part of that process.

Lee Lavis was part of the Veterans for Peace delegation that held that series of meetings with republicans last year, and also part of the recent panel discussion in London. In the 1990s, pre-ceasefire and afterwards, Lavis served on two tours in Northern Ireland with the 1st Battalion Staffordshire Regiment. "The Army does things very black-and-white – enemy and good guy, and I was a good guy," he said. "I saw every single member of the nationalist community as my enemy."

He has travelled a long distance in his thinking and questioning. . . In his own words, he became "the nail sticking out of the wood". One of his meetings last year was with a group of republican women, including Eibhlin Glenholmes and Breige Brownlee.

"It was the most difficult meeting and the most fraught . . . very, very tense," Lavis recalls. Those in the room were from the different sides of the conflict, and today's talking does not remove the many wounds of the past, how they hurt each other.

Brownlee remembers it beginning with "arms folded", it being "very, very emotional", and, at times, even "aggressive". But it was also "a most enlightening engagement". "You are better talking across the table, rather than anything going on under the table," she said.

And Lavis believes, however difficult, these conversations are essential. "You could really see the power of this work to change preconceived ideas. You saw that being deconstructed through that meeting," he said.

If these conversations were easy or cosy, they would change nothing. They have to be about asking and answering the difficult questions.

. . . Lavis says the dialogue with republicans is "not looking for sackcloth and ashes from us or them". Rather, it is about achieving some better understanding of each other. "I believe it stimulates further conversations," he said. "It breaks down barriers, removing that reduced view we have of each other." And he believes the contacts also deliver "the symbolic importance of former combatants talking". "For the British soldiers, it gives them closure on a part of their life that was traumatic," he said. "The process, for us, removes the balaclavas and, for them, it removes our helmets and camouflage cream. It humanises everything."

And so, the talking arrived on that stage in London. "The British soldiers there explained why they joined the Army," Seanna Walsh said. "And Pat [Magee] and myself were talking about the circumstances that gave rise to us going out to resist the British Army on our streets."

Recently, in Belfast, Deputy First Minister Martin McGuinness urged further "uncomfortable conversations" towards reconciliation, and Walsh sees this dialogue with Veterans for Peace in that frame. "It's about binding the wounds of war, attempting to re-build a society and a future for our children that is different from the lives of conflict and prison that we lived," he said. And for Breige Brownlee, this continuing dialogue is about "breaking down suspicions . . . breaking down the barriers". "Conversations have to be taken out of the corners and out of the rooms," she said.

. . . And why is it important? Because not long ago, this type of interaction would have been considered unthinkable.

Another British Army veteran, Kieran Devlin, posted a comment on that online article. He wrote: "Perhaps the most difficult conversation yet to be had doesn't belong to ex-combatants. It belongs to middle-class unionism. This section of society is comfortable, accepting the narrative that the boundaries of right and wrong are clearly defined and, more importantly, they know on which side they belong. The history of Ireland didn't begin in 1969 and, with this in mind, I believe that, if fault and blame are left outside the meeting room, great progress can be made."

These are conversations between people who fought from very different trenches. They could find many reasons not to talk with each other. They could go and look at different rolls of honour, rolls of hurt and rolls of the dead. They could look at the names, at what happened and refuse to engage. Yet they are talking, with "fault and blame" left outside the door. This is a sign of a maturing peace. Yet that maturity is what is often missing in sections and spheres of our politics. It is not a conversation about apology – but about learning, understanding and hearing the other without having to surrender or sell-out or shelve one's own story. It is both about what happened and why it should not be repeated, and all of the stories in these conversations are jigsaw pieces in the bigger picture.

Michael Culbert, Coiste na nIarchimí, writing for this book

Looking back at my own attitudinal changes, it really is quite amazing. In the 1970s, life was relatively simple. We knew who the enemy was – the State and its apparatus – and we attacked it in whatever way we could. That meant its personnel – British military and police; its property, thus the bombings; even those identified with actively supporting [it] in other ways – loyalists mobilised by the British for killings in our communities.

Not nice, but that is how it was. There were the church leaders, and peace people – [on] all sides – at all times (with a few honourable exceptions) condemning the IRA, never the British. So, we turned our ears from them, ignored them and got on with it.

I recall too my own attitudes, particularly towards the British military. Never a thought about their feelings, never even considering if they wanted to be here, or indeed if they were afraid. Absolutely no thought [for] their families, children, partners or parents. That was probably because I simply did not see them as people, only objects to be targeted. In simplistic terms, I saw the locally recruited – UDR, RUC – in a different light from the main British Army personnel. The latter were simply "the Brits", in a clump as it were. The more body bags going across the sea, the better their Government would know the cost of occupation. Little did we know how little their politicians cared about those young men and women, lured by hints of exotic travel and adventure, and trapped in a sangar in south Armagh or on target patrol in Belfast.

The UDR and RUC were different. To me, they were Irish and should not have been supporting the colonial masters. They lived and socialised here and, in many cases, were more accessible for targeting. Basically, the thinking could be summed up [as]: "We could be shot on sight, therefore, so can they".

But we all change as circumstances change. My belief is that none of us is as we were. We know more now than then, as we have had so many experiences and interactions which have blended ideas and attitudes. Today, with the political process now inclusive of republicans and the State apparatus no longer "an enemy", it has been relatively easy to slip into the interactions essential for collective well-being.

For me, as a republican, politically we have not yet got what we want in the long term, but then again, this state is no longer the unionist monolith it was. As a republican though, I do not see my life as an activist as over. The war was not for its own sake, and I did not participate in order to drop out once the armed struggle ended. In fact today was what it was all for – to forge ahead in the world of politics, with the former enemy now merely the opposition. And it is much harder than the previous life.

If we are not going to fight them, we have to talk with them – how else to bring about change, other than constant dialogue? We talk regularly with PSNI on matters relating to our communities – to work with them and to hold them to account for their failings. We interact with former loyalists and go to schools, etc., to explain to young people our pasts. We now work closely with former members of the British Army, and also visit schools, community groups – all in order to humanise the people who were engaged in the conflict. I feel strongly that we, who were engaged in the conflict, need to take major steps to show leadership in ways that clearly demonstrate to the public that we are also now engaged in real conflict resolution, and truly want to build for a better future for all.

Michael Culbert takes us from that brutal simplicity of conflict into the complexity and challenges of peace-building. His is a frank assessment, an honest assessment, of "war": not taking time to think about the enemy, "never even considering if they wanted to be here or, indeed, if they were afraid". Then he delivers what many will consider a cold assessment: "The more body bags going across the sea, the better their government would know the cost of occupation." Again, it is an honest statement about what war and conflict are about – enemies and killing – with a sense of the coldness of that, and of how dehumanising it all becomes and became.

Read that one sentence from Culbert on those who condemned the IRA: "We turned our ears from them, and got on with it." Is that what today's dissidents are doing? In conflict, in the fight, people do not see people. Enemies see enemies. They follow orders and instructions, until there are new or different orders and instructions. That is what happens in war, and what happened here. The ceasefires – republican and loyalist – and then the ending of the Army's decades-long Operation Banner, and the demilitarisation and decommissioning that took things away from the battlefield and into a different place and phase. Then, people had to see the other, think about the other; about all that had happened, and about what needed to happen next.

Peace-building is different. It is difficult and it demands a lot: the "real conflict resolution" effort that Culbert describes and that building "for a better future for all". That won't happen if nothing is done about the past, if it is only ever dug up for investigation and never properly understood; if we are as blind in the peace as enemies were in the wars. Doing nothing perpetuates division, and leaves wounds open and seeping. There is learning and an example in this dialogue between military veterans and former IRA prisoners: we see that there are many truths and narratives that come together to make the stories of the different pasts. If we think seriously about what happened, why it happened, and who was involved, then we should never have to ask, "for whom the bell tolls".

END THOUGHT

"She was a Light in the Darkness"

"Without commitment by the IRA to participate in a legacy process, there can be no loyalist involvement either."
Winston Irvine of the Progressive Unionist Party, writing for this book.

"For many thousands of people living in Northern Ireland, and indeed beyond, that tick on the ballot paper also marked an end of hope – a hope for justice, hope for answers."
Artist Colin Davidson, writing for this book.

"She fought her own struggle every day to survive and succeed, and she did so remarkably well for 40 years since our father's death . . . Thank you, Mum, for shining so bright."
Alice Reid, paying tribute to her mother Maureen, whose husband James was killed in a pub bombing in 1976.

As this book was being written and researched, the story dominating the headlines once more was of politics, and Stormont struggling. There was yet another crisis. A battle over budgets, welfare reform and the financial viability of the political institutions, escalated when police made an assessment of IRA involvement in the killing of a Belfast man Kevin McGuigan. It was seen as a reprisal for the earlier murder of Gerard Jock Davison, once one of the most senior IRA leaders in the city. And what happened? In 2015, 21 years after the original IRA and loyalist ceasefires, Secretary of State Theresa Villiers asked a panel to review police and MI5 intelligence relating to paramilitary structures, role and purpose. The resulting report pointed to the continued existence of leaderships and structures – IRA and loyalist – and the talk turned once again to transition and transformation, yet another strategy and more monitoring.

We have been down this road many times. It has all been said and heard before. More than 15 years prior to this latest crisis, another Secretary of State, Mo Mowlam conducted a review of the IRA ceasefire, after a killing and arms importation; she ultimately concluded that the ceasefire had not broken down, and nor was it disintegrating. In the rush to history, those in governments and high politics ran through and past many issues, including demobilisation or how to achieve the final exit of republican and loyalist organisations. So, this has become part of today's conversation, part of the unfinished peace. Perhaps it is too late – and perhaps there will be no such thing as a "final curtain", in terms of a complete standing down of all those leaderships and structures. But whatever happens on this and in politics generally, now or later, the unanswered past is still here: people are still hurting, and the questions and the arguments persist. The past will not go away quietly.

In the latest negotiations, Stormont was saved by an agreement which included a way forward on welfare issues and a strategy designed to end paramilitarism. Then, First Minister Peter Robinson set out his retirement plans. This is how politics moves and changes. But a process on legacy issues became a battle over draft legislation and an argument over national security – and ended again without agreement: the fifth process, including Eames/Bradley, in which there was no tangible end result. In my mind, this strengthens the argument that governments and politicians here need to step back from the past and leave it to independent others. A government cannot be a neutral observer or facilitator in this kind of process. It is a player with questions to answer, and much to protect and shield. Nor can you properly shape a legacy structure without knowing the contributions of others. Will the IRA be prepared to enter an "answering-process" on the past? Will the loyalists? We still don't know.

To date, loyalists have not been part of the latest talks and conversations. In a statement in October 2015, they made a pitch to be involved in those negotiations. This statement in itself represented a confirmation of the continued structural existence of the three organisations that, 21 years earlier, had come together to announce the ceasefire of the Combined Loyalist Military Command. This time, the declaration spoke of "re-committing to the principles of the Belfast Agreement", and offered the assurance: "We eschew all violence and criminality". Jonathan Powell, Tony Blair's chief-of-staff in the Downing Street years, attended the media event in Belfast, at which the formation of a new Loyalist Communities Council was announced. The initiative pointed towards the next steps in conflict transformation, and, in Powell's words offered "a last best chance" to address unresolved loyalist issues.

Winston Irvine, Progressive Unionist Party

The legacy of the conflict in Northern Ireland, with its many victims and survivors from all community backgrounds, can only properly be dealt with in a context of providing a stable, secure and peaceful future. This means we all must be committed to a fair and democratic society in which everyone – including combatant and non-combatant loyalists, republicans and others – feels able to make a positive contribution. In designing a legacy process, the question [of] ensuring that an unresolved past does not prevent a move to a better future becomes fundamental. All sections of society must have a say and stake in how the past is interpreted, explained and memorised. Only when we have a comprehensive process that can accommodate all stories, multiple narratives and views, can we say that we are beginning to deal with the past. In developing any such legacy process, loyalists must be involved from the outset, both in terms of design and implementation.

If we are going to move together as a society, we all have a responsibility to participate in a process that deals with the past and we must be charitable in how we approach it. We must also be very mindful of the sensitivities in addressing the scale of suffering and pain caused by the conflict, but we must avoid reopening old wounds or re-energising embers of revenge and retribution. Any process that deals with the past must be inclusive. Nationalists must be afforded the same opportunity to participate in a legacy process as any other community. I believe this to be no different for the loyalist community too. If the intention is to design a process that is to become a viable solution to deal with the past, then loyalists must be at the table – to exclude loyalists from a legacy process is to ensure that such a process becomes unworkable. I believe that a legacy process must have the support of all sides before it legislates on the methods and objectives of information retrieval. Any process must be for the benefit of society as a whole, and not to the benefit of the few.

If any information-gathering and sharing process designed to deal with the unresolved matters of conflict is to have any hope of success, then the conditions for engagement must be clear and unequivocal. However envisaged, it must also be made clear what information is required through a legacy process, and why.

I believe we must avoid a possible escalation of fears and tensions, which risks returning us to the past rather than releasing us from it. It is also essential that we make clear what we are trying to achieve from a legacy process. If Northern Ireland is to avoid being dragged backwards towards conflict, rather than away from it, we must avoid a race to the bottom when dealing with and designing the past/legacy process.

Without IRA involvement in a process that deals with the past, I do not believe that loyalists would give countenance to any suggestion that the IRA has gone away and so cannot be subject to accountability. Without commitment by the IRA to participate in a legacy process, there can be no loyalist involvement either. We must be upfront and honest about what can be achieved through a legacy process. We must be realistic about what is possible when it comes to victims. The practice of playing with the hopes and fears of victims on both sides must end. With the passing on of people and time, there is no possibility of some kind of Nirvana for the victims and survivors of Northern Ireland's conflict. We must reset our minds and attitudes, in order to reflect the expectations and results that any process can deliver.

Perhaps a good starting point for any such process would be a collective acknowledgement by all sides – churches, loyalist and republican combatants, non-combatants, Governments, political parties and media – of responsibility for the past, and a commitment it will never happen again. In this respect, and in ensuring we can all move forward together, the question is best understood as: how do we take the past out of the future?

The movement away from conflict towards peace has been a long journey – much longer than many envisaged. In the waiting, wounds fester. For this book, my daughter Elle has taken photographs of people who have been hurt and are still hurting and who may hurt forever; photographs that show what bombs and bullets do. Just look at Alex Bunting and Peter Heathwood, and you see the past in the present. It doesn't go away when people draw lines. So, perhaps what we need to remember is that what happened, and what is still happening, is about people and about pain, and, in the words and the work of the acclaimed Belfast artist, Colin Davidson, there is the reminder that time doesn't always heal. With brushes and colours and craft and in the quietness of his art, Davidson made a big statement in his exhibition *Silent Testimony*. We see it in the eyes and the faces of his 18 portraits: people visited and hurt by the horror of conflict. The paintings do not need words to be heard; their silence says everything, and the voiceless speak.

Colin Davidson, Artist, writing for this book

There was an understanding that time was healing. Ever since the Belfast Agreement of Good Friday 1998, there had been a growing swell of voices, calling for a communal "moving-on". History was just that – history. Most of us ticked the "yes" box in the referendum that followed the Agreement.

In that simple stroke of the pen, there was a hope that we were putting the dark, murky, terrifying decades of what were known as "the Troubles" behind us. Most of us wished for the daily killings and bombings to stop, for the gruesome massacres to cease. We wished for life to be normal.

But time doesn't always heal. For many thousands of people living in Northern Ireland, and indeed beyond, that tick on the ballot paper also marked an end of hope. A hope for justice, hope for answers. Their personal "moving-on" was now impossible. For many, the natural human process of dealing with loss was interrupted, often never to restart. And in the years that followed, with the rhetoric of blame, histrionics and procrastination, heard together with the calls for healing, forgiveness and love, this significant section of our community has fallen voiceless. After all, what can they say? How can they be heard? The noise of the 'peace process' has swept us all along.

In his poignantly moving song, "The Island", Paul Brady sings of the futility of "trying to reach the future through the past". Brady, who penned these words in 1985, was commenting on the darkness of the time and on the fact that the act of killing did not make the prospect of ideals becoming reality any more likely. But, in painting the 18 portraits which make up my exhibition, *Silent Testimony*, I have come to view those in our community who suffered loss through the Troubles as, in a way, paying for everyone else's peace. And I wonder if, unlike 1985, the key to our future is in fact through our past.

Was the call for a communal "moving on" in 1998 premature? Did it actually miss the whole point? Do we all have to deal with the trauma, the hurt, the anger of bereavement and loss as individual human beings, not just as communities? In doing so, and in going through the painful process, might we even realise that communal closure is in fact as elusive as personal closure? Perhaps, in us even attempting to answer these questions together, we might find the key turning in the lock which binds our future.

Davidson's words are a reminder that those who have been hurt the most are then asked to give the most, as people and places and communities try to climb out of conflict and try to find that thing that we call peace. One of those he painted was Maureen Reid, whose story was one of the many lost in the news and headlines of past decades. Maureen's husband, James was killed in a pub bombing in 1976 and, in the hard years that followed, she struggled and triumphed in her battle to bring up ten children, doing so on a small widow's pension. Maureen passed away in 2015, but she is remembered now in the Davidson painting, in the roses planted in the garden at the WAVE Trauma Centre where she worked and, here, in the words and poem of one of her daughters. Alice's words are the last in this book – words that many will identify with; those many whose stories and experiences got lost in the fog of those bombs and bullets, and in the living and dying of the conflict years.

Alice Reid, James and Maureen's daughter

Mum was a very simple, down-to-earth person. She was also a proud and modest woman who rarely asked anyone for anything. She was much more content helping and giving. Pleasing people, pleased her. She loved a laugh and had a smile for everyone she met. Work was her middle name, and she had great inner strength.

She thought of herself as unintelligent ("a dunce"), but her own life lessons taught her to be strong and, in her own words, "a fighter". Yes, she was a victim but she was also a victor. Equally, in war and life, there are many soldiers. Mum was a soldier of life, who took up her own arms every day, to nurture and protect; she fought her own struggle every day to survive and succeed, and she did so remarkably well for 40 years since our father's death. She was a light in the darkness.

Thank you Mum, for shining so bright. You were and shall remain our beautiful hero. I heard her say, "I was a victim of The Troubles." I now wonder, what about The Troubles of the victims? (Pain, trauma, loss, grief, torment, devastation, injury, depression . . .) Mum was a true inspiration, and I hope the world gets to hear about her.

This is a poem Alice wrote in tribute to her mother:

Priceless

Imagine a mother of ten
Imagine her happiness then
Imagine the joy that she felt
Imagine the pride in her heart

Imagine him leaving that day
Imagine the last word they'd say
Imagine the time in between
Imagine her wash, cook and clean

Imagine her hearing the bang
Imagine the sirens that sang
Imagine her thoughts as she ran
Imagine her search for her man

Imagine her need to be there
Imagine her prayer after prayer
Imagine the sight so degrading
Imagine the hope that was fading

Imagine the moment she heard
Imagine how shocked and how scared
Imagine the words that destroyed her
Imagine her mind, all a blur

Imagine the pain in her body
Imagine the pain in her mind
Imagine the thought of tomorrow
Imagine the depths of her sorrow

Imagine her face for you
Imagine her face for me
Imagine the sadness she'd hide
Imagine all just set aside

Imagine the worry of ten
Imagine her rest: where and when?
Imagine the work in her hands
Imagine her schedule, her plans

Imagine her teaching each day
Imagine her loving kind way
Imagine her comfort for years
Imagine her craic and her cheers

Imagine her loneliness long
Imagine the darkness til dawn
Imagine her doubt in herself
Imagine her life on the shelf

Imagine her gift of survival
Imagine her strength on arrival
Imagine her get-up-and-go
Imagine her sun, rain and snow

Imagine her struggle each day
Imagine the things she would say
Imagine her sickness was rough
Imagine she'd say, "It was tough"

Imagine her fun and her laughter
Imagine the woman, the grafter
Imagine her nerves made of steel
Imagine her love spun the wheel

Imagine the spuds and the dinner
Imagine her pies, all a winner
Imagine the mince by the pound
Imagine the knack she had found

Imagine her guts and her spirit
Imagine her anger, not near it
Imagine her faith and her living
Imagine her helping and giving

Imagine her sadness for years
Imagine the sting of her tears
Imagine a mother, a wife
Imagine a sentence for life

Imagine her loyalty strong
Imagine "a dunce", oh so wrong
Imagine her say, "I'm a fighter"
Imagine her smile, nothing brighter

Imagine to know her we're blessed
Imagine her work, her success
Imagine a mother of ten
Imagine she's at peace, Amen.

Alice Reid

Index